¹ In the beginning was information

¹In the beginning was information

A Scientist Explains
the Incredible Design
in Nature

Dr. Werner Gitt

First Master Books printing, February 2006
Fourth printing, February 2017

Master Books, Inc., P.O. Box 726, Green Forest, AR 72638.
Master Books® is a division of the New Leaf Publishing Group, Inc.

ISBN-13: 978-0-89051-461-0
Library of Congress Number: 2005934372

Cover by Left Coast Design, Portland, Oregon

Unless otherwise noted, all Scripture is from the New International Version of the Bible.

Please consider requesting that a copy of this volume be purchased by your local library system.

For information regarding author interviews, please contact the publicity department at (870) 438-5288.

Printed in the United States of America

Please visit our website for other great titles:
www.masterbooks.net

Master
Books®
A Division of New Leaf Publishing Group
www.masterbooks.net

Dedicated to Rona and Jörn

CONTENTS

Preface 11

Preface to the English Edition 13

  1 Preliminary Remarks about the Concept of Information 15

Part 1: Laws of Nature

  2 Principles of Laws of Nature 27

      2.1   The Terminology Used in the Natural
              Sciences 27

      2.2   The Limits of Science and the Persistence
              of Paradigms 30

      2.3   The Nature of Physical Laws 31

      2.4   The Relevance of the Laws of Nature 38

      2.5   The Classification of the Laws of Nature 40

      2.6   Possible and Impossible Events 43

Part 2: Information

  3 Information Is a Fundamental Entity 49

      3.1   Information: A Fundamental Quantity 49

      3.2   Information: A Material or a Mental
              Quantity? 50

      3.3   Information: Not a Property of Matter! 52

  4 The Five Levels of the Information Concept 55

      4.1   The Lowest Level of Information:
              Statistics 58

      4.2   The Second Level of Information:
              Syntax 60

      4.3   The Third Level of Information:
              Semantics 71

4.4   The Fourth Level of Information:
Pragmatics 74

4.5   The Fifth Level of Information:
Apobetics 76

5 Delineation of the Information Concept 83

6 Information in Living Organisms 89

6.1   Necessary Conditions for Life 90

6.2   The Genetic Code 93

6.3   The Origin of Biological Information 97

6.4   Materialistic Representations and Models
of the Origin of Biological Information 99

6.5   Scientists against Evolution 104

7 The Three Forms in which Information Appears 107

8 Three Kinds of Transmitted Information 111

9 The Quality and Usefulness of Information 115

10 Some Quantitative Evaluations of Semantics 119

11 Questions Often Asked about the Information
Concept 123

Part 3: Application of the Concept of Information to the Bible

12 Life Requires a Source of Information 135

13 The Quality and Usefulness of Biblical Information 139

14 Aspects of Information as Found in the Bible 143

14.1   God as Sender — Man as Recipient 143

14.2   Man as Sender — God as Recipient 153

14.3   The Highest Packing Density of
Information 156

15 The Quantities Used for Evaluating Information
and Their Application to the Bible 159

16 A Biblical Analogy of the Four Fundamental
     Entities — Mass, Energy, Information,
     and Will 163

Appendix

A1 The Statistical View of Information 171

    A1.1 Shannon's Theory of Information 171

    A1.2 Mathematical Description of Statistical
          Information 179

    A1.2.1 The Bit: Statistical Unit of Information............ 179

    A1.2.2 The Information Spiral....................................... 184

    A1.2.3 The Highest Packing Density of
             Information.. 194

    A1.3 Evaluation of Communication Systems 196

    A1.4 Statistical Analysis of Language 198

    A1.5 Statistical Synthesis of Language....................... 204

A2 Language: The Medium for Creating,
     Communicating, and Storing Information......... 209

    A2.1 Natural Languages... 209

    A2.1.1 General Remarks on the Structure of
             Human Language....................................... 210

    A2.1.2 Complexity and Peculiarities of
             Languages.. 213

    A2.1.3 The Origin of Languages................................... 216

    A2.1.4 Written Languages... 218

    A2.2 Special Languages Used in the Animal
          World.. 220

    A2.3 Does "Artificial Intelligence" Exist?.................... 223

A3 Energy 229

    A3.1 Energy, a Fundamental Quantity....................... 229

A3.2   Strategies for Maximizing the Utilization
          of Energy 233

A3.2.1   Utilization of Energy in Technological
          Systems 235

A3.2.2   Utilization of Energy in Biological
          Systems (Photosynthesis) 236

A3.3   The Consumption of Energy in
          Biological Systems: Strategies
          for Minimization 240

A3.4   Conservation of Energy in Biological
          Systems 243

A3.4.1   Animal "Chlorophyll" 244

A3.4.2   Animals with "Lamps" 245

A3.4.3   The Lung, an Optimal Structure 247

A3.4.4   The Flight of Migratory Birds 248

A3.4.4.1 The Flight of Migrating Birds: An
          Accurate Energy Calculation 248

A3.4.4.2 The Flight of Migrating Birds:
          A Navigational Masterpiece 253

References 255

Name Index 263

PREFACE

Theme of the book: The topic of this book is the concept of *information*, which is a fundamental entity on equal footing with matter and energy. Many questions have to be considered: What is information? How does information arise? What is the function of information? How is it encoded? How is it transmitted? What is the source of the information found in living organisms?

Information confronts us on all sides; newspapers, radio, and television bring new information daily, and information processing systems are found practically everywhere; for example, in computers, numerical control equipment, automatic assembly lines, and even car wash machines. It should be noted that the activities of all living organisms are controlled by programs comprising information.

Because information is required for all life processes, it can be stated unequivocally that information is an essential characteristic of all life. All efforts to explain life processes in terms of physics and chemistry only will always be unsuccessful. This is the fundamental problem confronting present-day biology, which is based on evolution.

Structure and purpose of this book: This book consists of three main parts and an appendix. In the first part, the nature of natural laws is discussed. This introduction is indispensable for the subsequent formulation and evaluation of information theorems.

The concept of information is clarified by means of many examples in the second and central part of the book. The basic principles are established by means of general theorems which are valid irrespective of the actual discipline. The purpose is to find laws of nature which hold for the fundamental entity known as information. With the aid of such theorems, it becomes possible to formulate conclusions for unknown situations, just as can be done in the case of laws of nature. In contrast to theorems about many other characteristic natural quantities (e.g., entropy), the theorems about information can be clearly illustrated and their validity is easy to demonstrate.

The purpose of this book is to formulate the concept of information as widely and as deeply as necessary. The reader will eventually be able to answer general questions about the origin of life as far as it is scientifically possible. If we can successfully formulate natural laws for information, then we will have found a new key for evaluating evolutionary ideas. In addition, it will become possible to develop an alternative model which refutes the doctrine of evolution.

The topics and theorems developed in the first two parts of the book are applied to the Bible in the third part. This provides a fresh way of unlocking the message of the Bible.

Readership: The first target group of this book is those who have a scientific inclination; especially information and communication scientists and linguists. The concept of information is highly relevant for these scientists as well as for theologians, and the given examples cover a wide range of disciplines. For the sake of ease of understanding, chapters which contain many formulas are placed in the appendix, and complex relationships are illustrated graphically.

Appendix: Questions which are closely linked to the concept of information (e.g., Shannon's theory and artificial intelligence), but would distract the reader's attention, are discussed in the fairly comprehensive appendix. The concept of energy receives ample attention, because energy plays a similarly important role in technology and in living organisms, as does information.

The title of the book: The title refers to the first verse of the Gospel written by John: "In the beginning was the Word. . . ." This book continually emphasizes the fact that information is required for the start of any controlled process, but the information itself is preceded by the prime source of all information. This is exactly what John has written, since "the Word" refers to the person who is the Prime Cause.

General remarks: References to literary sources are indicated by the first letter of the author followed by a serial number, enclosed in square brackets. If there is a "p" and a second number in the reference, this indicates page number(s).

Acknowledgments and thanks: After I had discussed the manuscript with my wife, it was also edited by Dr. Martin Ester

(München), Dipl.- Inform.; Daniel Keim (München); Dr. Volker Kessler (Vierkirchen), Dipl.- Inform.; Thomas Seidl; and Andreas Wolff. I am sincerely grateful for all their suggestions and amplifications.

PREFACE TO THE ENGLISH EDITION

As author, I am delighted that my book is now available in English. Prof. Dr. Jaap Kies (South Africa) was responsible for the arduous task of translating the book into his mother tongue. Dr. Carl Wieland, together with Russell Grigg (Australia), proofread the translation thoroughly. I would like to thank all of those involved for their work in bringing this book into being. May it be a help to those who are seeking and asking questions, as well as to those who already believe.

CHAPTER 1 Preliminary Remarks about the Concept of Information

By way of introduction, we shall consider a few systems and repeatedly ask the question: What is the reason that such a system can function?

1. The web of a spider: In Figure 1 we see a section of a web of a spider, a *Cyrtophora* in this case. The mesh size is approximately 0.8 x 1.2 mm. The circle in the upper picture indicates the part which has been highly magnified by an electron microscope to provide the lower picture. The design and structure of this web is brilliant, and the spider uses the available material extremely economically. The required rigidity and strength are obtained with a minimal amount of material. The spiral threads do not merely cross the radial ones, and the two sets are not attached at the points of intersection only. Rather, they run parallel over a small distance, where they are tied or "soldered" together with very fine threads.

Every spider is a versatile genius: It plans its web like an architect, and then carries out this plan like the proficient weaver it is. It is also a chemist who can synthesize silk employing a computer controlled manufacturing process, and then use the silk for spinning. The spider is so proficient that it seems to have completed courses in structural engineering, chemistry, architecture, and information science, but we know that this was not the case. So who instructed it? Where did it obtain the specialized knowledge? Who was its adviser? Most spiders are also active in recycling. They eat their web in the morning, then the material is chemically processed and re-used for a new web.

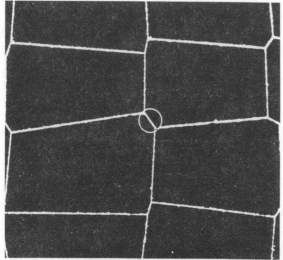

Figure 1:
The web of a
Cyrtophora
spider.

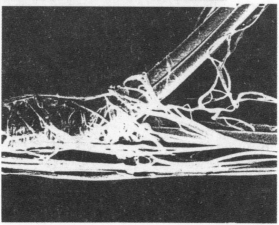

The answer to the question of why everything works in this way is unequivocally that *information* plays an essential role.

2. The spinnerets of *Uroctea*: The spinning nipples of *Uroctea* spiders are shown in Figure 2 under high magnification. The female has 1,500 spinnerets, only a few of which appear in Figure 2, where threads can be seen emerging from two of them. Silk having the required tensile strength is produced in the "factories" located directly below the spinnerets. All these complex processes are computer controlled, and all the required equipment is highly miniaturized. How is it possible that such a complex and minutely detailed manufacturing process can be

0,01 mm

Figure 2: The spinnerets of *Uroctea*.

carried out without mishap? Because the system contains a controlling program which has all the required processing information (see chapter 7).

3. The *Morpho rhetenor* butterfly: The South American butterfly, *Morpho rhetenor*, is depicted in Figure 3 under various magnifications so that the detailed structure of its wing scales can be seen (*Scientific American*, vol. 245, Nov. 1981, p. 106). The wings exhibit marvelous colorful patterns; metallic blue above (top left) and brown underneath (top right). The wings were analyzed for pigmentation, but none was found. How can this colorful beauty then be explained?

The detailed structure of the wings becomes apparent in three magnification steps, namely 50 x, 350 x, and 20,000 x. At the lower magnifications, the structure resembles roof tiles, but when the magnification is 20,000, the secret is revealed. The structure is quite extraordinary: a

Morpho rhetenor

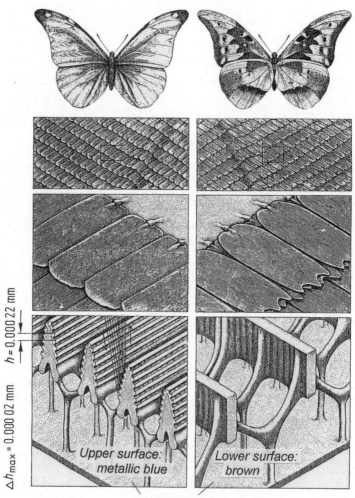

Magnification: 20,000 times

Figure 3: The South American butterfly *Morpho rhetenor* with wing surface sections under different magnifications.

regular grid of precisely constructed wedge-shaped ridges spaced at intervals of about 0.00022 mm. This pattern is repeated so accurately that the maximum deviation is only 0.00002 mm. No earthly workshop specializing in miniaturization would be able to make one single wing scale with this required precision. What is the purpose of this marvelous structure?

A certain physical effect is utilized here in a marvelous way. It can be explained in terms of a simple example: When one drops two stones in a pool, concentric waves spread out from each point of impact. At some points these waves cancel out, and at other points they enhance one another. This effect is known as interference, and it is exactly this effect which causes the observed colors. When light rays from the sun impinge on the stepped grid, some colors are canceled out and other colors are enhanced. The grid spacing and the wavelengths of the incident light are precisely tuned in to one another.

How did this marvelous structure arise where everything is geared to a special physical effect? Once again the answer is information!

4. The development of human embryos: The wonders which occur during the nine-month gestation period are unsurpassable. During the first four weeks of the new life, billions of cells are formed, and they arrange themselves according to a fascinating plan to shape the new human being. Around the 15th day, a dramatic new development occurs: the first blood vessels appear. A few days later another wonderful event takes place: Within the tiny breast of the 1.7 mm long embryo two blood vessels join to form the heart, which begins to pump blood through the miniscule body before the end of the third week. The tiny new heart provides the developing brain with blood and oxygen. In the fourth month, the heart of the fetus[1] already pumps almost 8 gallons (30 liters) of blood per day, and at birth this volume will be 92 gallons (350 liters).

In the embryonic stage, lungs, eyes, and ears develop, although they are not used yet. After two months, the embryo is only three to four centimeters long. It is so small that it could literally fit inside a walnut shell, but even at this stage all organs are already present. During the following months the organs increase in size and assume

---

1. After 12 weeks, no new organs are formed. When organo-genesis (= embryo-genesis = the growth and differentiation of cells at the sites of new organs during the first 12 weeks) is concluded, the embryo is referred to as a fetus, and its further growth is known as fetal development.

their eventual shape. Various stages of human embryonic and fetal development are shown in Figure 4 [B3]:

> **Part A:** A four-week-old embryo which is 4.2 mm long: 1 - boundary between back and abdomen, 2 - incipient shoulder groove, 3 - liver bulge, 4 - heart bulge, 5 - eye, 6 - thin and thick part of the navel funnel, 7 - Anulis umbilicalis, 8 - Anulis umbilicalis impar, 9 - coccyx.
>
> **Part B:** The embryo at four weeks when it is 4.2 mm long.
>
> **Part C:** The nervous system of a two-month-old embryo which is 17.7 mm long: 1 - Telencephalon (= the front part of the first brain bubble), 2 - optical nerve, 3 - Cerebellum, 4 - Medulla oblongata, 5 - Lobus olfactorius (sense of smell), 6 - Nervus ulnaris (elbow), 7 - Nervus obturatorius (hip region), 8 - Nervus plantaris lateralis (outer foot-sole) and Nervus suralis (calf).
>
> **Part D:** Fetus of 75 mm, shown inside the uterus: 1 - Placenta, 2 - Myometrium (= muscular wall of the womb), 3 - amniotic membrane. The amniotic fluid has been removed.

How is it possible that embryonic development does not entail a disorderly growth of cells, but is systematic and purposeful according to a set timetable? A precise plan, in which all stages are programmed in the finest detail, underlies all these processes. In this case also, information is the overall guiding factor.

5. **The organ-playing robot:** Would it be possible for a robot to play an organ? In Figure 5, we see exactly this. This Japanese robot, called Vasubot, even enthralls music lovers. It has two hands and two feet which are able to manipulate the manuals and the pedals, and it reads sheet music by means of a video camera. The notes are then converted to the required hand and foot motions. This robot can read and play any piece of music immediately without first having to practice it. The reason for this ability is the information given in a program, together with all the required mechanisms. If the program is removed, the robot cannot do anything. Again, we observe that information is the essential ingredient.

CONSEQUENCES

After having considered a few very diverse systems, we may conclude that the built-in information is the common factor. None of

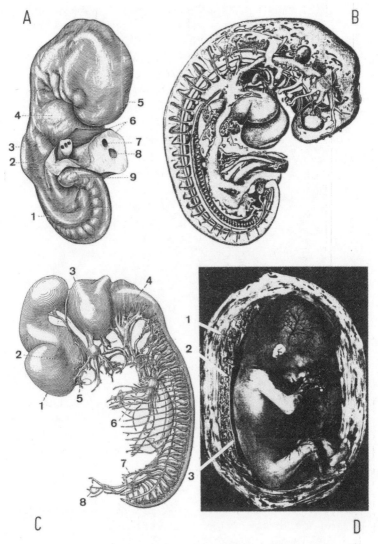

Figure 4: Various developmental stages of a human embryo.

these systems could operate if the stored information was deleted. For a better understanding of processes occurring in living as well as in inanimate systems, we have to study the concept of information in detail. A professor of informatics at Dortmund briefly formulated a basic theorem, with which we could agree:

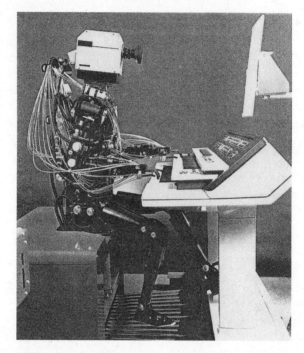

Figure 5: This organ-playing robot was exhibited at EXPO '85 in Japan. It was developed by Professor Ichiro Kato of Wasedo University, and was built by Sumitomo Electronic Industries. The robot is now on show in the official Japanese government building EXPO '85 (tsukuba). This illustrates the capabilities of robot technology, but this system cannot do anything which has not been pre-programmed.

"Anybody who can identify the source of information, has the key for understanding this world"[2] (or: "He who can give an account of the origin of information holds in his hands the key to interpret this world").

---

2. However, I would like to add the following condition. It is not clear from the statement whether God is referred to, or whether He is excluded. The question of the source of the information is acknowledged to be of fundamental importance, but even if the question about the source of the information has been answered logically and correctly, one would not be able to really understand this world without acknowledging the Spirit of God. If the Bible really is the Book of Truth, as stated in many ways (e.g., John 17:17), then it is the key for understanding the world.

The book *The Character of Physical Law*, by the American physicist Richard P. Feynman, may be regarded as a classic in the field of physics. The following is quoted from its preface [F1, p 172]: "The age in which we live is the age in which we are discovering the fundamental laws of nature, and that day will never come again." In the field of physics, most laws have probably been discovered and formulated since then. However, in regard to the fundamental quantity information, we are still squarely in the process of discovery. Based on previous work [G4, G5, G7, G8, G9, G17, G18] we will formulate in this book several theorems on information which are similar to laws of nature. For the purpose of appreciating the scope and meaning of the developed theorems, some fundamental properties of the natural laws are discussed in the next chapter.

PART 1:

Laws of Nature

CHAPTER 2 Principles of Laws of Nature

2.1 THE TERMINOLOGY USED IN THE NATURAL SCIENCES

Through the natural sciences, the world around us is observed for the purpose of discovering the rules governing it. Experimentation and observation (e.g., measuring and weighing) are the basic "modus operandi." Hans Sachsse, who specialized in natural philosophy and chemistry, described (natural) science as "a census of observational relationships which cannot say anything about first causes or the reasons for things being as they are; it can only establish the regularity of the relationships." The observational material is organized systematically, and the principles derived from it are formulated in the most general terms possible (e.g., construction of machines). Questions about the origin of the world and of life, as well as ethical questions, fall outside the scope of science, and such questions cannot be answered scientifically. Conclusions about matters that do fall within the scope of (natural) science can be formulated with varying degrees of certainty. The certainty or uncertainty of the results can be expressed in various ways.

Law of Nature: If the truth of a statement is verified repeatedly in a reproducible way so that it is regarded as generally valid, then we have a natural law. The structures and phenomena encountered in the real world can be described in terms of the laws of nature in the form of principles which are universally valid. This holds for both their chronological development and their internal structural relationships. The laws of nature describe those phenomena, events and results which occur in the interplay between matter and energy. For these reasons, psychological emotions like love, mourning, or joy, and philosophical questions, are excluded from the natural sciences. Statements about natural events can be classified according to the degree of certainty, namely: models, theories, hypotheses, paradigms, speculations, and fiction. These categories are now discussed.

Model: Models are representations of reality. Only the most important properties are reflected, and minor or unrecognized aspects are not covered. Models are important because of their illustrativeness. A model is a deliberate but simplified representation of reality and it describes observed structures in a readily understandable way. It is possible to have more than one model for a given reality, and, because it is by nature provisional and simple, any model can always be improved upon.

Theory (Greek *theoría* = view, consideration, investigation): Theories endeavor to explain facts in a unified representation of models and hypotheses. To put it briefly, a theory is a scientific statement based on empirical findings. Since empirical results are seldom final, theories are of a provisional nature, and the inherent hypothetical element inevitably causes uncertainty — in the best case, a statement can be made in terms of specific probabilities. Theories are therefore a means of tying observed facts together, and the best theories are those which attain this objective with the least number of inconsistencies.

Hypothesis (Greek *hypóthesis* = assumption, conjecture, supposition): A hypothesis is an unverified scientific conjecture which contains speculations, and which amplifies an incomplete empirical result, or provisionally explains some fact. Any new hypothesis must be based on facts, and it may not contradict the known laws of nature. If a hypothesis serves as a methodological guide when a new research project is undertaken, it is known as a working hypothesis. When observational facts support a hypothesis, the probability of its being true is increased, but if ONE contradicting fact is uncovered, the hypothesis must be rejected (falsification). As early as the 17th century, Blaise Pascal (1623–1662) said that we could be certain that a hypothesis is false if ONE SINGLE derived relationship contradicts any observed phenomenon.

Paradigm (Greek *parádeigma* = example, sample): When a certain theory (or a system of hypotheses, or a world view) pervades entire fields of research or an entire scientific era, it is known as a paradigm. Such a view then dictates the scope for specific researches and delineates the presuppositions used for explaining individual phenomena. If a system of hypotheses has been derived from presuppositions dictated by a world view, it usually cannot be reconciled with the available facts. Typical examples are geocentricity (refuted by Copernicus), and phlogiston chemistry (disproved by Lavoisier in 1774). It is hoped that this book will help to uproot the current evolutionary paradigm.

Speculation: When a statement is based purely on discussion, fantasy, imagination, or contemplation, and does not correspond to reality, it is speculation, or merely an intellectual game. Because no actual experimentation is involved, it is easy to make undiscoverable mistakes. In thought experiments, difficulties can easily be evaded, undesirable aspects can be suppressed, and contradictions can be deftly concealed. Thought experiments can probably raise questions, but cannot answer any; only actual experimentation can provide answers. In this sense, the "hypercycle" proposed by Manfred Eigen is pure speculation [G10, p. 153–155]. Mere speculation without experimentation and observation is not science, neither is pure deduction from arbitrary presuppositions, nor is a biased selection of observations. Even the most abstract theory should not lose contact with reality and experimentation; it must be empirically verifiable.[3] Thought experiments as well as deductions from philosophical postulates not based on observation are speculations.

Fiction (Latin *fictio* = fabrication, story): A fiction is either a deliberate or an unintentional fantasy which is not based on reality. Sometimes a false assumption (fiction) can be introduced deliberately for the purpose of clarifying a scientific problem methodologically.

---

3. Verification (Latin *verus* = true, *facere* = make):Verification means that a statement is tested experimentally. The result of such a verification is not generally valid, however. It holds strictly only for cases which have actually been confirmed, because the possibility that hitherto unknown counter examples may exist cannot be excluded. If one contradictory case is found, then the statement is rejected (falsified!). This can also be expressed as follows: It is not possible to verify a theory; a theory can only be falsified. A theory is good if it could be falsified very easily, and when it survives all open criticisms and tests, it can be accepted.

2.2 THE LIMITS OF SCIENCE AND THE PERSISTENCE OF PARADIGMS

We have discussed different categories of laws of nature and can now realize that many statements are often formulated with far too much confidence and in terms which are far too absolute. Max Born (1882–1970), a Nobel laureate, clearly pointed this out with respect to the natural sciences [B4]:

> Ideas like absolute correctness, absolute accuracy, final truth, etc. are illusions which have no place in any science. With one's restricted knowledge of the present situation, one may express conjectures and expectations about the future in terms of probabilities. In terms of the underlying theory, any probabilistic statement is neither true nor false. This liberation of thought seems to me to be the greatest blessing accorded us by present-day science.

Another Nobel laureate, Max Planck (1858–1947), deplored the fact that theories which have long ago become unacceptable are doggedly adhered to in the sciences [P3, p 13]:

> A new scientific truth is usually not propagated in such a way that opponents become convinced and discard their previous views. No, the adversaries eventually die off, and the upcoming generation is familiarized anew with the truth.

This unjustified adherence to discarded ideas was pointed out by Professor Wolfgang Wieland (a theoretical scientist, University of Freiburg, Germany) in regard to the large number of shaky hypotheses floating around [W4, p 631]:

> Ideas originally formulated as working hypotheses for further investigation, possess an inherent persistence. The stability accorded established theories (in line with Kuhn's conception), is of a similar nature. It only appears that such theories are tested empirically, but in actual fact observations are always explained in such a way that they are consistent with the pre-established theories. It may even happen that observations are twisted for this purpose.

The persistence of a paradigm which has survived the onslaught of reality for a long time, is even greater [W4, p 632]:

> "When it comes to collisions between paradigms and empirical reality, the latter usually loses, according to Kuhn's findings. He based his conclusions on the history of science and not on science theory. However, the power of the paradigm is not unlimited. . . . There are stages in the development of a science when empirical reality is not adapted to fit the paradigm; during such phases different paradigms compete. Kuhn calls these stages scientific revolutions. . . . According to Kuhn's conception it is a fable that the reason why successful theories replace previous ones is because they perform better in explaining phenomena. The performance of a theory can be measured historically in quite different terms, namely the number of its sworn-in adherents." Much relevant scientific data is lost because of the dictatorship of a false paradigm, since deviating results are regarded as "errors in measurement" and are therefore ignored.

A minimal requirement for testing whether a theory should be retained, or whether a hypothesis should not yet be discarded, or that a process could really work, is that the relevant laws of nature should not be violated.

2.3 THE NATURE OF PHYSICAL LAWS

A fundamental metaphysical law is that of causality. This means that every event must have a cause, and that under the same circumstances a certain cause always has the same effects. For a better understanding of the laws of nature we will now discuss some basic aspects which are important for the evaluation and application of events and processes:

N1: The laws of nature are based on experience. It is often asserted that the laws of nature are proven theorems, but we have to emphasize that the laws of nature cannot be proved! They are only identified and formulated through observation. It is often possible to formulate conclusions in exact mathematical terms, ensuring precision, brevity, and generality. Even though numerous mathematical theorems (except the initial axioms) can be proved,[4] this is not the

---

4. Provability: The German mathematician David Hilbert (1862–1943) held the optimistic view that every mathematical problem could be resolved in the sense that a solution could be found, or that it could be proved that a solution

case for the laws of nature. A mathematical formulation of an observation should not be confused with a proof. We affirm: the laws of nature are nothing more than empirical statements. They cannot be proved, but they are nevertheless valid.

The fundamental law of the conservation of energy is a case in point. It has never been proved, because it is just as unprovable as all other laws of nature. So why is it universally valid? Answer: Because it has been shown to be true in millions of experiences with reality. It has survived all real tests. In the past, many people believed in perpetual motion, and they repeatedly invested much time and money trying to invent a machine that could run continuously without a supply of energy. Even though they were NEVER successful, they rendered an important service to science. Through all their ideas and efforts, they demonstrated that the energy law cannot be circumvented. It has been established as a fundamental physical law with no known exceptions. The possibility that a counter example may be found one day cannot be excluded, even if we are now quite sure of its truth. If a mathematical proof of its truth existed, then each and every single non-recurrent possible deviation from this natural law could be excluded beforehand.

The unprovability of the laws of nature has been characterized as follows by R.E. Peierls, a British physicist [P1, p 536]:

> Even the most beautiful derivation of a natural law . . . collapses immediately when it is refuted by subsequent research. . . . Scientists regard these laws as being what they are: Formulations derived from our experiences, tested, tempered, and confirmed through theoretical predictions and in new situations. Together with subsequent improvements, the formulations would only be accepted as long as they are suitable and useful for the systematization, explanation, and understanding of natural phenomena.

---

was impossible, for example the quadrature (squaring) of a circle. He therefore said in his famous talk in Königsberg (1930) that there were no unsolvable problems: "We must know, we will know." Kurt Gödel (1906–1978), the well-known Austrian mathematician, rejected this view. He showed that, even in a formal system, not all true theorems could be proved. This statement, called the first incompleteness theorem of Gödel, was quite a revolutionary result. Because of the far-reaching effects for mathematics and for science theory, Heinrich Scholz called Gödel's work "A critique of pure reason from the year 1931."

N2: The laws of nature are universally valid. The theorem of the unity of nature is an important scientific law. This means that the validity of the laws of nature is not restricted to a certain limited space or time. Such a law is universally valid in the sense that it holds for an unlimited number of single cases. The infinitude of these single cases can never be exhausted by our observations. A claim of universal validity for an indefinite number of cases can immediately be rejected when one single counter example is found.[5]

In our three-dimensional world the known laws of nature are universally valid, and this validity extends beyond the confines of the earth out through the entire physical universe, according to astronomical findings. When the first voyages to the moon were planned, it was logically assumed that the laws identified and formulated on earth, were also valid on the moon. The laws of energy and of gravity were used to compute the quantities of fuel required, and when man landed on the moon, the assumption of universal validity was found to be justified. The law of the unity of nature (the universal validity of laws of nature) will hold until a counter example is found.

N3: The laws of nature are equally valid for living beings and for inanimate matter. Any law which is valid according to N2 above, includes living beings. Richard P. Feynman (1918–1988), Nobel laureate for physics (1965), writes [F1, p 74]:

---

5. Amendments to formulated laws of nature: An established natural law loses its universal validity when one single counter example is found. However, it is often only necessary to change the formulation to describe the actual law more precisely. We should therefore distinguish between the actual law as it operates in nature, and its formulation in human terms. More precise formulations do not invalidate an "approximately formulated law," but do provide a better description of reality. In the following two cases, the original formulations were too narrow, and had to be revised:

Example 1: The classical laws of mechanics lost their validity when appreciable fractions of the speed of light were involved. They were extended by the more precise special theory of relativity, because the relativistic effects could not be observed when velocities were small. The laws of classical mechanics are a good enough approximation for general purposes (e.g., construction of machines), but, strictly speaking, their original formulations were incorrect.

Example 2: The law of conservation of mass had to be reformulated to become a general law of the conservation of mass and energy, when nuclear reactions were involved (loss of mass, $E = m \times c^2$). Nevertheless, the law of mass conservation is a potent law of nature.

The law for conservations of energy is as true for life as for other phenomena. Incidentally, it is interesting that every law or principle that we know for "dead" things, and that we can test on the great phenomenon of life, works just as well there. There is no evidence yet that what goes on in living creatures is necessarily different, so far as the physical laws are concerned, from what goes on in non-living things, although the living things may be much more complicated.

All measurements (sensory organs), metabolic processes, and transfers of information in living organisms strictly obey the laws of nature. The brilliant concepts realized in living beings, are based on refined and very ingenious implementations of the laws of nature. For example, the sensitivity of human hearing attains the physically possible limits by means of a combination of determining factors [G11, p 85 – 88]. The laws of aerodynamics are employed so masterfully in the flight of birds and insects, that similar performance levels have not yet been achieved in any technological system (see Appendix A3.4.4).

N4: The laws of nature are not restricted to any one field of study. This theorem is actually redundant in the light of N2 and N3, but it is formulated separately to avoid any possibility of misunderstanding.

The energy conservation law was discovered by the German doctor and physicist Julius Robert Mayer (1814–1878) during an extended voyage in the tropics. He was a medical officer and he formulated this law when contemplating the course of organic life. Although it was discovered by a medical officer, nobody considered the possibility of restricting the validity of this theorem to medical science only. There is no area of physics where this theorem has not been decisive in the clarification of relationships. It is fundamental in all technical and biological processes.

The second law of thermodynamics was discovered by Rudolf Clausius in 1850 during the course of technological research. He formulated it for thermodynamic processes, but this theorem is also valid far beyond all areas of technology. Even the multiplicity of interactions and conversions in biological systems proceed according to the requirements of this law of nature.

Later in this book we will formulate several theorems on information, but the reader should not labor under the impression that their validity is restricted to the areas of informatics or technology. On the contrary, they have the same impact as laws of nature, and are therefore universally applicable in all cases where information is involved.

N5: The laws of nature are immutable. All known observations indicate that the laws of nature have never changed. It is generally assumed that the known laws are constant over time, but this is also merely an observation that cannot be proven.

Comment: Of course, He who has invented and established the laws of nature is also able to circumvent them. He is Lord of the laws of nature, and in both the Old and the New Testaments we find numerous examples of such events (see theorem N10b).

N6: The laws of nature are simple. It should be noted that the laws of nature can mostly be formulated in very simple terms. Their effects are, however, often complex, as may be seen in the following example. The law of gravity has been described as the most important generalization which human intellect has been fortunate enough to discover. It states that two bodies exert a force on each other which is inversely proportional to the square of their distance and directly proportional to the product of their masses. It can be formulated mathematically as follows:

$$F = G \times m_1 \times m_2 / r^2$$

The force F is given by a constant (the so-called gravitational constant, G) multiplied by the product of the two masses m_1 and m_2, divided by the square of the distance r. In addition, it can be mentioned that the effect of a force on an object is to accelerate it. This means that the velocity of an object acted on by a force changes faster when its mass is smaller. Now almost everything worth knowing about the law of gravity has been said. When this law is used to compute the orbits of the planets, it immediately becomes clear that the effects of a simple natural law can be very complex. When the relative motions of three bodies are analyzed in terms of this law, the mathematical formulations become quite intractable.

Faraday's law of electrolysis states that the quantity of matter separated out during electrolysis, is proportional to the electrical current and to its duration (e.g., electroplating with copper or gold). This formulation may seem to be very mathematical, but what it really means is that one unit of charge is required to separate one atom from the molecule it belongs to.

Conclusion: Laws of nature may be expressed and formulated verbally to any required degree of precision. In many cases, it is possible and convenient to formulate them mathematically as well. As Feynman states [F1, p 41]: "In the last instance mathematics is nothing more than a logical course of events which is expressed in formulas." Sir James H. Jeans (1877–1946), the well-known British mathematician, physicist, and astronomer, said [F1, p 58]: "The Great Architect seems to be a mathematician."

N7: The laws of nature are (in principle) falsifiable. To be really meaningful, a theorem must be formulated in such a way that it could be refuted if it was false. The fact that the laws of nature can be formulated the way they are cannot be ascribed to human ingenuity, but is a result of their being established by the Creator. After a law has been formulated, we discover that it could in principle very easily be negated if invalid. This is what makes these laws so important and accords them their great range of applicability.

There is a German saying which goes like this: "When the cock crows on the dungheap, the weather will change, or it will remain as it is." This statement cannot be falsified, therefore it is worthless. In contrast, the energy conservation law is very susceptible to falsification: "Energy cannot be created, neither can it be destroyed." The formulation is strikingly simple and it seems to be very easy to refute. If it was not valid, one could devise an experiment where the before and after energy equilibria did not balance. Nevertheless, it has not yet been possible to come up with one single counter example. In this way, a theorem which is based on observation is accepted as a law of nature.

N8: The laws of nature can be expressed in various ways. Different ways of expression can be employed for any given natural law, depending on the mode of application. If the question is whether an expected result could be obtained or not, it would be advantageous to describe it in the form of an impossibility theorem, and when calculations are involved, a mathematical formulation is preferable. The energy law could be formulated in one of four different ways, depending on the circumstances:

a) Energy cannot be created from nothing; neither can it be destroyed.

b) It is impossible to construct a machine which can work perpetually once it has been set in motion, without a continuous supply of energy (b follows directly from a).

c) E = constant (The energy of a system is constant.)

d) dE/dt = 0

(The balance of the total of all energies E of a system does not change, meaning that the derivative of energy versus time is zero.)

N9: The laws of nature describe reproducible results. When a natural law has been identified as such, its validity could be established anew in each and every case where it is applicable. Reproducibility is an essential characteristic of the laws of nature. One could drop a stone as often as you like from various heights and the law of gravity would always be obeyed. It is thus possible to make predictions about the behavior and interrelationships of things by means of the laws of nature. The laws of nature are eventually established through continual verification.

The nine above-mentioned general but fundamental theorems about the nature of the laws of nature, N1 to N9, have all been derived from experience. Their correctness cannot be proved, but can be tested repeatedly in the real world. We now formulate a tenth theorem which depends, however, on the personal view of the user. For this reason we present two different versions, theorems N10a and N10b. In the one case, the existence of God is denied, and in the second case, He is accepted as the Prime Cause. Both views are equally a question of belief and conviction. In the case of any given model, we have to decide which one of the two assumptions would be more useful.

N10a: Natural events can be explained without God. This assumption can be used in all cases where the laws of nature are applied to existing or planned systems. An analysis of the energy equilibrium when ice melts is an example of an existing system, while an example of a planned system is the building of a new space vehicle. In actual fact, most effects of the laws of nature can be explained and computed without reference to God (e.g., free fall). All attempts to explain the origin of life by means of models where God as initiator is ignored are based on theorem N10a.

It is necessary to formulate an important alternative theorem for those who acknowledge the God of the Bible, namely, when did the laws of nature begin to operate, and what is God's position in regard to these laws? These questions cannot be solved through observation, and we require some knowledge of the Bible as background.

N10b: The present laws of nature became operational when creation was completed. The laws of nature are a fundamental component of the world as we know it, and they indicate that the Creator sustains all things (Col. 1:17, Heb. 1:3). These laws were installed during the six creation days, and thus cannot be regarded as prerequisites for creation, since they themselves were also created. It is very emphatically denied that God's creative acts could be explained in terms of the present laws of nature. At the end of the six days of creation, everything was complete — the earth, the universe, the plants, animals, and man: "By the seventh day God had finished the work he had been doing" (Gen. 2:2).

If one tried to explain the actual creative acts in terms of the laws of nature, one would very soon be trapped in an inextricable net of speculations. This holds both for creationists and for supporters of evolution. The latter endeavor to explain the origin of life by means of laws of nature, but nobody has yet been able to do this! We therefore conclude: All the laws of nature have only been in operation since the completion of creation.

If God is the Creator of the laws of nature, then He himself is not subject to them. He can use them freely, and can, through His omnipotence, limit their effects or even nullify them. The miracles described in the Bible are extraordinary events where the effects of particular laws of nature were completely or partially suspended for a certain period or in a certain place. When Jesus walked on the water (Matt. 14:22–33), He, as the Son of God and Lord of everything, nullified the law of gravity. We read in Matthew 24:29 that "the heavenly bodies will be shaken"(this could also be translated as "the forces of the heavens will be shaken") when Jesus comes again. In the language of physics, this means that the present finely tuned equilibria of the various kinds of forces in the universe will be changed by the Creator, with the result that the orbits of the earth and the moon will become entangled and the stars will seem to move erratically: "The earth reels like a drunkard, it sways like a hut in the wind" (Isa. 24:20).

The moment that historical questions (e.g., about the origin of the world and of life) or future events (like the end of the earth) are considered, then N10a is entirely useless.

2.4 THE RELEVANCE OF THE LAWS OF NATURE

R1: The laws of nature provide us with a better understanding of natural phenomena and events. Without the laws of nature we would have had a very limited knowledge of the physical, chemical, astronomical, and biological processes occurring in the world around us. The progress of science mostly relies on the fact that fundamental principles are identified and classified, even when different effects are studied.

R2: The laws of nature enable us to make predictions. Because of N5 and N9, the expected course of observed processes can be predicted. Exactly because of this certainty, it is in many cases possible to compute beforehand what will happen. If, for example, a stone is dropped, one can calculate what its speed will be after two seconds.

R3: The laws of nature make technological development possible. All engineering constructions and all technical manufacturing processes are based on the laws of nature. The reason why the construction of a bridge, a car, or an aircraft can be planned in advance, is that the relevant laws of nature are known. Without knowledge of the laws of nature, there could have been neither chemical nor pharmaceutical industries.

R4: By means of the laws of nature, it is possible to determine beforehand whether an envisaged process would be realizable or not. This is a very important application of the laws of nature. Some time ago I received a comprehensive piece of work consisting of many diagrams, calculations, and explanations, from an inventor with the request that the proposed construction should be checked. This person envisioned an extremely complex system of pumps and pipes which would be able to drive a hydraulic motor. It was, however, immediately clear, without my having to do any calculations or tests, that such an arrangement could never work, because it violated the energy law. In many cases, the laws of nature enable one to make conclusions beforehand without having to study the details.

R5: The laws of nature are applicable to cases formerly unknown. The fact that the laws of nature can be transferred to new cases is of special importance. Up to the present time, nobody has been able to imitate the process of photosynthesis which takes place in every blade of grass. If and when such an endeavor may eventually be planned, then all proposed methods which violate any one of the laws could be rejected in advance. Any such design could be eliminated as useless in the conceptual phase. In addition, past results which were accepted in the light of some paradigm, could also be evaluated. Is it, for example, possible that information could have originated in a postulated primeval soup? This question is discussed further in chapter 6.

R6: One can employ a known natural law to discover another

one. It has happened time and again in the history of science that a new law has been discovered using the validity of a known law. If the law of gravity had not been known, then the behavior of the moons of Jupiter could not have been investigated properly. Observations of their motions made it possible to compute the speed of light, which is an important physical constant.

The orbits of the planets cannot be exactly elliptical (as would be required if the gravitational pull of the sun was the only force acting on them), as required by Newton's law, since they are not only under the gravitational influence of the sun, but they also affect one another gravitationally to a lesser extent. John Couch Adams (1819–1892), a British astronomer and mathematician, computed the expected perturbations caused by their mutual gravitational attractions, of the orbits of the then known major planets, Jupiter, Saturn, and Uranus. The French astronomer Urban J.J. Leverrier (1811–1877) also computed the deviations of these orbits from the perfect Kepler ellipses independently. It was found that Jupiter and Saturn "lived up to the expectations," but Uranus exhibited deviant behavior.

Relying on the validity of Newton's law, both astronomers were able to deduce the position of a hitherto unknown planet from these irregularities. Each of them then approached an observatory with the request to look for an unknown planet in such and such a celestial position. This request was not taken seriously at one observatory; they regarded it as absurd that a pencil-pusher could tell them where to look for a new planet. The other observatory responded promptly, and they discovered Neptune. Leverrier wrote to the German astronomer Johann Gottfried Galle (1812–1910), who then discovered Neptune very close to the predicted position.

2.5 THE CLASSIFICATION OF THE LAWS OF NATURE

When one considers the laws of nature according to the ways they are expressed, one discovers striking general principles which they seem to obey. The laws can accordingly be classified as follows.

Conservation theorems: The following description applies to this group of laws: A certain number, given in a suitable unit of measurement, can be computed at a specific moment. If this number is recomputed later after many changes may have occurred in nature, its value is unchanged. The best-known law in this category is the law of the conservation of energy. This is the most abstract and the most difficult of all the conservation laws, but at the same time it is the most useful one, since it is used most frequently. It is more difficult to understand than the laws about the conservation of mass (see footnote 5), of momentum, of rotational moment, or of electrical charge. One reason is that energy can exist in many different forms, like kinetic energy, potential energy, heat energy, electrical energy, chemical energy, and nuclear energy. In any given process, the involved energy can be divided among these forms in many different ways, and a number can then be computed for each kind of energy. The conservation law now states that the sum of all these numbers stays constant irrespective of all the conversions that took place during the time interval concerned. This sum is always the same at any given moment. It is very surprising that such a simple formulation holds for every physical or biological system, no matter how complex it may be.

Equivalence theorems: Mass and energy can be seen to be equivalent in terms of Einstein's famous formula $E = m \times c^2$. In the case of atomic processes of energy conversion (nuclear energy) there is a small loss of mass (called the deficit) which releases an equivalent amount of energy, according to Einstein's formula.

Directional theorems: From experience in this world we know that numerous events proceed in one sense only. A dropped cup will break. The converse event, namely that the cup will put itself together and jump back into our hand, never happens, however long we may wait. When a stone is thrown into a pool of water, concentric waves move outward on the surface of the water. This process can be described mathematically, and the resulting equations are equally valid for outward moving waves and for the imaginary case if small waves should start from the edge and move concentrically inward, becoming larger as they do so. This converse process has never been observed, although the first event can be repeated as often as we like.

For some laws of nature, the direction does not play any role (e.g., energy), but for others the process is unidirectional, like a one-way street. In the latter case, one can clearly distinguish between past and future. In all cases where friction is involved, the processes are irreversible; they proceed in one direction only. Examples of such laws are the law of entropy (see the appendix), the chemical principle of Le Chatelier (Henry-Louis Le Chatelier, French chemist, 1850–1936; see Q20 p. 128–130), and the law of mass action.

Impossibility theorems: Most laws of nature can be expressed in the form: "It is impossible that. . . ." The energy law for example, can be stated as follows: "It is impossible that energy can come into existence by itself." R. Clausius formulated the second law of thermodynamics as an impossibility: "Heat cannot of itself pass from a colder to a hotter body." The impossibility theorems are very useful, because they effectively distinguish between possible and impossible events. This type of scientific formulation will be encountered frequently when we come to the information theorems.

Geometrical impossibilities can also be devised. Three different geometric representations appear in Figure 6, but such bodies are just as impossible to construct as it is to expect results that are precluded by laws of nature.

Laws which describe processes: If the future (prognosis) or the past (retrognosis) states of a system can be described when the values of the relevant variables are known for at least one moment in time, such a formulation is known as a process law. A typical physical example is the description of radioactive decay.

Co-existence laws: These describe the simultaneous existence of the properties of a system. The formula describing the state changes of an ideal gas, p x v = R x T, is a typical physical co-existence law. The values of the three quantities, pressure p, specific volume v, and absolute temperature T, comprise a complete description of the "state" of an ideal gas. This means that it does not depend on the previous history of the gas, and neither does it depend on the way the present pressure or the present volume has been obtained. Quantities of this type are known as state variables.

Limit theorems: Limit theorems describe boundaries that

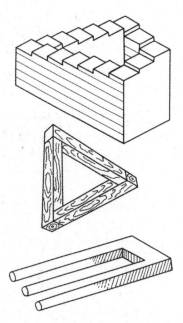

Figure 6: Geometrically impossible bodies.

cannot be overstepped. In 1927, the German physicist Werner Heisenberg (1901–1976) published such a theorem, namely the so-called uncertainty principle of Heisenberg. According to this principle, it is impossible to determine both the position and the velocity of a particle exactly at a prescribed moment. The product of the two uncertainties is always greater than a specific natural constant, which would have been impossible if the uncertainties were vanishingly small. It follows, for example, that certain measurements can never be absolutely exact. This finding resulted in the collapse of the structure of the then current 19th century deterministic philosophy. The affirmations of the laws of nature are so powerful that viewpoints which were held up to the time they are formulated, may be rapidly discarded.

Information theorems: In conclusion, we mention that there is a series of theorems which should also be regarded as laws of nature, although they are not of a physical or a chemical nature. These laws will be discussed fully in this book, and all the previously mentioned criteria, N1 to N9, as well as the relevance statements R1 to R6, are also valid in their case.

2.6 POSSIBLE AND IMPOSSIBLE EVENTS

The totality of all imaginable events and processes can be divided into two groups as in Figure 7, namely,

a) possible events
b) impossible events.

Possible events occur under the "supervision" of the laws of nature, but it is in general not possible to describe all of them completely. On the other hand, impossible events could be identified by means of the so-called impossibility theorems.

Impossible events can be divided into two groups, those which are "fundamentally impossible," and those which are "statistically impossible." Events which contradict, for example, the energy law, are impossible in principle, because this theorem even holds for individual atoms. On the other hand, radioactive decay is a statistical law which is subject to the probability theorems, and cannot be applied to individual atoms, but in all practical cases, the number of atoms is so immense that an "exact" formulation can be used, namely $n(t) = n_0 x e^{-k x t}$. The decay constant k does not depend on temperature, nor on pressure, nor on any possible chemical bond. The half-life T is given by the formula $T = \ln 2/k$; this indicates the time required for any given quantity n_0 to diminish to half as much, $n_0/2$. Since we are dealing with statistical events, one might expect that less than half the number of atoms or appreciably more then half could have decayed at time T. However, the probability of deviation from this law is so close to zero that we could regard it as statistically impossible. It should be clear that impossible events are neither observable nor recognizable nor measurable. Possible events have in general either been observed, or they are observable. However, there are other possible events about which it can be said that they

- cannot or cannot yet be observed (e.g., processes taking place in the sun's interior)
- are in principle observable, but have never been observed

Thus far, we have only discussed natural events, but now we can apply these concepts to technological processes (in the widest sense of the word, comprising everything that can be made by human beings). The following categories are now apparent:

1. possible processes
   1.1 already implemented
   1.2 not yet implemented, but realizable in principle

2. impossible processes: proposed processes of this kind are fundamentally unrealizable, because they are precluded by laws of nature.

The distinctions illustrated in Figure 7 follow from a comparison of possible events in nature and in technology, namely:

a) processes which occur only in nature, but have not (yet) been realized technologically (e.g., photosynthesis, the storage of information on DNA molecules, and life functions);
b) processes occurring in nature which are also technologically realizable (e.g., industrial synthesis of organic substances);
c) processes which have been technologically implemented, but do not occur in nature (e.g., synthesis of artificial materials).

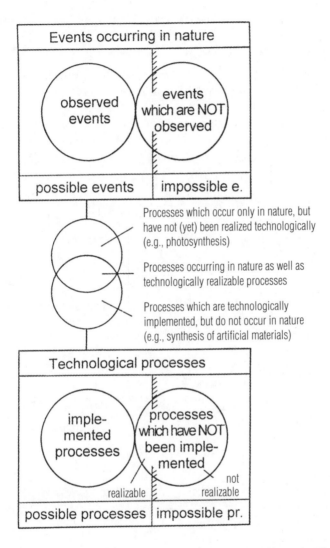

Figure 7: Possible and impossible events in nature and in technological processes.

○ THE NATURAL LAWS CAN BE USED
AND ARE USED AS A foundation
OR STARTING POINT FOR A
NEW Hypothesis AND OR
EXP. THE BIBLE CAN BE
USED AS the Starting Pt /Foundation
of our Life...

○ A NATURAL LAW Just is & cannot
BE PROVEN ONLY EXPERIMENTED.
THE BIBLE Just is, PPL are trying
to PROVE it & DISPROVE it, but
why NOT EXPERIMENT.

PART 2:

Information

3 Information Is a
Fundamental Entity

3.1 INFORMATION: A FUNDAMENTAL QUANTITY

The trail-blazing discoveries about the nature of energy in the 19th century caused the first technological revolution, when manual labor was replaced on a large scale by technological appliances — machines which could convert energy. In the same way, knowledge concerning the nature of information in our time initiated the second technological revolution where mental "labor" is saved through the use of technological appliances — namely, data processing machines. The concept "information" is not only of prime importance for informatics theories and communication techniques, but it is a fundamental quantity in such wide-ranging sciences as cybernetics, linguistics, biology, history, and theology. Many scientists therefore justly regard information as the third fundamental entity alongside matter and energy.

Claude E. Shannon was the first researcher who tried to define information mathematically. The theory based on his findings had the advantages that different methods of communication could be compared and that their performance could be evaluated. In addition, the introduction of the bit as a unit of information made it possible to describe the storage requirements of information quantitatively. The main disadvantage of Shannon's definition of information is that the actual contents and impact of messages were not investigated. Shannon's theory of information, which describes information from a statistical viewpoint only, is discussed fully in the appendix (chapter

A1).

The true nature of information will be discussed in detail in the following chapters, and statements will be made about information and the laws of nature. After a thorough analysis of the information concept, it will be shown that the fundamental theorems can be applied to all technological and biological systems and also to all communication systems, including such diverse forms as the gyrations of bees and the message of the Bible. There is only one prerequisite — namely, that the information must be in coded form.

Since the concept of information is so complex that it cannot be defined in one statement (see Figure 12), we will proceed as follows: We will formulate various special theorems which will gradually reveal more information about the "nature" of information, until we eventually arrive at a precise definition (compare chapter 5). Any repetitions found in the contents of some theorems (redundance) is intentional, and the possibility of having various different formulations according to theorem N8 (paragraph 2.3), is also employed.

3.2 INFORMATION: A MATERIAL OR A MENTAL QUANTITY?

We have indicated that Shannon's definition of information encompasses only a very minor aspect of information. Several authors have repeatedly pointed out this defect, as the following quotations show:

> Karl Steinbuch, a German information scientist [S11]: "The classical theory of information can be compared to the statement that one kilogram of gold has the same value as one kilogram of sand."
>
> Warren Weaver, an American information scientist [S7]: "Two messages, one of which is heavily loaded with meaning and the other which is pure nonsense, can be exactly equivalent . . . as regards information."
>
> Ernst von Weizsäcker [W3]: "The reason for the 'uselessness' of Shannon's theory in the different sciences is frankly that no science can limit itself to its syntactic level."[6]
>
> The essential aspect of each and every piece of information

---

6. Many authors erroneously elevate Shannon's information theory to the syntactic level. This is, however, not justified in the light of appendix A1, since it comprises only the statistical aspects of a message, without regard to syntactic rules.

is its mental content, and not the number of letters used. If one disregards the contents, then Jean Cocteau's facetious remark is relevant: "The greatest literary work of art is basically nothing but a scrambled alphabet."

At this stage we want to point out a fundamental fallacy that has already caused many misunderstandings and has led to seriously erroneous conclusions, namely the assumption that information is a material phenomenon. The philosophy of materialism is fundamentally predisposed to relegate information to the material domain, as is apparent from philosophical articles emanating from the former DDR (East Germany) [S8 for example]. Even so, the former East German scientist J. Peil [P2] writes: "Even the biology based on a materialistic philosophy, which discarded all vitalistic and metaphysical components, did not readily accept the reduction of biology to physics. . . . Information is neither a physical nor a chemical principle like energy and matter, even though the latter are required as carriers."

Also, according to a frequently quoted statement by the American mathematician Norbert Wiener (1894–1964) information cannot be a physical entity [W5]: "Information is information, neither matter nor energy. Any materialism which disregards this, will not survive one day."

Werner Strombach, a German information scientist of Dortmund [S12], emphasizes the nonmaterial nature of information by defining it as an "enfolding of order at the level of contemplative cognition."

The German biologist G. Osche [O3] sketches the unsuitability of Shannon's theory from a biological viewpoint, and also emphasizes the nonmaterial nature of information: "While matter and energy are the concerns of physics, the description of biological phenomena typically involves information in a functional capacity. In cybernetics, the general information concept quantitatively expresses the information content of a given set of symbols by employing the probability distribution of all possible permutations of the symbols. But the information content of biological systems (genetic information) is concerned with its 'value' and its 'functional meaning,' and thus with the semantic aspect of information, with its quality."

Hans-Joachim Flechtner, a German cyberneticist, referred to the fact that information is of a mental nature, both because of its contents and because of the encoding process. This aspect is, however, frequently underrated [F3]: "When a message is composed, it involves the coding of its mental content, but the message itself is not concerned about whether the contents are important or unimportant, valuable, useful, or meaningless. Only the recipient can evaluate the message after decoding it."

3.3 INFORMATION: NOT A PROPERTY OF MATTER!

It should now be clear that information, being a fundamental entity, cannot be a property of matter, and its origin cannot be explained in terms of material processes. We therefore formulate the following fundamental theorem:

> **Theorem 1:** The fundamental quantity information is a non-material (mental) entity. It is not a property of matter, so that purely material processes are fundamentally precluded as sources of information.

Figure 8 illustrates the known fundamental entities — mass, energy, and information. Mass and energy are undoubtedly of a material-physical nature, and for both of them important conservation laws play a significant role in physics and chemistry and in all derived applied sciences. Mass and energy are linked by means of Einstein's equivalence formula, $E = m \times c^2$. In the left part of Figure 8, some of the many chemical and physical properties of matter in all its forms are illustrated, together with the defined units. The right hand part of Figure 8 illustrates nonmaterial properties and quantities, where information, I, belongs.

What is the causative factor for the existence of information? What prompts us to write a letter, a postcard, a note of felicitation, a diary, or a comment in a file? The most important prerequisite is our own volition, or that of a supervisor. In analogy to the material side, we now introduce a fourth fundamental entity, namely "will" (volition), W. Information and volition are closely linked, but this relationship cannot be expressed in a formula, because both are of a nonmaterial (mental, intellectual, spiritual) nature. The connecting arrows indicate the following: Information is always based on the will of a sender who issues the information. It is a variable quantity depending on intentional conditions. Will itself is also not constant, but can in its turn be influenced by the information received from another sender. Conclusion:

Theorem 2: Information only arises through an intentional, volitional act.

It is clear from Figure 8 that the nonmaterial entity, information, can influence the material quantities. Electrical, mechanical, or chemical quantities can be steered, controlled, utilized, or optimized by means of intentional information. The strategy for achieving such control is always based on information, whether it is a cybernetic manufacturing technique, instructions for building an economical car, or the utilization of electricity for driving a machine. In the first

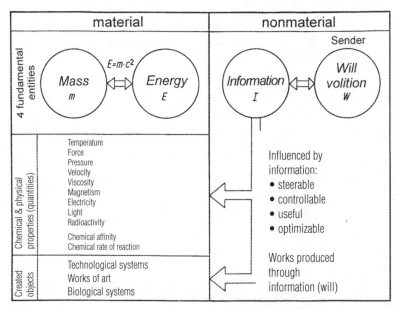

Figure 8: The four fundamental entities are mass and energy (material) and information and will (nonmaterial). Mass and energy comprise the fundamental quantities of the physical world; they are linked through the well-known Einstein equation, $E = m \times c^2$. On the nonmaterial side we also have two fundamental entities, namely information and volition, which are closely linked. Information can be stored in physical media and used to steer, control, and optimize material processes. All created systems originate through information. A creative source of information is always linked to the volitional intent of a person; this fact demonstrates the nonmaterial nature of information.

place, there must be the intention to solve a problem, followed by a conceptual construct for which the information may be coded in the form of a program, a technical drawing, or a description, etc. The next step is then to implement the concept. All technological systems as well as all constructed objects, from pins to works of art, have been produced by means of information. None of these artifacts came into existence through some form of self-organization of matter, but all of them were preceded by establishing the required information. We can now conclude that information was present in the beginning, as the title of this book states.

Theorem 3: Information comprises the nonmaterial foundation for all technological systems and for all works of art.

What is the position in regard to biological systems? Does theorem 3 also hold for such systems, or is there some restriction? If we could successfully formulate the theorems in such a way that they are valid as laws of nature, then they would be universally valid according to the essential characteristics of the laws of nature, N2, N3, and N4.

CHAPTER 4 The Five Levels of the
Information Concept

Figure 9 is a picture of icons cut in stone as they appear in the graves of pharaohs and on obelisks of ancient Egypt. The question is whether these pictures represent information or not. So let us check them against the three necessary conditions (NC) for identifying information (discussed in more detail in paragraph 4.2):

NC 1: A number of symbols are required to establish information. This first condition is satisfied because we have various different symbols like an owl, water waves, a mouth, reeds, etc.

NC 2: The sequence of the symbols must be irregular. This condition is also satisfied, as there are no regularities or periodic patterns.

Figure 9:
Egyptian hieroglyphics.

NC 3: The symbols must be written in some recognizable order, such as drawn, printed, chiseled, or engraved in rows, columns, circles, or spirals. In this example, the symbols appear in columns.

It now seems possible that the given sequence of symbols might comprise information because all three conditions are met, but it could also be possible that the Egyptians simply loved to decorate their monuments. They could have decorated their walls with hieroglyphics,[7] just like we often hang carpets on walls. The true nature of these symbols remained a secret for 15 centuries because nobody could assign meanings to them.

This situation changed when one of Napoleon's men discovered a piece of black basalt near the town of Rosetta on the Nile in July 1799. This flat stone was the size of an ordinary dinner plate and it was exceptional because it contained inscriptions in three languages: 54 lines of Greek, 32 lines of Demotic, and 14 lines of hieroglyphics. The total of 1,419 hieroglyphic symbols includes 166 different ones, and there are 468 Greek words. This stone, known as the Rosetta Stone (Figure 10),

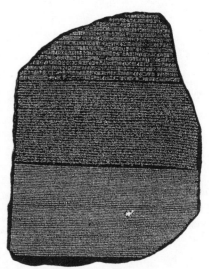

Figure 10: The Rosetta Stone.

is now in the possession of the British Museum in London. It played a key role in the deciphering of hieroglyphics, and its first success was the translation of an Egyptian pictorial text in 1822.[8]

Because the meaning of the entire text was found, it was established that the hieroglyphics really represented information. Today, the meanings of the hieroglyphic symbols are known, and anybody who knows this script is able to translate ancient Egyptian texts. Since

7. Greek *hierós* = sacred; *glyptós* = chiselled, cut; *glyphike téchne* = the art of carving (in stone); *hieroglyphiká* = sacred writing signs of ancient Egyptian pictorial writing.

8. Decoding of hieroglyphics: The Greek text was easy to read and to translate, and already in Cairo it was found to be an homage to King Ptolemy inscribed by

Besser ist ein Scheffel, den dir Gott gibt, als 5000 in Unrecht.

Halte deine Zunge frei von böser Rede, dann machst du dich bei
den Leuten beliebt.

Hüte dich, einen Elenden zu berauben und einem Schwachen
Gewalt anzutun.

Figure 11: A computer printout of some proverbs (in German) translated into hieroglyphics. Translation of the German text: It is better to receive one helping from God, than 5,000 dishonestly. Do not speak evil, then you will be loved by everybody. Take care that you do not rob a distressed person, nor do violence to somebody in poor health.

the meaning of the codes is known, it is now possible to transcribe English text into hieroglyphics, as is shown in Figure 11, where the corresponding symbols have been produced by means of a computer/plotter system.

This illustrative example has now clarified some basic principles about the nature of information. Further details follow.

---

priests of Memphis in the year 196 B.C. With the obvious assumption that the contents of all three texts were identical, it appeared to be possible to decipher the pictorial writing, symbol by symbol. This assumption proved to be correct, but the decoding process took quite some time, since a 1,400-year-old presupposition stood in the way. Horapollon, an Egyptian living in the fourth century, described hieroglyphics as being a purely pictorial script, as it indeed seemed to be. But this assumption resulted in some grotesque findings. When studying the Demotic text, a Swedish linguist, Åkerblad, recognized all the proper names appearing in the Greek version, as well as the words for "temple" and "Greeks." Subsequently, Thomas Young, a medical physicist, recognized the names Berenice and Cleopatra in the cartouches (the symbol groups appearing in the ovals in the sixth line from the top in Figure 10). Instead of looking for pictorial symbols, Young boldly suggested that the pictures were phonetic symbols representing sounds or letters. But he was just as reluctant as everybody else to pursue this idea — another example of the inhibiting effect that presuppositions have on the truth. The eventual breakthrough was made by the French founder of Egyptology, Jean Francois Champollion (1790–1832). He correlated single hieroglyphic symbols with the corresponding Greek letters appearing in the names Ptolemy and Cleopatra, and could then begin with the deciphering.

4.1 THE LOWEST LEVEL OF INFORMATION: STATISTICS

When considering a book B, a computer program C, or the human genome (the totality of genes), we first discuss the following questions:

- How many letters, numbers, and words make up the entire text?
- How many single letters does the employed alphabet contain (e. g. a, b, c . . . z, or G, C, A, T)?
- How frequently do certain letters and words occur?

To answer these questions, it is immaterial whether we are dealing with actual meaningful text, with pure nonsense, or with random sequences of symbols or words. Such investigations are not concerned with the contents, but only with statistical aspects. These topics all belong to the first and lowest level of information, namely the level of statistics.

As explained fully in appendix A1, Shannon's theory of information is suitable for describing the statistical aspects of information, e.g., those quantitative properties of languages which depend on frequencies. Nothing can be said about the meaningfulness or not of any given sequence of symbols. The question of grammatical correctness is also completely excluded at this level. Conclusions:

Definition 1: According to Shannon's theory, any random sequence of symbols is regarded as information, without regard to its origin or whether it is meaningful or not.

Definition 2: The statistical information content of a sequence of symbols is a quantitative concept, measured in bits (binary digits).

According to Shannon's definition, the information content of a single message (which could be one symbol, one sign, one syllable, or a single word) is a measure of the probability of its being received correctly. Probabilities range from 0 to 1, so that this measure is always positive. The information content of a number of messages (signs for example) is found by adding the individual probabilities as required by the condition of summability. An important property of information according to Shannon is:

Theorem 4: A message which has been subject to interference or "noise," in general comprises more information than an error-free message.

This theorem follows from the larger number of possible alternatives in a distorted message, and Shannon states that the information content of a message increases with the number of symbols (see equation 6 in appendix A1). It is obvious that the actual information content cannot at all be described in such terms, as should be clear from the following example: When somebody uses many words to say practically nothing, this message is accorded a large information content because of the large number of letters used. If somebody else, who is really knowledgeable, concisely expresses the essentials, his message has a much lower information content.

Some quotations concerning this aspect of information are: French President Charles De Gaulle (1890–1970), "The ten commandments are so concise and plainly intelligible because they were compiled without first having a commission of inquiry." Another philosopher said, "There are about 35 million laws on earth to validate the ten commandments." A certain representative in the American Congress concluded, "The Lord's Prayer consists of 56 words, and the Ten Commandments contain 297 words. The Declaration of Independence contains 300 words, but the recently published ordinance about the price of coal comprises no fewer than 26,911 words."

Theorem 5: Shannon's definition of information exclusively concerns the statistical properties of sequences of symbols; meaning is completely ignored.

It follows that this concept of information is unsuitable for evaluating the information content of meaningful sequences of symbols. We now realize that an appreciable extension of Shannon's information theory is required to significantly evaluate information and information processing in both living and inanimate systems. The concept of information and the five levels required for a complete description are illustrated in Figure 12. This diagram can be regarded as a nonverbal description of information. In the following greatly extended description and definition, where real information is concerned, Shannon's theory is only useful for describing the statistical level (see chapter 5).

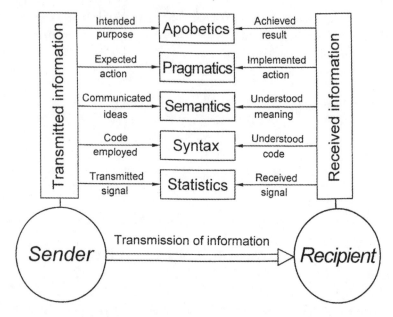

Figure 12: The five aspects of information. A complete characterization of the information concept requires all five aspects — statistics, syntax, semantics, pragmatics, and apobetics, which are essential for both the sender and the recipient. Information originates as a language; it is first formulated, and then transmitted or stored. An agreed-upon alphabet comprising individual symbols (code), is used to compose words. Then the (meaningful) words are arranged in sentences according to the rules of the relevant grammar (syntax), to convey the intended meaning (semantics). It is obvious that the information concept also includes the expected/implemented action (pragmatics), and the intended/achieved purpose (apobetics).

4.2 THE SECOND LEVEL OF INFORMATION: SYNTAX

When considering the book B mentioned earlier, it is obvious that the letters do not appear in random sequences. Combinations like "the," "car," "father," etc. occur frequently, but we do not find other possible combinations like "xcy," "bkaln," or "dwust." In other words:

• Only certain combinations of letters are allowed (agreed-upon) English words. Other conceivable combinations do not belong to the language. It is also not a random process when words are arranged in sentences; the rules of grammar must be adhered to.

Both the construction of words and the arrangement of words in sentences to form information-bearing sequences of symbols, are subject to quite specific rules based on deliberate conventions[9] for each and every language.

> **Definition 3:** Syntax is meant to include all structural properties of the process of setting up information. At this second level, we are only concerned with the actual sets of symbols (codes) and the rules governing the way they are assembled into sequences (grammar and vocabulary) independent of any meaning they may or may not have.

Note: It has become clear that this level consists of two parts, namely:

A) Code: Selection of the set of symbols used.
B) The syntax proper: inter-relationships among the symbols.

A) The Code: The System of Symbols Used for Setting Up Information

A set of symbols is required for the representation of information at the syntax level. Most written languages use letters, but a very wide range of conventions exists: Morse code, hieroglyphics, international flag codes, musical notes, various data processing codes, genetic codes, figures made by gyrating bees, pheromones (scents) released by insects, and hand signs used by deaf-mute persons.

Several questions are relevant: What code should be used? How many symbols are available? What criteria are used for constructing the code? What mode of transmission is suitable? How could we determine whether an unknown system is a code or not?

The number of symbols: The number of different symbols q, employed by a coding system, can vary greatly, and depends strongly on the purpose and the application. In computer technology, only two switch positions are recognized, so that binary codes were created which are comprised of only two different symbols. Quaternary codes, comprised of four different symbols, are involved in all living organisms. The reason why four symbols represent an optimum in this case is

---

9. In the case of all artificial and formal languages these conventions were laid down deliberately. The origin of natural languages is discussed in appendix A2, "Origin of Languages."

discussed in chapter 6. The various alphabet systems used by different languages consist of from 20 to 35 letters, and this number of letters is sufficient for representing all the sounds of the language concerned. Chinese writing is not based on elementary sounds, but pictures are employed, every one of which represents a single word, so that the number of different symbols is very large. Some examples of coding systems with the required number of symbols are:

- Binary code (q = 2 symbols, all electronic DP codes)
- Ternary code (q = 3, not used)
- Quaternary code (q = 4, e.g., the genetic code consisting of four letters: A, C, G, T)
- Quinary code (q = 5)
- Octal code (q = 8 octal digits: 0, 1, 2, . . . , 7)
- Decimal code (q = 10 decimal digits: 0, 1, 2, . . . , 9)
- Hexadecimal code[10] (q = 16 HD digits: 0, 1, 2, . . . , E, F)
- Hebrew alphabet (q = 22 letters)
- Greek alphabet (q = 24 letters)
- Latin alphabet (q = 26 letters: A, B, C, . . . , X, Y, Z)
- Braille (q = 26 letters)
- International flag code (q = 26 different flags)
- Russian alphabet (q = 32 Cyrillic letters)
- Japanese Katakana writing (q = 50 symbols representing different syllables)
- Chinese writing (q > 50,000 symbols)
- Hieroglyphics (in the time of Ptolemy: q = 5,000 to 7,000; Middle Kingdom, 12th Dynasty: q = approximately 800)

Criteria for selecting a code: Coding systems are not created arbitrarily, but they are optimized according to criteria depending on their use, as is shown in the following examples:

• Pictorial appeal (e.g., hieroglyphics and pictograms)
• Small number of symbols (e.g., Braille, cuneiform script, binary code, and genetic code)

---

10. Hexadecimal system: This is used for representing numbers with base 16 and the word is a hybrid derived from both Greek and Latin: Greek hexa = 6, Latin decem = 10. Another more suitable word is sedecimal (Latin sedecim = 16), or "hexadecadic" from the Greek word for 16.

- Speed of writing (e.g., shorthand)
- Ease of writing (e.g., cuneiform)
- Ease of sensing (e.g., Braille)
- Ease of transmission (e.g., Morse code)
- Technological legibility (e.g., universal product codes and postal bar codes)
- Ease of detecting errors (e.g., special error detecting codes)
- Ease of correcting errors (e.g., Hamming code and genetic code)
- Ease of visualizing tones (musical notes)
- Representation of the sounds of natural languages (alphabets)
- Redundance for counteracting interference errors (various computer codes and natural languages; written German has, for example, a redundancy of 66 %)
- Maximization of storage density (genetic code)

The choice of code depends on the mode of communication. If a certain mode of transmission has been adopted for technological reasons depending on some physical or chemical phenomenon or other, then the code must comply with the relevant requirements. In addition, the ideas of the sender and the recipient must be in tune with one another to guarantee certainty of transmission and reception (see Figures 14 and 15). The most complex setups of this kind are again found in living systems. Various existing types of special message systems are reviewed below:

- Acoustic transmission (conveyed by means of sounds):
  - Natural spoken languages used by humans
  - Mating and warning calls of animals (e.g., songs of birds and whales)
  - Mechanical transducers (e.g., loudspeakers, sirens, and fog horns)
  - Musical instruments (e.g., piano and violin)

- Optical transmission (carried by light waves):
  - Written languages
  - Technical drawings (e.g., for constructing machines and buildings, and electrical circuit diagrams)
  - Technical flashing signals (e.g., identifying flashes of lighthouses)
  - Flashing signals produced by living organisms (e.g., fireflies and luminous fishes)
  - Flag signals

- Punched cards, mark sensing
- Universal product code, postal bar codes
- hand movements, as used by deaf-mute persons, for example
- body language (e.g., mating dances and aggressive stances of animals)
- facial expressions and body movements (e.g., mime, gesticulation, and deaf-mute signs)
- dancing motions (bee gyrations)

• Tactile transmission (Latin tactilis = sense of touch) (signals: physical contact):
- Braille writing
- Musical rolls, barrel of barrel-organ

• Magnetic transmission (carrier: magnetic field):
- magnetic tape
- magnetic disk
- magnetic card

• Electrical transmission (carrier: electrical current or electromagnetic waves):
- telephone
- radio and TV

• Chemical transmission (carrier: chemical compounds):
- genetic code (DNA, chromosomes)
- hormonal system

• Olfactory transmission (Latin olfacere = smelling, employing the sense of smell) (carrier: chemical compounds):
- scents emitted by gregarious insects (pheromones)

• Electro-chemical transmission:
- nervous system

How can a code be recognized? In the case of an unknown system, it is not always easy to decide whether one is dealing with a real code or not. The conditions required for a code are now mentioned and explained, after having initially discussed hieroglyphics as an example. The following are necessary conditions (NC), all three of which must be fulfilled simultaneously for a given set of symbols to be a code:

NC 1: A uniquely defined set of symbols is used.

NC 2: The sequence of the individual symbols must be irregular.

Examples: −.− − −.− * − − * * . − .. −   (aperiodic)
                                                                qrst werb ggtzut

Counter examples:

− − −...− − −...− − −...− − −...   (periodic)
− − − − − − − − − − − − − −   (the same symbol
r r r r r r r r r r r r r r r r r r   constantly repeated)

NC 3: The symbols appear in clearly distinguishable structures (e.g., rows, columns, blocks, or spirals).

In most cases a fourth condition is also required:

NC 4: At least some symbols must occur repeatedly.

Examples: Maguf bitfeg fetgur justig amus telge.
                    Der grüne Apfel fällt vom Baum.
                    The people are living in houses.

It is difficult to construct meaningful sentences without using some letters more than once.[11] Such sentences are often rather grotesque, for example:

Get nymph; quiz sad brow; fix luck (i, u used twice, j, v omitted).

---

11. Pangrams: A pangram is a sentence comprising all the letters of the alphabet, where each letter is used once only. No such sentence is known in German; it should contain exactly 30 letters: a, b, c, . . . , z, as well as ß, ä, ö, and ü. Sentences comprised of a few more than 30 letters have been constructed, but they are often rather artificial.

   Examples of English sentences which contain all 26 letters, but with some letters repeated, are:
   – How quickly daft jumping zebras vex. (30 letters)
   – The five boxing wizards jump quickly. (31 letters)
   – Pack my box with five dozen liquor jugs. (32 letters)
   – The quick brown fox jumps over a lazy dog. (33 letters)
   A German example:
   – Quer vorm Jagdplatz mixt Baby Klöße für Schwäne. (40 letters)
   A French example:
   – Voyez le brick geant que j'examine près du wharf. (39 letters)

In a competition held by the Society for the German Language, long single words with no repetitions of letters were submitted. The winner, comprised of 24 letters, was: Heizölrückstoßabdämpfung (Note that a and ä for example, are regarded as different letters because they represent different sounds.)

There is only one sufficient condition (SC) for establishing whether a given set of symbols is a code:

> SC 1: It can be decoded successfully and meaningfully (e.g., hieroglyphics and the genetic code).

There are also sufficient conditions for showing that we are NOT dealing with a code system. A sequence of symbols cannot be a code, if:

a) it can be explained fully on the level of physics and chemistry, i.e., when its origin is exclusively of a material nature. Example: The periodic signals received in 1967 by the British astronomers J. Bell and A. Hewish, were thought to be coded messages from space sent by "little green men." It was, however, eventually established that this "message" had a purely physical origin, and a new type of star was discovered: pulsars.

or

b) it is known to be a random sequence (e.g., when its origin is known or communicated). This conclusion also holds when the sequence randomly contains valid symbols from any other code.

Example 1: Randomly generated characters: AZTIG KFD MAUER DFK KLIXA WIFE TSAA. Although the German word "MAUER" and the word "WIFE" may be recognized, this is not a code according to our definition, because we know that it is a random sequence.

Example 2: In the Kornberg synthesis (1955) a DNA polymerazae resulted when an enzyme reacted with Coli bacteria. After a considerable time, two kinds of strings were found:

1) alternating strings:

    ... TATATATATATATATATATATATAT ...
    ... ATATATATATATATATATATATATA ...

2) homopolymere strings:

... GGGGGGGGGGGGGGGGGGGGGGGG ...
... CCCCCCCCCCCCCCCCCCCCCCCC ...

Although both types of strings together contained all the symbols employed in the genetic code, they were nevertheless devoid of information, since necessary condition (NC) 2 is not fulfilled.

The fundamentals of the "code" theme were already established by the author in the out-of-print book having the same name as the present one [G5, German title: *Am Anfang war die Information*]. A code always represents a mental concept and, according to our experience, its assigned meaning always depends on some convention. It is thus possible to determine at the code level already whether any given system originated from a creative mental concept or not.

We are now in a position to formulate some fundamental empirical theorems:[12]

Theorem 6: A code is an essential requirement for establishing information.

Theorem 7: The allocation of meanings to the set of available symbols is a mental process depending on convention.[13]

Theorem 8: If a code has been defined by a deliberate convention, it must be strictly adhered to afterward.

12. The German system of postal codes: theorems 6 to 11, can be illustrated in the case of the well-known postal code system. A five-figure numerical system was introduced in Germany in July 1993. The country was divided into 26,400 delivery zones. Large mail users who received more than 2,000 postal articles per day, were given their own numbers, and 16,500 postal codes were allocated to post box clients. The first digit identifies the region (e.g., 1 for the Berlin area, 2 Hamburg, and 8 München) and the second digit usually indicates a major city. Digits 3 to 5 then identify the local postal zone. A team of experts, being the sender, allocated the available numbers (theorem 7). According to theorem 9, these codes must be known to both the sender and the recipient, and to achieve this, the most massive printing effort in history produced 40 million postal code directories, each having 1,000 pages and weighing about 4.5 pounds (2 kg). These were then made available to all households. The coding system was established after comprehensive consultation (it had to be well designed, and it was a mental process as required by theorem 11).

13. Mental process, intelligent inventor: It should be emphasized that matter as such is unable to generate any code. All experiences indicate that a thinking being voluntarily exercising his own free will, cognition, and creativity is required. Helmut Gipper, a German linguist, defined thought as follows [G3, p 261]: "The mental activity of a living being can be regarded as thought when he succeeds in saving and in a practical way employing empirical data obtained

Theorem 9: If the information is to be understood, the particular code must be known to both the sender and the recipient.

Theorem 10: According to Theorem 6, only structures which are based on a code can represent information. This is a necessary but not sufficient condition for the establishment of information.

Theorem 11: A code system is always the result of a mental process (see footnote 14) (it requires an intelligent origin or inventor).

The expression "rejoice" appears in different languages and coding systems in Figure 13. This leads to another important empirical theorem:

Theorem 12: Any given piece of information can be represented by any selected code.

Comment: Theorem 12 does not state that a complete translation is always possible. It is an art to suitably translate and express metaphors, twists of logic, ambiguities, and special figurative styles into the required language.

It is possible to formulate fundamental principles of information even at the relatively low level of codes by means of the above theorems. If, for example, one finds a code underlying any given system, then one can conclude that the system had a mental origin. In the case of the hieroglyphics, nobody suggested that they were caused by a purely physical process like random mechanical effects, wind, or erosion; Theorem 11 is thus validated.

The following is a brief list of some properties common to all coding systems:

---

through his senses, as made possible by his biological capabilities and the structure of his brain. He should also be able to freely organize the data in the form of if-then relationships, derive simple conclusions, and find solutions to problems. Thought should thus not be confused with the instinctive abilities of animals which have no freedom to make decisions. Freedom of choice is pre-supposed. Neither the weaving of their webs by spiders, nor the construction of honeycombs by bees or their so-called 'gyration language' has anything to do with cognition, however complex, meaningful, and marvelous these abilities may be. These instinctive acts are fixed, allowing no or only minor variation in the framework provided."

- A code is a necessary prerequisite for establishing and storing information.
- Every choice of code must be well thought out beforehand in the conceptual stage.
- Devising a code is a creative mental process.
- Matter can be a carrier of codes, but it cannot generate any codes.

B) The Actual Syntax

Definition 4: The actual syntax describes the construction of sentences and phrases, as well as the structural media required for their formation. The set of possible sentences of a language is defined by means of a formalized or formalizable assemblage of rules. This comprises the morphology, phonetics, and vocabulary of the language.

The following questions are relevant:

გიხაⴌⴌცⴌ6

أفرحوا

Радуйтесь

džiaukitės

örüljetek

verbly julle

rejoice

Figure 13: Different codes expressing the same meaning. The word "rejoice" is represented by means of a selection of different coding systems: Georgian, Arabic, Russian, Lithuanian, Hungarian, Czech, and English (Braille, Morse code, shorthand).

a) Concerning the sender:
  – Which of the possible combinations of symbols are actual defined words of the language (lexicon and notation)?
  – How should the words be arranged (construction of the sentences, word placement, and stylistics), linked with one another, and be inflected to form a sentence (grammar)?
  – What language should be used for this information?
  – Which special modes of expression are used (stylistics, aesthetics, precision of expression, and formalisms)?
  – Are the sentences syntactically correct?

b) Concerning the recipient:
  – Does the recipient understand the language? (Understanding the contents is not yet relevant.)

The following two sample sentences illustrate the syntax level once again:

A: The bird singed the song.
B: The green freedom prosecuted the cerebrating house.

Sentence B is perfectly correct syntactically, but it is semantically meaningless. In contrast, the semantics of sentence A is acceptable, but its syntax is erroneous.

By the syntax of a language is meant all the rules which describe how individual language elements could and should be combined. The syntax of natural languages is much more complex (see appendix A2) than that of formal artificial languages. The syntactic rules of an artificial language must be complete and unambiguous because, for example, a compiler program which translates written programs into computer code cannot call the programmer to clarify semantic issues.

Knowledge of the conventions applying to the actual encoding as well as to the allocation of meanings is equally essential for both the sender and the recipient. This knowledge is either transferred directly (e.g., by being introduced into a computer system or by being inherited in the case of natural systems), or it must be learned from scratch (e.g., mother tongue or any other natural language).

No person enters this world with the inherited knowledge of some language or some conceptual system. Knowledge of a language is acquired by learning the applicable vocabulary and grammar as they have been established in the conventions of the language concerned.

4.3 THE THIRD LEVEL OF INFORMATION: SEMANTICS

When we read the previously mentioned book B, we are not interested in statistics about the letters, neither are we concerned with the actual grammar, but we are interested in the meaning of the contents. Symbol sequences and syntactic rules are essential for the representation of information, but the essential characteristic of the conveyed information is not the selected code, neither is it the size, number, or form of the letters, or the method of transmission (in writing, or as optical, acoustic, electrical, tactile or olfactory signals), but it is the message being conveyed, the conclusions, and the meanings (semantics). This central aspect of information plays no role in storage and transmission, since the cost of a telegram, for example, does not depend on the importance of the message, but only on the number of letters or words. Both the sender and the recipient are mainly interested in the meaning; it is the meaning that changes a sequence of symbols into information. So now we have arrived at the third level of information, the semantic level (Greek *semantikós* = characteristic, significance, aspect of meaning).

Typical semantic questions are:

a) Concerning the sender:
   - What are the thoughts in the sender's mind?
   - What meaning is contained in the information being formulated?
   - What information is implied in addition to the explicit information?
   - What means are employed for conveying the information (metaphors, idioms, or parables)?

b) Concerning the recipient:
   - Does the recipient understand the information?
   - What background information is required for understanding the transmitted information?
   - Is the message true or false?
   - Is the message meaningful?

Theorem 13: Any piece of information has been transmitted by somebody and is meant for somebody. A sender and a recipient are always involved whenever and wherever information is concerned.

Comment: Many kinds of information are directed to one single recipient (like a letter) and others are aimed at very many recipients (e.g., a book, or newspaper). In exceptional cases, the information never reaches the recipient (e.g., a letter lost in the mail).

It is only at the semantic level that we really have meaningful information, thus we may establish the following theorem:

Theorem 14: Any entity, to be accepted as information, must entail semantics; it must be meaningful.

Semantics is an essential aspect of information, because the meaning is the only invariant property. The statistical and syntactical properties can be altered appreciably when information is represented in another language (e.g., translated into Chinese), but the meaning does not change.

Meanings always represent mental concepts, therefore we have:

Theorem 15: When its progress along the chain of transmission events is traced backward, every piece of information leads to a mental source, the mind of the sender.

Sequences of letters generated by various kinds of statistical processes are shown in Figure 38 (appendix A1.5). The programs used for this purpose were partially able to reproduce some of the syntactic properties of the language, but in the light of Theorems 16 and 17 these sequences of letters do not represent information. The next theorem enables one to distinguish between information and non-information:

Theorem 16: If a chain of symbols comprises only a statistical sequence of characters, it does not represent information.

Information is essentially linked to a sender (a mental source of information) according to Theorems 13 and 15. This result is independent of whether the recipient understands the information or not. When researchers studied Egyptian obelisks, the symbols were seen as information long before they were deciphered, because it was obvious that they could not have resulted from random processes. The meaning of the hieroglyphics could not be understood by any contemporaries (recipients) before the Rosetta Stone was found in

1799, but even so, it was regarded as information. The same holds for the gyrations of bees which were only understood by humans after being deciphered by Karl von Frisch. In contrast, the genetic code is still mostly unknown, except for the code allocations between the triplets and the amino acids.

All suitable ways of expressing meanings (mental substrates, thoughts, or nonmaterial contents of consciousness) are called languages. Information can be transmitted or stored in material media only when a language is available. The information itself is totally invariant in regard to the transmission system (acoustic, optical, or electrical) as well as the system of storage (brain, book, data processing system, or magnetic tape). This invariance is the result of its nonmaterial nature. There are different kinds of languages:

1. Natural languages used for communication: at present there are approximately 5,100 living languages on earth.
2. Artificial communication languages and languages used for signaling: Esperanto, deaf-mute languages, flag codes, and traffic signs.
3. Formal artificial languages: logical and mathematical calculi, chemical symbols, musical notation, algorithmic languages, programming languages like Ada, Algol, APL, BASIC, C, C++, Fortran, Pascal, and PL/1.
4. Special technical languages: building and construction plans, block diagrams, diagrams depicting the structure of chemical compounds, and electrical, hydraulic, and pneumatic circuit diagrams.
5. Special languages found in living organisms: genetic languages, bee gyrations, pheromonal languages of various insects, hormonal languages, signaling systems in the webs of spiders, the language of dolphins, and instincts (e.g., the migration routes of birds, salmon, and eels). As is explained in appendix A2, the latter examples should rather be regarded as communication systems.

A common property of all languages is that defined sets of symbols are used, and that definite agreed-upon rules and meanings are allocated to the single signs or language elements. Every language consists of units like morphemes, lexemes, expressions, and entire sentences (in natural languages), that serve as carriers of meaning (formatives). Meanings are internally assigned to the formatives of a language, and both the sender and the recipient should be in accord about these meanings. The following can be employed for encoding meanings in natural languages: morphology, syntax (grammar and stylistics), phonetics, intonation, and gesticulation, as well as numerous other supplementary aids like homonyms, homophones, metaphors, synonyms, polysemes, antonyms, paraphrasing, anomalies, metonymy, and irony, etc.

Every communication process between sender and recipient consists of formulating and understanding the sememes (Greek sema = sign) in one and the same language. In the formulation process, the information to be transmitted is generated in a suitable language in the mind of the sender. In the comprehension process, the symbol combinations are analyzed by the recipient and converted into the corresponding ideas. It is universally accepted that the sender and the recipient are both intelligent beings, or that a particular system must have been created by an intelligent being (Figures 23 and 24, chapter 7).

4.4 THE FOURTH LEVEL OF INFORMATION: PRAGMATICS

Let us again consider book B mentioned initially to help us understand the nature of the next level. There is a Russian saying that "The effect of words can last one hour, but a book serves as a perpetual reminder." Books can have lasting effects. After one has read a software manual, for example, one can use the described system. Many people who read the Bible are moved to act in entirely new ways. In this regard, Blaise Pascal said, "There are enough passages in Scripture to comfort people in all spheres of life, and there are enough passages that can horrify them." Information always leads to some action, although, for our purposes, it is immaterial whether the recipient acts according to the sender's wishes, responds negatively, or ignores it. It often happens that even a concise but striking promotional slogan for a washing powder can result in a preference for that brand.

Up to the semantic level, the purpose the sender has with the transmitted information is not considered. Every transmission of information indicates that the sender has some purpose in mind for the recipient. In order to achieve the intended result, the sender describes the actions required of the recipient to bring him to implement the desired purpose. We have now reached an entirely new level of information, called pragmatics (Greek *pragmatike* = the art of doing the right thing; taking action).

Some examples of pragmatic aspects are:[14]

a) Concerning the sender:
   – What actions are desired of the recipient?
   – Has a specific action been formulated explicitly, or should it be implicit?
   – Is the action required by the sender to be taken in only one predetermined way, or is there some degree of freedom?

b) Concerning the recipient:
   – To what extent does the received and understood meaning influence the behavior of the recipient?
   – What is the actual response of the recipient?

Theorem 17: Information always entails a pragmatic aspect.

The pragmatic aspect could:

   – be unnegotiable and unambiguous without any degree of freedom, e.g., a computer program, activities in a cell, or a military command;
   – allow a limited freedom of choice, like instinctive acts of animals;
   – allow considerable freedom of action (only in the case of human beings).

Note: Even if there is considerable variation in the pragmatics resulting from the semantics, it does not detract anything from the validity of Theorem 17.

When language is used, it does not simply mean that sentences are jumbled together, but that requests, complaints, questions, instructions,

---

14. Minister for semantics: Former U.S. President Harry S. Truman (1884–1972) once wrote the following facetious circular: "I have recently appointed a Minister for Semantics — a very important portfolio. His task is to provide me with expressions that appear to be heavy with meaning, to teach me how one can say yes and no in one sentence without becoming entangled in contradictions, to work out a word combination which will make me appear to be against inflation in San Francisco, and supporting inflation in New York, and, finally, to show me how one could wrap oneself in silence but still tell all. You will agree that such a man would save me a lot of trouble" (source: *Reader's Digest*, February 1993, p. 168). Truman did not realize that he was actually looking for a Minister for Pragmatics (or even Apobetics). He was mainly concerned with the workings of his mind, but he placed it at least one level too low — on the semantic level.

teachings, warnings, threats, and commands are formulated to coerce the recipient to take some action. Information was defined by Werner Strombach [S12] as a structure which achieves some result in a receiving system. He thus referred to the important aspect of taking action.

We can distinguish two types of action:

a) Fixed:
   – programmed actions (e.g., mechanical manufacturing processes, the operation of data processing programs, construction of biological cells, respiration, blood circulation, and the functioning of organs)
   – instinctive acts (behavior of animals)
   – trained actions (e.g., police dogs, and circus performances involving lions, elephants, horses, bears, tigers, dogs, seals, dolphins, etc.)

b) Flexible and creative:
   – learned activities like social manners and manual skills
   – sensible actions (humans)
   – intuitive actions (humans)
   – intelligent actions based on free will (humans)

All the activities of the recipient can depend on information that has previously been conceptualized by the sender for the intended purpose. On the other hand, intelligent actions that do not derive from a sender are also possible.

A relevant theorem is the following:

> **Theorem 18:** Information is able to cause the recipient to take some action (stimulate, initialize, or implement). This reactive functioning of information is valid for both inanimate systems (e.g., computers or an automatic car wash) as well as living organisms (e.g., activities in cells, actions of animals, and activities of human beings).

4.5 THE FIFTH LEVEL OF INFORMATION: APOBETICS

We consider book B for the last time to illustrate one further level of information. Goethe once said, "Certain books seem to have been written not so much to enable one to learn something, but to show that the author knew something." This reason for writing a book, which is of course not worth emulating, does, however, express something of fundamental importance: The sender has some purpose for the recipient. The purpose of a promotional slogan is that the manufacturing firm can have a good turnover for the year. In the New Testament, John mentions a completely different purpose for his information: "I write these things to you who believe in the name of the Son of God so that you may know that you have eternal life" (1 John 5:13). We conclude that some purpose is pursued whenever information is involved.

We now realize that any piece of information has a purpose, and have come to the last and highest level of information, namely apobetics (the teleological aspect, the question of the purpose; derived from the Greek apobeinon = result, success, conclusion). The term "apobetics" was introduced by the author in 1981 [G4] to conform to the titles of the other four levels. For every result on the side of the recipient there is a corresponding conceptual purpose, plan, or representation in the mind of the sender. The teleological aspect of information is the most important, because it concerns the premeditated purpose of the sender. Any piece of information involves the question: "Why does the sender communicate this information, and what result does he want to achieve for or in the recipient?" The following examples should elucidate this aspect:

- The male bird calls a mate by means of his song, or he establishes his territory.
- Computer programs are written with a purpose (e.g., solution of a set of equations, inversion of matrices, or to manipulate some system).
- The manufacturer of chocolate A uses a promotional slogan to urge the recipient to buy his brand.
- The Creator gave gregarious insects a pheromonal language for the purpose of communication, for example to identify intruders or indicate the location of a new source of food.
- Man was gifted with a natural language; this can be used for communicating with other people, and to formulate purposes.
- God gives us a purpose in life through the Bible; this is discussed more fully in Part 3 of this book.

Examples of questions concerning apobetics, are:

a) Concerning the sender:
- – Has an unambiguous purpose been defined?
- – What purpose is intended for the recipient?
- – Can this purpose be recognized directly, or could it only be deduced indirectly?

b) Concerning the recipient:
- – What purpose is achieved through the actions of the recipient?
- – Does the result obtained in the recipient correspond to the purpose which the sender had in mind?
- – Did the recipient find a purpose which the sender had not intended (e.g., the evaluation of historical documents could serve a purpose which was never thought of by the author)?

The sender's intention can be achieved in various ways by the recipient:

- – completely (doing exactly what the sender requested)
- – partly
- – not at all
- – doing exactly the opposite

The response to an unambiguously formulated purpose (e.g., computer program, commands given personally, or promotional material) could be any one of these different actions. The purpose could, however, not even be mentioned, or could not have been imagined by the sender (e.g., documents with trivial contents surviving from previous centuries which provide researchers with important clues not intended by the original author).

In this case also we can formulate significant empirical theorems:

Theorem 19: Every piece of information is intentional (the teleological aspect).[15]

Theorem 20: The teleological aspect of information is the most important level, since it comprises the intentions of the

15. Information on tombstones: In the sense of Theorem 19 it does not matter whether the originally intended purpose or a different one has been achieved. It should become clear from the following episode that even the information found on tombstones could have a far-reaching effect. Some years ago a Ghanaian professor who visited Braunschweig to complete his doctorate in architecture told me about a cemetery near Accra. The crosses planted on the

sender. The sum total of the four lower levels is that they are only a means for attaining the purpose (apobetics).

Note: The teleological aspect may often overlap and coincide with the pragmatic aspect to a large extent, but it is theoretically always possible to distinguish the two.

Theorem 21: The five aspects of information (statistics, syntax, semantics, pragmatics, and apobetics) are valid for both the sender and the recipient. The five levels are involved in a continuous interplay between the two.

Theorem 22: The separate aspects of information are interlinked in such a way that every lower level is a necessary prerequisite for the realization of the next one above it.

Whenever the teleological aspect is minimized or deliberately ignored, we should be aware of the fact that Theorem 19 is violated. Evolutionary doctrine deliberately denies any purposefulness that might be apparent. In the words of G.G. Simpson, an American zoologist, "Man is the result of a materialistic process having no purpose or intent; he represents the highest fortuitous organizational form of matter and energy."

In this respect, one more theorem is required:

Theorem 23: There is no known natural law through which matter can give rise to information, neither is any phys-

---

graves of the first Christian missionaries are still there, and it is clear from the inscribed dates that they succumbed from tropical diseases within a few days after their arrival. Superficially, it could be said that the efforts of those people were in vain. God ended their lives before they had a chance to proclaim one sentence of the gospel and there were no visible results. But this Ghanaian friend said that he had been moved by the silent witnessing of those crosses to take a decisive step in faith. It became clear to him that God must have blessed those men with so much love that they went out without regard to their own safety to tell others of this love. It is clear that God's way is often different from our expectations. What might appear futile in our time stream, is fruitful and permanent in God's kairos. The purpose of the missionaries was to win Africans for Christ, and after a long time somebody did fulfill this purpose. Now he witnesses for the gospel to many students in his mother tongue. In their hour of death, those missionaries could not have had an inkling that their purpose would eventually be realized.

ical process or material phenomenon known that can do this.

Synopsis: It should be clear that information is a multi-layered concept. Shannon's theory embraces only a very small fraction of the real nature of information, as can easily be ascertained in terms of the five levels that we discussed. Contradictory statements and erroneous conclusions of many authors are a result of discussing information without being clear about the relevant level, nor whether the appropriate level lends itself to wide ranging conclusions. It is, for example, not possible to find answers about the origin of biological systems, when one only considers the statistical level. Even when impressive mathematical formulations are forthcoming, they will bring no clarification if they are restricted to the level of Shannon's theory. Well-founded conclusions are only possible when the sender/recipient problem is treated fully at all five information levels.

All of the Theorems 1 to 23 formulated thus far, as well as Theorems 24 to 30, which will follow, are based on empirical reality. They may thus be regarded as natural laws, since they exhibit the characteristics of natural laws as explained in chapter 2. These theorems have been tested in real situations (compare Theorem N1 in paragraph 2.3). Any natural law can be rejected the moment a single counter example is found, and this also holds for these information theorems. After many talks by the author at colleges and universities, both abroad and at home, no researcher could mention one single counter example. In one case, somebody said that it might be possible that one of these theorems could be negated a few million years in the future, when a counter example may be found. My answer was that it was possible, as in the case of all natural laws. However, even if one or more of the theorems could be nullified by a counter example after a few million years, we still have to accept them and live with them now.

The seven most important results are repeated once more:

- There can be no information without a code.
- Any code is the result of a free and deliberate convention.
- There can be no information without a sender.
- Any given chain of information points to a mental source.
- There can be no information without volition (will).
- There can be no information unless all five hierarchical levels are involved: statistics, syntax, semantics, pragmatics, and apobetics.
- Information cannot originate in statistical processes.

These seven theorems can also be formulated as impossibility theorems, as has been shown in paragraph 2.5 for practically all laws of nature:

- It is impossible to set up, store, or transmit information without using a code.
- It is impossible to have a code apart from a free and deliberate convention.
- It is impossible that information can exist without having had a mental source.
- It is impossible for information to exist without having been established voluntarily by a free will.
- It is impossible for information to exist without all five hierarchical levels — statistics, syntax, semantics, pragmatics, and apobetics.
- It is impossible that information can originate in statistical processes.

We still have to describe a domain of definition for all these theorems; this will be done in the next chapter.

Figure 14 may serve the purpose of ordering the proposed theorems. Three phenomena are represented hierarchically, namely matter, information, and life, with matter at the lowest level. All known natural laws belong here (e.g., conservation of energy, strength of materials, and electric charge). According to Theorem 1, information is not a property of matter, and thus requires a next higher level. All information theorems belong to this level. The highest level is that of life. Natural laws belonging to this level may be called life theorems. A fundamental theorem at this level was formulated by Louis Pasteur (1822–1895), and it has not yet been contradicted by any experiment: "Life can only come from life." The following statements can be made about the three hierarchical levels shown in Figure 14:

- * Information is nonmaterial, but it requires material media for storage and transmission.
- * Information is not life, but the information in cells is essential for all living beings. Information is a necessary prerequisite for life.
- * Life is nonmaterial, and it is not information, but both entities, matter and information, are essential for life.

Because of the philosophical bias, both information and life itself are regarded as purely material phenomena in the evolutionary view. The origin and the nature of life is reduced to physical-chemical causes. In the words of Jean B. de Lamarck (1744–1829), "Life is merely a physical phenomenon. All manifestations of life are based on mechanical, physical, and chemical causes, being properties of organic matter" (*Philosophie Zoologique*, Paris, 1809, Vol. 1, p. 104 f). The German evolutionist Manfred Eigen expressed a similar view [E2, p. 149]: "The logic of life originates in physics and chemistry." His pupil, Bernd-Olaf Küppers, paved the way for molecular Darwinism, but the present author has already responded to this materialistic view [G14, p. 90–92]. All such ideas have in common that biological facts are interwoven with subjective representations which cannot be justified scientifically. The information theorems formulated in this book, should enable the reader to distinguish between truth and folly.

The code systems used for communication in the animal kingdom have not been "invented" by them, but were created fully functional according to Figure 24.

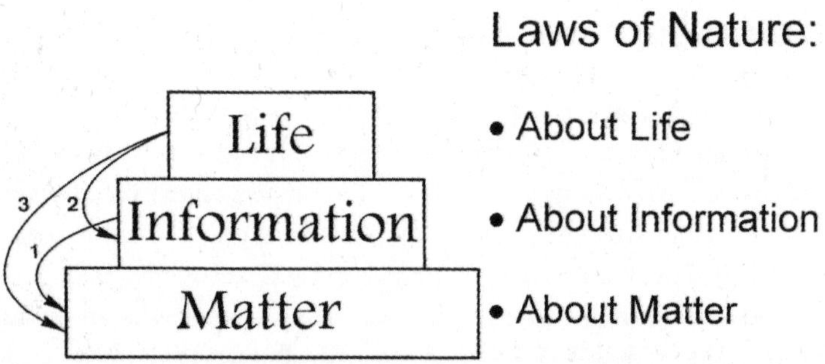

Figure 14: Certain natural laws are valid for each of the three hierarchical levels; the main concern of this book is the information theorems. The meaning of the arrows are:
1. Information requires matter for storage and transmission.
2. Life requires information.
3. Biological life requires matter as necessary medium. Information and matter fall far short in describing life, but life depends on the necessary conditions prevailing at the lower levels.

CHAPTER 5 Delineation of the Information Concept

The question now arises as to the region in which the derived theorems are valid. Do they only hold for computers, or also above and beyond that in all technological domains? Are living systems included or not?

What is the position with regard to unknown systems which we might like to evaluate? Are there criteria which enable us to determine beforehand whether the theorems may be applied, or whether we have left the domain of validity? We thus require an unambiguous definition.

We have already considered a number of examples which we have tacitly included in the domain, namely a computer program, a book, flag codes, and hieroglyphics. What about the crystalline structure of a metal or a salt, or of a snowflake, all of which become visible under magnification? The starry skies are investigated by means of telescopes and we obtain "information" about the stars in this way. A detective gathers "information" at the scene of a crime and deduces circumstantial evidence from meaningful clues. A paleontologist may observe the mussel-bearing shale in a geological layer. The scientist "studies the book of nature" and obtains new knowledge in this way. New technological regularities are discovered, and, when formulated, they comprise a lot of information. Now which of the above examples belong to our domain?

Every scientific definition of a concept requires precise formulation, as in everyday communications. A definition serves to fix matters, but it also brings limitations. The same holds for the information concept.

To be able to define a domain, we require a peculiar property of information, namely its representational function. Information itself is never the actual object or fact, neither is it a relationship (event or idea), but the encoded symbols merely represent that which is discussed. Symbols of extremely different nature (see paragraph 4.2) play a substitutionary role with regard to reality or a system of thought. Information is always an abstract representation of something quite different. For example, the symbols in today's newspaper represent an event which happened yesterday; this event is not contemporaneous, moreover, it might have happened in another country and is not at all present where and when the information is transmitted. The genetic letters in a DNA molecule represent the amino acids which will only be constructed at a later stage for subsequent incorporation into a protein molecule. The words appearing in a novel represent persons and their activities.

We can now formulate two fundamental properties of information:

Property 1: Information is not the thing itself, neither is it a condition, but it is an abstract representation of material realities or conceptual relationships, like problem formulations, ideas, programs, or algorithms. The representation is in a suitable coding system and the realities could be objects, or physical, chemical, or biological conditions. The reality being represented is usually not present at the time and place of the transfer of information, neither can it be observed or measured at that moment.

Property 2: Information always plays a substitutionary role. The encoding of reality is a mental process.

It is again clear from Property 2 that information cannot be a property of matter; it is always an intellectual construct (see Theorems 1 to 3, paragraph 3.3). An intelligent sender who can abstractly encode reality is required.

Both the above salient properties now enable us to delineate the information concept unambiguously. Figure 15 (page 86) clearly illustrates the domains of information (A) and non-information (B and C). Whenever any reality is observed directly by seeing, hearing, or measuring, then that process falls outside our domain. Whenever a coding system which represents something else is employed, then we are inside our domain A, and then all the mentioned theorems are completely valid as laws of nature. The following basic definition has now been established:

> **Definition D5:** The domain A of definition of information includes only systems which encode and represent an abstract description of some object or idea as illustrated in Figure 15. This definition is valid in the case of the given examples (book, newspaper, computer program, DNA molecule, or hieroglyphics), which means that these lie inside the described domain. When a reality is observed directly, this substitutionary and abstract function is absent, and examples like a star, a house, a tree, or a snowflake do not belong to our definition of information (Part B). The proposed theorems are as valid as natural laws inside the domain we have just defined.

It should be noted that the DNA molecule with its genetic information lies inside the domain A. We shall see later that this is a true coding system. Three chemical letters comprise the code for a certain amino acid, but the acid itself is not present, neither spatially nor temporally, as required by Property 1; it is not even present elsewhere. The actual acid is only synthesized at a later stage, according to the code which substitutes for it.

The energy law is valid and exists regardless of our knowledge about it. It only became information after it had been discovered and formulated by means of a coding system (everyday language or formulas). Information thus does not exist by itself — it requires cognitive activity to be established.

We can now formulate another information theorem:

> **Theorem 24:** Information requires a material medium for storage.

If one writes some information with chalk on a blackboard, the chalk is the material carrier. If it is wiped off, the total quantity of chalk is still there, but the information has vanished. In this case, the

Three possible domains for the Definition of Information

What is the best one?

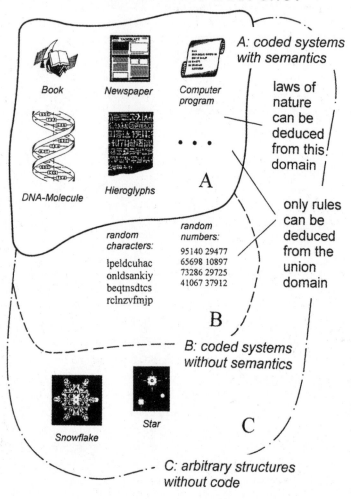

Figure 15: Part A is the domain of definition of information (see Definition D5 for an explanation). In this domain, all the laws of nature about information are valid. The domains B and C fall outside of the definition domain. B represents random characters or random numbers and therefore also lies outside.

chalk was a suitable material medium, but the essential aspect was the actual arrangement of the particles of the chalk. This arrangement was definitely not random — it had a mental origin. The same information that was written on the blackboard could also have been written on a magnetic diskette. Certain tracks of the diskette then became magnetized, and also in this case there is a carrier for the information as stated by Theorem 24. The quantity of material involved is appreciably less than for the chalk and blackboard, but the amount of material is not crucial. Moreover, the information is independent of the chemical composition of the storage medium. If large neon letter signs are used for displaying the same information, then the amount of material required is increased by several orders of magnitude.

CHAPTER 6 Information in Living Organisms

There is an extreme multiplicity of life forms around us, and even a simple unicellular organism is much more complex and purposefully designed than anything that human inventiveness can produce. Matter and energy are basic prerequisites for life, but they cannot be used to distinguish between living and inanimate systems. The central characteristic of all living beings is the "information" they contain, and this information regulates all life processes and procreative functions. Transfer of information plays a fundamental role in all living organisms. When, for example, insects carry pollen from one flower to another, this is in the first place an information-carrying process (genetic information is transferred); the actual material employed is of no concern. Although information is essential for life, information alone does not at all comprise a complete description of life.

Man is undoubtedly the most complex information-processing system existing on earth. The total number of bits handled daily in all information-processing events occurring in the human body is 3×10^{24}. This includes all deliberate as well as all involuntary activities, the former comprising the use of language and the information required for controlling voluntary movements, while the latter includes the control of the internal organs and the hormonal systems. The number of bits being processed daily in the human body is more than a million times the total amount of human knowledge stored in all the libraries of the world, which is about 10^{18} bits.

6.1 NECESSARY CONDITIONS FOR LIFE

The basic building blocks of living beings are the proteins, which consist of only 20 different amino acids. These acids have to be arranged in a very definite sequence for every protein. There are inconceivably many possible chains consisting of 20 amino acids in arbitrary sequences, but only some very special sequences are meaningful in the sense that they provide the proteins which are required for life functions. These proteins are used by and built into the organism, serving as building materials, reserves, bearers of energy, and working and transport substances. They are the basic substances comprising the material parts of living organisms and they include such important compounds as enzymes, anti-bodies, blood pigments, and hormones. Every organ and every kind of life has its own specific proteins and there are about 50,000 different proteins in the human body, each of which performs important functions. Their structure as well as the relevant "chemical factories" in the cells have to be encoded in such a way that protein synthesis can proceed optimally, combining the correct quantities of the required substances.

The structural formulas of the 20 different amino acids which serve as chemical building blocks for the proteins found in all living beings, appear in the book *In sechs Tagen vom Chaos zum Men-schen* [G10, p. 143]. If a certain specific protein must be manufactured in a cell, then the chemical formula must be communicated to the cell as well as the chemical procedures for its synthesis. The exact sequence of the individual building blocks is extremely important for living organisms, so that the instructions must be in written form. This requires a coding system as well as the necessary equipment which can decode the information and carry out the instructions for the synthesis. The minimal requirements are:

- According to Theorem 6, a coding system is required for compiling information, and this system should be able to identify uniquely all the relevant amino acids by means of a standard set of symbols which must remain constant.
- As required by Theorems 14, 17, and 19, for any piece of information, this information should involve precisely defined semantics, pragmatics, and apobetics.
- There must be a physical carrier able to store all the required information in the smallest possible space, according to Theorem 24.

The names of the 20 amino acids occurring in living beings and their internationally accepted three-letter abbreviations are listed in Figure 16 (e.g., Ala for alanine). It is noteworthy that exactly this code with four different letters is employed; these four letters are arranged in "words" of three letters each to uniquely identify an amino acid. Our next endeavor is to determine whether this system is optimal or not.

Amino acid	Genetic code	Abbr
Alanine	GCA GCC GCG GCU	Ala
Arginine	AGA AGG CGA CGC CGG CGU	Arg
Asparagine	AAC AAU	Asn
Aspartic acid	GAC GAU	Asp
Cysteine	UGC UGU	Cys
Glutamine	CAA CAG	Gln
Glutamic acid	GAA GAG	Glu
Glycine	GGA GGC GGG GGU	Gly
Histidine	CAC CAU	His
Isoleucine	AUA AUC AUU	Ile
Leucine	CUA CUC CUG CUU UUA UUG	Leu
Lysine	AAA AAG	Lys
Methionine	AUG	Met
Phenylalanine	UUC UUU	Phe
Proline	CCA CCC CCG CCU	Pro
Serine	AGC AGU UCA UCC UCG UCU	Ser
Threonine	ACA ACC ACG ACU	Thr
Tryptophan	UGG	Try
Tyrosine	UAC UAU	Tyr
Valine	GUA GUC GUG GUU	Val
STOP sign	UAA UAG UGA	

Figure 16: The 20 amino acids which are present in living systems, given in alphabetic order, together with their international three-letter abbreviations. The code combinations (triplets) which give rise to the relevant acid are indicated in the right-hand column.

The storage medium is the DNA molecule (deoxyribonucleic acid), which resembles a double helix as illustrated in Figure 17. A DNA fiber is only about two millionths of a millimeter thick, so that it is barely visible with an electron microscope. The chemical letters A, G, T, and C are located on this information tape, and the amount of

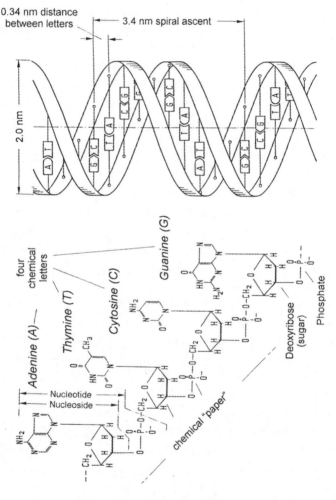

Figure 17: The way in which genetic information is stored. At the left, the "chemical paper" is shown in the form of a long sugar-phosphate chain with the four chemical letters, A, T, C, and G. The actual structure and dimensions of a DNA molecule can be seen at the top.

information is so immense in the case of human DNA that it would stretch from the North Pole to the equator if it was typed on paper, using standard letter sizes. The DNA is structured in such a way that it can be replicated every time a cell divides in two. Each of the two daughter cells must have identically the same genetic information after the division and copying processes. This replication is so precise, that it can be compared to 280 clerks copying the entire Bible sequentially each one from the previous one, with, at most, one single letter being transposed erroneously in the entire copying process.

When a DNA string is replicated, the double strand is unwound, and at the same time a complementary strand is constructed on each separate one, so that, eventually, there are two new double strands identical to the original one. As can be seen in Figure 17, A is complementary to T, and C to G.

One cell division lasts from 20 to 80 minutes, and during this time the entire molecular library, equivalent to one thousand books, is copied correctly.

6.2 THE GENETIC CODE

We now discuss the question of devising a suitable coding system. For instance, how many different letters are required and how long should the words be for optimal performance? If a certain coding system has been adopted, it should be strictly adhered to (theorem 8, par 4.2), since it must be in tune with extremely complex translation and implementation processes. The table in Figure 19 comprises only the most interesting 25 fields, but it can be extended indefinitely downward and to the right. Each field represents a specific method of encoding, for example, if n = 3 and L = 4, we have a ternary code with 3 different letters. In that case, a word for identifying an amino acid would have a length of L = 4, meaning that quartets of 4 letters represent one word. If we now want to select the best code, the following requirements should be met:

- The storage space in a cell must be a minimum, so that the code should economize on the required material. The more letters required for each amino acid, the more material is required, as well as more storage space.
- The copying mechanism described above requires n to be an even number. The replication of each of the two strands of DNA into complementary strands thus needs an alphabet having an

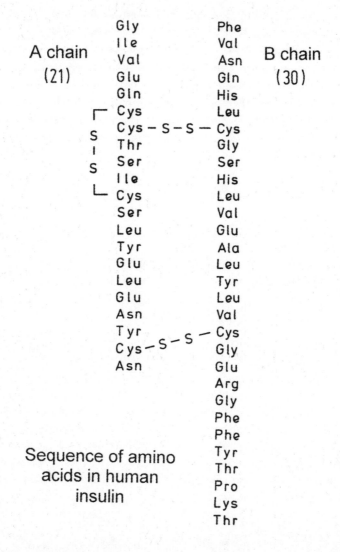

Figure 18: The chemical formula of insulin. The A chain consists of 21 amino acids and the B chain is comprised of 30 amino acids. Three of the 20 amino acids present in living organisms, are absent (Asp, Met, Try), two occur six times (Cys, Leu), one five times (Glu), three occur four times (Gly, Tyr, Val), etc. The two chains are linked by two disulphide bridges. Insulin is an essential hormone, its main function being to maintain the normal sugar content of the blood at 3.9 to 6.4 mmol/l (70–115 mg/dl).

even number of letters. For the purpose of limiting copying errors during the very many replication events, some redundance must be provided for (see appendix A 1.4).

– The longer the employed alphabet, the more complex the implementing mechanisms have to be. It would also require more material for storage, and the incidence of copying errors would increase.

In each field of Figure 19, the number of possible combinations for the different words appears in the top left corner. The 20 amino acids require at least 20 different possibilities and, according to Shannon's theory, the required information content of each amino acid could be calculated as follows: For 20 amino acids, the average information content would be $i_A \equiv i_W \equiv ld\ 20 = \log 20/\log 2 = 4.32$ bits per amino acid (ld is the logarithm with base 2).

If four letters (quartets) are represented in binary code (n = 2), then (4 letters per word)x(1 bit per letter) = 4 bits per word, which is less than the required 4.32 bits per word. This limit is indicated by the hatched boundary in Figure 19. The six fields adjacent to this line, numbered 1 to 6, are the best candidates. All other fields lying further to the right could also be considered, but they would require too much material for storage. So we only have to consider the six numbered cases.

It is, in principle, possible to use quintets of binary codes, resulting in an average of 5 bits per word, but the replication process requires an even number of symbols. We can thus exclude ternary code (n = 3) and quinary code (n = 5). The next candidate is binary code (No. 2), but it needs too much storage material in relation to No. 4 (a quaternary code using triplets), five symbols versus three implies a surplus of 67%. At this stage, we have only two remaining candidates out of the large number of possibilities, namely No. 4 and No. 6. And our choice falls on No. 4, which is a combination of triplets from a quaternary code having four different letters. Although No. 4 has the disadvantage of requiring 50% more material than No. 6, it has advantages which more than compensate for this disadvantage, namely:

– With six different symbols, the recognition and translation requirements become disproportionately much more complex than with four letters, and thus requires much more material for these purposes.

– In the case of No. 4, the information content of a word is 6 bits per word, as against 5.17 bits per word for No. 6. The resulting redundancy is thus greater, and this ensures greater accuracy for the transfer of information.

Conclusion: The coding system used for living beings is optimal from an engineering standpoint. This fact strengthens the argument that it was a case of purposeful design rather than fortuitous chance.

L = Word Length = Number of Letters per Word / n = Number of Different Letters	$L = 2$	$L = 3$	$L = 4$	$L = 5$	$L = 6$
	Doublet	Triplet	Quartet	Quintet	Sextet
	\multicolumn{5}{c}{Word Length $L \longrightarrow$}				
Binary Code $n = 2$ $i_B = \mathrm{ld}\,n = 1$ bit	$m = n^L = 4$ $i_W = L\,\mathrm{ld}\,n$ 2bit/word	$2^3 = 8$ 3bit/word	$2^4 = 16$ 4bit/word	$2^5 = 32$ 5bit/word	$2^6 = 64$ 6bit/word
Ternary Code $n = 3$ $i_B = 1.585$ bit	$3^2 = 9$ 3,170	$3^3 = 27$ 4,755	$3^4 = 81$ 6,340	$3^5 = 243$ 7,925	$3^6 = 729$ 9,510
Quarternary Code $n = 4$ $i_B = 2$ bit	$4^2 = 16$ 4,0	$4^3 = 64$ 6,0	$4^4 = 256$ 8,0	$4^5 = 1024$ 10,0	$4^6 = 4096$ 12,0
Quinary Code $n = 5$ $i_B = 2.322$ bit	$5^2 = 25$ 4,644	$5^3 = 125$ 6,966	$5^4 = 625$ 9,288	$5^5 = 3125$ 11,610	$5^6 = 15625$ 13,932
Senary Code $n = 6$ $i_B = 2.585$ bit	$6^2 = 36$ 5,170	$6^3 = 216$ 7,755	$6^4 = 1296$ 10,340	$6^5 = 7776$ 12,925	$6^6 = 46656$ 15,510

(Left side vertical label: Length of the alphabet n)

$i_B = \mathrm{ld}\,n$ Information content of *one* word [bit/word]
$i_W = L\,\mathrm{ld}\,n$ Information content of *one* letter [bit/letter]
$m = n^L$ Number of possible combinations to make one word with the length L by n different letters

Figure 19: The theoretical possibility of constructing a code consisting of words of equal length. Every field (block) represents a definite coding system as indicated by the number of different letters n, and the word length L.

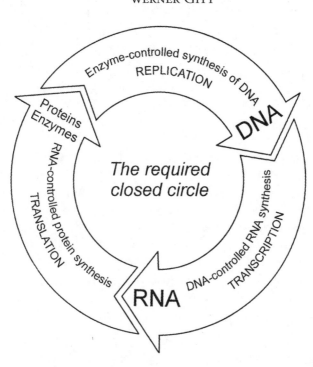

Figure 20: A simplified representation of the cyclic information-controlled process occurring in living cells. The translation is based on pragmatics, but it is involved in the cyclic process of semantic information, since the DNA synthesis can only take place under enzymatic catalysis. This sketch clearly illustrates that such a cyclic process must have been complete right from the start, and could not have originated in a continuous process. The structure of this example of a complex information transfer system also corresponds to Figure 24.

6.3 THE ORIGIN OF BIOLOGICAL INFORMATION

We find a unique coding system and a definite syntax in every genome.[16] The coding system is composed of four chemical symbols for the letters of the defined alphabet, and the syntax entails triplets representing certain amino acids. The genetic syntax system also uses structural units like expressors, repressors, and operators, and thus extends far beyond these two aspects (4 symbols and triplet words).

---

16. Genome (Greek *génos* = generation, kind, inheritance): the simple (haploid) complement of chromosomes of a cell; the totality of all the genes of a cell.

It is not yet fully understood. It is known that the information in a cell goes through a cyclic process (Figure 20), but the semantics of this process is not (yet) understood in the case of human beings. The locations of many functions of chromosomes or genes are known, but we do not yet understand the genetic language. Because semantics is involved, it means that pragmatics also have to be fulfilled. The semantics are invariant, as can be seen in the similarity (not identity!) of uni-ovular twins. If one carefully considers living organisms in their entirety as well as in selected detail, the purposefulness is unmistakable. The apobetics aspect is thus obvious for anybody to see; this includes the observation that information never originates by chance, but is always conceived purposefully.

The substitutionary function of information is also satisfied (see Definition D5 in chapter 5), since the triplets in the DNA molecule represent those amino acids that will be synthesized at a later stage for incorporation into proteins (the amino acids themselves are not present). We can now establish an important theorem:

> **Theorem 25:** Biological information is not an exceptional kind of information, but it differs from other systems in that it has a very high storage density and that it obviously employs extremely ingenious concepts.

In accordance with the theorems formulated in chapters 3 to 5, in particular the impossibility theorems at the end of chapter 4, it is clear that the information present in living organisms requires an intelligent source. Man could not have been this source, so the only remaining possibility is that there must have been a Creator. We can now formulate the following theorems:

> **Theorem 26:** The information present in living beings must have had a mental source.

A corollary of Theorem 26 is:

> **Theorem 27:** Any model for the origin of life (and of information) based solely on physical and/or chemical processes, is inherently false.

In their school textbook, R. Junker and S. Scherer establish a basic type that must have been "ready-made" [J3]. This result, which requires the information content of living beings to be complete right from the beginning, is biologically sound. The derived theorems about the nature of information fit this model.

6.4 MATERIALISTIC REPRESENTATIONS AND MODELS OF THE ORIGIN OF BIOLOGICAL INFORMATION

The question "How did life originate?" which interests us all, is inseparably linked to the question "Where did the information come from?" Since the findings of James D. Watson (*1928) and Francis H.C. Crick (*1916), it was increasingly realized by contemporary researchers that the information residing in the cells is of crucial importance for the existence of life. Anybody who wants to make meaningful statements about the origin of life would be forced to explain how the information originated. All evolutionary views are fundamentally unable to answer this crucial question.

The philosophy that life and its origin are purely material phenomena currently dominates the biological sciences. Following are the words of some authors who support this view.

Jean-Baptiste de Lamarck (1744–1829), a French zoologist and philosopher, wrote, "Life is nothing but a physical phenomenon. All life features originate in mechanical, physical, and chemical processes which are based on the properties of organic matter itself" (*Philosophie Zoologique*, Paris, 1809, Vol. 1).

The German microbiologist R.W. Kaplan holds a similar materialistic view [K1]: "Life is effected by the different parts of a system which work together in a certain way. . . . Life can be completely explained in terms of the properties of these parts and their inevitable interactions. . . . The origin of life can be explained in terms of hypotheses describing fully the sequence of events since the origin of protobionts, and the fact that all these events could be deduced from physical, chemical, and other laws which are valid for material systems."

Manfred Eigen (*1927), a Nobel laureate of Göttingen, discusses questions about life from the molecular biology view, with as point of departure the unwarranted postulate that natural laws controlled the origin of life. In his work on the self-organization of matter [E1], he uses an impressive array of formulas, but does not rise above the level of statistical information. This voluminous work is thus useless and does not answer any questions about the origin of information and of life. He writes in [E2, p 55], "Information arises from non-information."

This statement is nothing but a confession of materialism, and it fails the tests required by reality.

Franz M. Wuketits defines the target readership of his book [W8] as follows: ". . . not only biologists and theoretical scientists, but in equal measure scientists and philosophers, and everybody who is interested in the adventures of contemporary science." He then presents a so-called "evolutionary theoretical science," claiming to initiate a new Copernican revolution. Up to the present time, great scientific results were obtained by means of observation, measuring, and weighing, as was done for example by Copernicus, Galilei, Newton, Einstein, Born, and Planck. In his system, Wuketits follows the backward route: His point of departure is to assume that evolution is true, so that all natural phenomena have to be interpreted through these spectacles. He writes in the introduction of his book [W8, p. 11–12]:

> The fundamental truth of biological evolution is accepted beforehand, yes, we assume in advance that the principle of evolution is universally valid, that it is just as valid in the pre-organic domain as in the organic, and that it can be extended to the spheres of psychology, sociology, and culture. If we accept that the evolutionary view also holds for the human mind and cognition, then evolutionary ideas can also be applied to the analysis of those phenomena which are usually regarded as belonging to theoretical science. As a result this view then becomes relatively more important in the evaluation of the progress of scientific research. We thus arrive at an evolutionary theory of science, a theory of human knowledge which relates to an evolutionary establishment of itself.

If such statements were based on a sufficient body of facts, then one might perhaps agree with the conclusions, but the reverse process was followed: All phenomena of nature are placed under the all-encompassing evolutionary umbrella. Scientists who submit themselves to such a mental corset and support it uncritically, degrade themselves to mere vassals of a materialistic philosophy. Science should, however, only be subservient to the truth, and not to pre-programmed folly. Evolutionary theory bans any mention of a planning Spirit as a purposeful First Cause in natural systems, and endeavors to imprison all sciences in the straightjacket called the "self-organization of matter." Wuketits supports evolutionary theory with a near ideological fervor, and accuses everybody of fable mongering who claims to be scientific and speak of "planning spirits" or of a "designer" in nature. He wishes to ban thoughts of "finality" and of "final and purposeful causes" from science and from the domain of all serious schools of thought.

An appreciable fraction of all scientists who concern themselves with cosmological questions and with questions of origins, support the evolutionary view, to such an extent that the well-known American bio-informaticist Hubert P. Jockey [J1] bemoans the fact that the literature in this area is blandly and totally supportive. He writes in the *Journal of Theoretical Biology* [vol. 91, 1981, p. 13]:

> Since science does not have the faintest idea how life on earth originated. . . . it would only be honest to confess this to other scientists, to grantors, and to the public at large. Prominent scientists speaking ex cathedra, should refrain from polarizing the minds of students and young productive scientists with statements that are based solely on beliefs.

The doctrine of evolution is definitely not a viable scientific *leitmotiv* (guiding principle); even the well-known theoreticist Karl Popper [H1], once characterized it as a "metaphysical research program." This assertion is just as noteworthy as it is honest, because Popper himself supports evolution.

We now discuss some theoretical models which suggest that information can originate in matter.

Cumulative selection (Latin *cumulare* = gather): Richard Dawkins, a British neo-Darwinist, revives the historical example of the typewriter-thrumming monkeys (see appendix A1.5) and replaces them with "computer monkeys." As shown in Figure 21, he begins with a random sequence of 28 letters [D2 p. 66–67] and seeks to demonstrate how a predetermined phrase selected from Shakespeare, "Methinks it is like a weasel," can be derived through mutation and selection. The random initial sequence with the required number of letters is copied repeatedly, allowing for random copying errors (representing mutations). The computer program checks all the "daughter" sentences and selects that one which most resembles the target sentence. The process is subsequently repeated for the resulting "winning sentences," until eventually, after 43 "generations," the goal is reached.

There is a spate of new Jesus books which constantly present strange new and false ideas contrary to the New Testament. Prof. Klaus

Berger of the Heidelberg School of Theology remarked (1994): "Please buy and read such a book, then you will realize what degree of gullibility is ascribed to you." With equal zeal, Dawkins publishes his easily detectable fallacies about the way information originates. It is therefore necessary to discuss his representation fully so that you, the reader, can see what feeble-mindedness is ascribed to you.

In the initial pages of his book, Dawkins [D2, p. 13] softens the reader to the purposelessness of living structures: "Biology is the study of complex matters that appear to have been designed purposefully." Further along he selects a target sentence and his entire program is designed toward this goal. This game can be played with any random initial sequence and the goal will always be reached, because the programming is fixed. Even the number of letters is given in advance. It is obvious that no information is generated; on the contrary, it has been predetermined. B.O. Küppers plays a similar evolution game [K3]: The predetermined target word is "evolutionstheorie" appearing twice (see the right hand part of Figure 21). It should be clear from Theorem 27 that random processes cannot give rise to information.

Genetic algorithms: The so-called "genetic algorithms" are yet another way of trying to explain how information could originate in matter [F5, M4]. The combination of words is deliberately chosen from biology and numerical mathematics to suggest that evolutionary events are described mathematically. What is actually involved is a purely numerical method used for the optimization of dynamic processes. This method can be used to find, by repeated approximations, the maximum value of an analytic function numerically (e.g., $f(x,y) = yx - x^4$), or the optimal route of a commercial traveler. The effects of mutation and selection can thus be simulated by computer. Using predetermined samples of bits (sequences of noughts and ones), each position is regarded as a gene. The sample is then modified (mutated) by allowing various genetic operators to influence the bit string (e.g., crossover). A "fitness function," assumed for the process of evolution, is then applied to each result. It should be pointed out that this genetic algorithm is purely a numerical calculation method, and definitely not an algorithm which describes real processes in cells. Numerical methods cannot describe the origin of information.

Evolutionary models for the origin of the genetic code: We find proposals for the way the genetic code could have originated in very many publications [e.g., O2, E2, K1], but up to the present time, nobody has been able to propose anything better than purely imaginary models. It has not yet been shown empirically how information can arise in matter, and, according to Theorem 11, this will never happen.

Dawkins's example:
Initial sequence:
WDLMNLT DTJBKWIRZREZLMQCO P
Predetermined target sentence:
METHINKS IT IS LIKE A WEASEL

First test:
Gen. 01   WDLMNLT DTJBKWIRZREZLMQCO P
Gen. 02   WDLTMNLT DTJBSWIRZREZLMQLO P
Gen. 10   MDLDMNLS ITJISWHRZREZ MECS P
Gen. 20   MELDINLS IT ISWPRKE Z WECSEL
Gen. 30   METHINGS IT ISWLIKE B WECSEL
Gen. 40   METHINKS IT IS LIKE I WEASEL
Gen. 43   METHINKS IT IS LIKE A WEASEL

Second test:
Gen. 01   Y YVMQKZPFJXWVHGLAWFVCHHQXYOPY
Gen. 10   Y YVMQKSPFTXWSHLIKEFV HQYSPY
Gen. 20   YETHINKSPITXISHLIKEFA WOYSEY
Gen. 30   METHINKS IT ISSLIKE A WEFSEY
Gen. 40   METHINKS IT ISBLIKE A WEASES
Gen. 50   METHINKS IT ISJLIKE A WEASEO
Gen. 60   METHINKS IT IS LIKE A WEASEP
Gen. 64   METHINKS IT IS LIKE A WEASEL

Küppers's example:
Initial sequence:
ELWWSJILAKLAFTYJ:/ELWWSJILAKLAFTYJ:/
Predetermined target sentence:
EVOLUTIONSTHEORIE/ (twice)

Gen. 01   ELWWSJILAKLAFTYJ:/ELWWSJILAKLAFTYJ:/
ELYWSJILAK?AFTYJ:/ELWOSBCSEKLAJSYK:/
ELWOSBCKEKLKUTII:/ELWOTBCKYKLIFTYJ:/
ELWOSBDKEKLAJTYt:/ELWOTBCKZKLIJTYJ:

Gen. 05   EVQLVDGONS?THEOQUI/EVOKVDGONSLHE.QIC/
ETOLVDGONS?HEOQIE/EVOLVDGONS?LUOQUC/
EVQLVDGONC?HEOQIE/EVOLVDIONKLHEKQIC/
EVOLVDGONSLHEOQIC/EVOLVDGONS?HEOQIE/
EVOLVEDONSLHEOQIC/EVOLVDGONS?HEOQIE

Gen. 30   EVOLUTIONSTHEORIE/EVOLUTIONSTHEORIE/
EVOLUTIONSTHEORIE/EVOLUTIONSTHEORIE/
EVOLUTIONSTHEORIE/EVOLVDIONSTHEORIE/
EVOLUTIONSTHEORIE/EVOPUTIONSTHEORIE/
EVOLUTIONSTHEORIE:JE/EVOPUTIONSTHEORIE/
EVOLVTIONSTHEORIE/EVO?UTIONSKXHEORI

Figure 21: Molecular-Darwinistic representations of the origin of information according to R. Dawkins and B.O. Küppers.

6.5 SCIENTISTS AGAINST EVOLUTION

Fortunately, the number of scientists who repudiate evolutionary views and dilemmas is increasing. This number includes internationally renowned experts, of whom some quotations follow. In *New Scientist*, the British astrophysicist Sir Fred Hoyle, one of today's best known cosmologists, expresses his concern about the customary representations under the title "The Big Bang in Astronomy" [H4, p. 523–524]:

> But the interesting quark transformations are almost immediately over and done with, to be followed by a little rather simple nuclear physics, to be followed by what? By a dull-as-ditchwater expansion which degrades itself adiabatically until it is incapable of doing anything at all. The notion that galaxies form, to be followed by an active astronomical history, is an illusion. Nothing forms, the thing is as dead as a door-nail. . . . The punch line is that, even though outward speeds are maintained in a free explosion, internal motions are not. Internal motions die away adiabatically, and the expanding system becomes inert, which is exactly why the big-bang cosmologies lead to a universe that is dead-and-done-with almost from its beginning.

These views correspond with the findings of Hermann Schneider, a nuclear physicist of Heidelberg, who has critically evaluated the big-bang theory from a physical viewpoint. He concludes [S5]: "In the evolution model the natural laws have to describe the origin of all things in the macro and the micro cosmos, as well as their operation. But this overtaxes the laws of nature."

Fred Hoyle makes the following remarks about the much-quoted primeval soup in which life supposedly developed according to evolutionary expectations [H4, p 526]:

> I don't know how long it is going to be before astronomers generally recognize that the combinatorial arrangement of not even one among the many thousands of biopoymers on which life depends could have been arrived at by natural processes here on the earth. Astronomers will have a little difficulty at understanding this because they will be assured by biologists that it is not so, the biologists having been assured in their

turn by others that it is not so. The "others" are a group of persons who believe, quite openly, in mathematical miracles. They advocate the belief that tucked away in nature, outside of normal physics, there is a law which performs miracles.

In his book *Synthetische Artbildung (The Synthetic Formation of Kinds)*, Professor Dr. Heribert Nilsson, a botanist at Lund University in Sweden, describes evolutionary doctrine as an obstacle which prevents the development of an exact biology:

> The final result of all my researches and discussions is that the theory of evolution should be discarded in its entirety, because it always leads to extreme contradictions and confusing consequences when tested against the empirical results of research on the formation of different kinds of living forms and related fields. This assertion would agitate many people. Moreover: my next conclusion is that, far from being a benign natural-philosophical school of thought, the theory of evolution is a severe obstacle for biological research. As many examples show, it actually prevents the drawing of logical conclusions from even one set of experimental material. Because everything must be bent to fit this speculative theory, an exact biology cannot develop.

Professor Dr. Bruno Vollmert of Karlsruhe, an expert in the field of macro-molecular chemistry, has shown that all experiments purporting to support evolution miss the crux of the matter [V1]:

> All hitherto published experiments about the poly-condensation of nucleotides or amino acids are irrelevant to the problem of evolution at the molecular level, because they were based on simple monomers, and not on "primeval soups" derived from Miller experiments. But poly-condensation experiments with primeval soups or the dissolved mix of substances of them are just as superfluous as attempts to construct perpetual motion machines.

A French Nobel laureate, A. Lwoff [L2], pointed out that every organism can only function in terms of the complex net of available information:

An organism is a system of interdependent structures and functions. It consists of cells, and the cells are made of molecules which have to cooperate smoothly. Every molecule must know what the others are doing. It must be able to receive messages and act on them.

When considering the source of this information, we can now formulate the following theorem which is based on research of many thousands of man-years:

Theorem 28: There is no known law of nature, no known process, and no known sequence of events which can cause information to originate by itself in matter.

This was also the conclusion of the seventh "International Conference on the Origins of Life" held together with the fourth congress of the "International Society for the Study of the Origin of Life (ISSOL)" in Mainz, Germany. At such occasions, scientists from all over the world exchange their latest results. In his review of the congress, Klaus Dose [D3] writes: "A further puzzle remains, namely the question of the origin of biological information, i.e., the information residing in our genes today." Not even the physical building blocks required for the storage of the information can construct themselves: "The spontaneous formation of simple nucleotides or even of poly-nucleotides which were able to be replicated on the pre-biotic earth should now be regarded as improbable in the light of the very many unsuccessful experiments in this regard."

As early as 1864, when Louis Pasteur addressed the Sorbonne University in Paris, he predicted that the theory of the spontaneous generation of living cells would never recover from the fatal blow delivered by his experiments. In this regard, Klaus Dose makes an equally important statement: "The Mainz report may have an equally important historical impact, because for the first time it has now been determined unequivocally by a large number of scientists that all evolutionary theses that living systems developed from poly-nucleotides which originated spontaneously, are devoid of any empirical base."

CHAPTER 7 The Three Forms in which Information Appears

Information accosts us from all sides and presents itself over a wide range of manifestations:

- From messages pounded out by drums in the jungle to telephone conversations by means of communications satellites.
- From the computer-controlled processes for producing synthetic materials to the adaptive control of rolling mills.
- In printed form from telephone directories to the Bible.
- From the technical drawings which specify the construction of a gas-driven engine to the circuit diagram of a large scale integrated computer chip.
- From the hormonal system of an organism to the navigational instincts of migrating birds.
- From the genome of a bacterium to the genetic information inherited by humans.

In addition to the five essential levels of information mentioned in chapter 4 (statistics, syntax, semantics, pragmatics, and apobetics), it is also advantageous to consider a three-fold vertical division of types of information:

1. Constructional/creative information: This includes all information which is used for the purpose of producing something. Before anything can be made, the originator mobilizes his intelligence, his supply of ideas, his know-how, and his inventiveness to encode his concept in a suitable way. There are many types of encoded blueprints, e.g., technical drawings for the construction of a machine, a cake recipe, details of the chemical processes for synthesizing polyvinyl chloride, an electrical circuit diagram, or the genetic information required for the construction of a living cell.

The criteria for evaluating the searched-for solution are found both in the conceptual stage (semantic aspect of the information) and in the sophistication of the implementation (pragmatics). One or more of the following catchwords characterize these criteria, depending on the situation, as shown in Figure 22: underlying functional concept, degree of inventiveness, cleverness of the method of solution, achieved optimality, input strategy, brevity of construction time, applied technology, suitable programming, and degree of miniaturization (e.g., economical use of material and energy). The quality of the visible results (apobetics) can be evaluated in terms of the achieved goal, the efficiency of the input, the ingenuity of the operation, and the certainty of correct functioning (e.g., low susceptibility to interference).

2. Operational information: All concepts having the purpose of maintaining some "industry" in the widest sense of the word are included under this kind of information. Many systems require operational information in the form of programs, for proper functioning. These programs are indispensable and ensure that the preconceived processes run as expected. A barrel-organ cannot function without the required cylinder, and the human body is viable only when the conceptual information is provided with all the interactions carried by the nervous system to and from the brain and all the bodily organs. The amount of information streaming through the deliberate as well as all involuntary activities of the human body is about 3×10^{24} bits per day. When this is compared with the total quantity of information stored in all the libraries of the world — 10^{18} bits — we make an astounding discovery: The quantity of information processed in our bodies during the course of one day, is one million times greater then all the knowledge represented in the books of the world.

Further examples of operational information as found in technology and in nature:

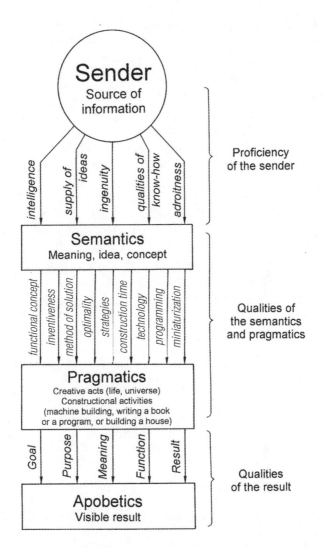

Figure 22: Qualitative properties of the sender and his information on the semantic, pragmatic, and apobetic levels. In this diagram we represent the qualitative properties of constructional/creative information, and include both the creative acts of God and human engineering concepts. It is obvious that there is a tight link between the qualitative aspects of the information and the capabilities of the sender. Similar qualitative properties can be formulated for the other two types of information, operational and communication information.

- the operating system of a computer (e.g., DOS programs),
- the program controlling a robot or a process computer,
- warning systems for airplanes and ships,
- pheromone languages of insects,
- bee dancing (see Figure 39 in appendix A2),
- the hormonal system of the body, and
- operational information in the animal kingdom, which we call "instincts" because of our lack of knowledge about their codes and methods of transfer (e.g., the navigational system of migrating birds as described in appendix A3.4.4.2).

3. Communication information: This is composed of all other kinds of information, e.g., letters, books, phone calls, radio transmissions, bird songs, and the message of the Bible. The apobetic aspect of such information does not include the construction of a product, neither is it involved in maintaining some process. The goals are: transmission of a message, spreading joy, amusement, instruction, and personal confidences.

CHAPTER 8 Three Kinds of Transmitted Information

In our study of the nature of information we have come across various different distinguishing criteria:

a) Distinction according to aspect: statistics, syntax, semantics, pragmatics, and apobetics
b) Distinction according to purpose: constructional/creative information, operational, and communication information
c) Distinction according to direction of flow: transmitted or received information.

Yet another distinction could also be made regarding the sender and the quality of the information processing involved. There are three types:

1. Copied information: This is comprised of the identical propagation of existing information. No new information arises during copying, so that it is a mechanical process and not an intellectual one. The equipment and methods used for copying were created by the initiative of one or more minds, and the copying process itself is also a deliberate and purposeful action, but it can be done by a machine. Examples of copied information: Duplication of a computer program in a data processing system (e.g., magnetic tape, magnetic disk, and real memory), replication of DNA molecules in living cells, the second printing of a book without any changes or additions, making a photocopy, and reading an extract or a letter. Every piece of copied information must, however, have been created somewhere along the line.

2. Reproduced information: In the arts, there is a clear distinction between the original composer, poet, or writer, and the subsequent performers of such works. An actor did not create the acts or the text, but he does contribute by employing his own talents of intonation, mimicry, and creativity. Similarly, when a Mozart symphony or a Bach cantata is performed, the musicians play a reproductive role — they do not alter the work of the composer, but they might introduce individual effects. We thus define reproduced information as a semantic entity which is elaborated and adapted by the actual sender without modifying in any real sense the originally created information. All animal languages can be included in this category, because all allocated meanings are fixed. The acts of performing animals are reproductive and not creative. Computer software functions according to this principle, since all creative ideas like algorithms (methods of solution) and data structures had to be devised beforehand by the programmer and then implemented in the form of a written program. The various relevant parameters can be entered into a machine (computer) which does nothing more than reproduce the available information in the required form. Even the results obtained by means of AI programs (artificial intelligence; see appendix A2.3) are in the last instance nothing more than reproduced information. They may be quite complex and may appear to be "intelligent," but they cannot create information. Machines can reproduce information, since reproduction does not entail creative thought processes.

3. Creative information: This is the highest level of transmitted information: something new is produced. It does not involve copied or reproduced information. This kind of information always requires a personal mind exercising its own free will, as original source. This generally entails a nonmaterial intellectual process, which thus cannot be entrusted to a machine. Creative information can always be linked to a person who has cognitive capabilities, and it represents something new. We can now formulate the following special theorem:

> **Theorem 29:** Every piece of creative information represents some mental effort and can be traced to a personal idea-giver

who exercised his own free will, and who is endowed with an intelligent mind.

This theorem can also be expressed as follows:

Theorem 30: New information can only originate in a creative thought process.

Examples of creative information: designing a coding system, designing a language, untrammeled discourse by means of natural languages, creating a programming language, writing a book, writing an original scientific paper, program instructions in DNA molecules, and the setting up of blueprints for living beings.

Conclusions: It should now be clear where the follies of evolutionary views lie. If someone presents a model for explaining the origin of life, but he cannot say where the creative information characteristic of all life forms came from, then the crucial question remains unanswered. Somebody who looks for the origin of information only in physical matter ignores the fundamental natural laws about information; what is more, he scorns them. It is clear from the history of science that one can ignore the laws of nature for a limited time only.

There are only four different possible relationships between sender and recipient [G4], as illustrated in Figure 23. Only intelligent beings qualify as sender or recipient (God and man), or systems constructed by intelligent minds (e.g., man, other living beings, machines like

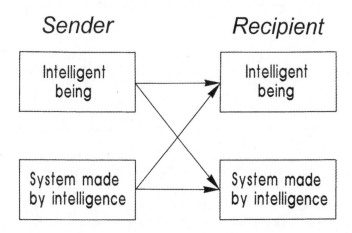

Figure 23: The four possible combinations of sender and recipient.

computers or communication systems, and storage media). The four possible communication channels are shown in Figure 23. According to Theorem 29, senders of creative information can only be personal beings, while machines may serve as senders of copied or reproduced information.

There also are cases where both the sender and the recipient are parts of a complete transmission system (Figure 24).

Example: In the system used for the transmission of exact (atomic) time in Germany, the atomic clock located at the Physikalisch-Technischen Bundesanstalt (Federal Institute of Physics and Technology) in Braunschweig, transmits the exact time over the transmitter designated as DCF77 in Mainflingen (near Frankfurt/Main). A specially designed code is employed (compare Theorems 6 to 11) and these signals can then be decoded by commercially available receiving equipment to provide time and date. Both the transmitter and the receiver are "systems created by intelligence" (the lower link in Figure 23). All the parts of this system have been produced by intelligent minds, as shown in Figure 24.

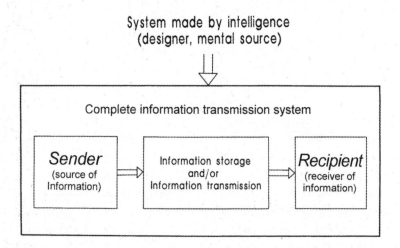

Figure 24: A complete transmission system in which sender and recipient are integrated. The entire system is based on conceptual ideas and always requires a mental source.

CHAPTER 9 The Quality and Usefulness of Information

Shannon's information theory can be regarded as an extension of probability theory. He takes the bit as the unit of measurement of information, and a book with 200 pages then contains twice as much information as one with 100 pages if the pages contain the same number of letters. Meaning is completely ignored. Wolfgang Feitscher gave a striking description of this situation: "When considering semantic information, we are like a chemist who can weigh substances, but cannot analyze them." In this sense, Shannon solved the problem of weighing information, but the analysis question is still untouched. To rise above Shannon's theory, it is necessary to define measures for semantic information which must be generally valid. We will now discuss some aspects which may pave the way for solving this difficult problem.

A semantic measure would not be a measure of quantity but of quality. It could happen that a book of several volumes may have a lower semantic evaluation than a thin brochure. A qualitative evaluation of information involves some parameters which depend very strongly on a subjective appraisal, and this has an appreciable aggravating effect on the problem. Figure 25 (page 117) depicts a graph of the semantic value of information with respect to its usefulness. There are five value levels.

1. Extremely important information: This is the highest level because of its high apobetics content (e.g., essential and vital information).

2. Important information: Information which is required for achieving some purpose (e.g., knowledge of planned routes, telephone numbers, address lists, and subject knowledge).

3. Valuable information: This includes information which is of general value in the sense of being informative, constructive, edifying, or amusing (e.g., daily news, weather reports, general increase of knowledge, and novelties).

4. Trivial information: Insignificant or meaningless information (e.g., already known or useless information, clichés, banalities, or small talk).

5. Harmful information: Information with negative consequences, leading to false results, misconceptions, and other negative effects (e.g., deliberate or erroneous misinformation, slander, cursing, agitation, false propaganda, charlatanry, malicious gossip, expletives, sectarian doctrines, unbiblical theology, pornographic, ideological, and astrological publications, and pulp magazines).

Valuable information (1 to 3) is accorded a positive sign, and worthless information (4 and 5) a negative sign, so that now we can regard information as a signable quantity. In the x direction (Figure 25) we distinguish between usable (positive) and useless (negative) information. We thus have four quadrants for evaluating information, characterized as follows.

First quadrant: This is the most important domain, since it is comprised of all information that is both useful and valuable. "Useful" means that the information is available and accessible and can in principle be implemented. On the one hand, usefulness is an objective property, but the concept of value concerns a person, an event, a plan, or a purpose, and it is always subjective.

Second quadrant: The information in this quadrant is also valuable, as in the case of the first quadrant, but it cannot be used. There are various possible reasons for this:

- It is not yet available (e.g., cure for cancer; a book on an important theme which has not yet been written).
- It cannot be located in the gigantic flood of information.
- The author has it available, but it has not yet been transmitted (published).
- It is not of topical interest any more.

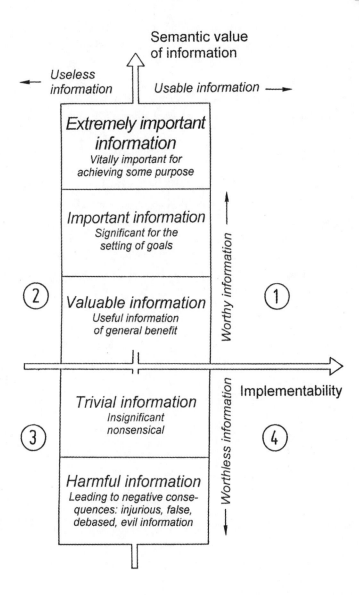

Figure 25: Graph representing the evaluation levels of the usability of semantic information. There is no indication of scale, so we are mainly dealing with a qualitative evaluation of semantic information. Valuable information is accorded a positive, and worthless information a negative, sign. Usable and useless information are also distinguished by their sign.

Third and fourth quadrants: This is the domain of worthless information. At the trivial level, this is comprised of meaningless or unordered information: insignificant, inane, or nonsensical information. In the amplified harmful form, information can be false (inadvertently), deliberately falsified, or evil, and can have negative effects. The fourth quadrant indicates that such information exists, while the third quadrant depicts information that is not yet available or accessible (e.g., trash literature which is unpublished). According to certain statistics an American youth at the end of his school career attended 11,000 school periods, watched TV for 22,000 hours, during which he heard 350,000 promotional slogans, and saw 20,000 murders. That has to have injurious effects. It is, in human terms, necessary to avoid the fourth quadrant, and, in technical terms, security measures must be taken to prevent damage (e.g., error-detecting codes in data processing systems, and control procedures for preventing instability in manufacturing processes).

CHAPTER **10** Some Quantitative
Evaluations of
Semantics

We can now begin to evaluate semantic information quantitatively, after having considered the essentials at the semantics level in the preceding chapters. Let us take the semantic value S to represent a quantitative evaluation of the quality of the information. Then six quantities can be used, namely semantic quality q, relevance r, timeliness a, accessibility z, existence e, and comprehensibility v. It is obvious from these concepts that we are considering the information from the point of view of the recipient and his subjective appraisal. These quantities are normalized on a scale from 0 to 1, and they are all positive, except for q which can also take on negative values, as should be clear from the previous chapter. These six variables are now discussed briefly.

1. Semantic quality q (a subjective concept, mainly concerns the recipient): This is used as a measure of the importance of the meaning of some information. Different qualities can be considered according to the goal and the kind of information. Some significant aspects of creative information in particular are depicted in Figure 22 (page 109). For a computer program, for example, the following criteria are relevant and crucial on the semantic level and in part at the pragmatic level:

– Efficacy of the applied algorithm (e.g., simple method of solution,

speed of convergence, and absence of instability).
- Minimal computing time (this can be a decisive cost factor when
  time has to be paid for).
- Portability, meaning that the program can also run on other
  computer systems.
- Reliability, meaning that the program has been tested
  comprehensively and is fully debugged so that the desired
  results will be obtained with a high degree of certainty.
- The programming language used.

The weight of each aspect depends on both objective and subjective evaluations. For inane or nonsensical information q is taken as zero, while for the best possible information q = 1.

2. Relevance r (subjective concept, mainly concerns the recipient): This aspect reflects individual interests in particular and it includes its relevance for achieving some purpose (e.g., an economical, a technical, or a strategic goal, collector's value, or life purpose). If r = 1 for person A, the same information can be totally irrelevant for B (r = 0). The weather forecasts for Australia are normally of no importance for somebody in Europe (r = 0), but their relevance can increase dramatically when that person is planning to go there. For a farmer, the agricultural news has a relevance completely different from the latest research results in physics. It is obvious that relevance depends entirely on the recipient. A gale and storm tide warning over the radio is highly relevant for inhabitants of a coastal island, while continental residents who live inland are not concerned. The main problem of relevance is to estimate it correctly. If relevance has been appraised erroneously, it might have catastrophic effects. There are innumerable cases in human history where wrong decisions were made on the grounds of a faulty appraisal of the relevance of information. The cost was astronomical in terms of lives and property.

3. Timeliness t (subjective concept, mainly concerns the recipient): It is in many cases necessary that relevant information should be available at the required moment. Newsworthiness is time-dependent, so that t = 0 for yesterday's news, and t = 1 for highly relevant information received at the right moment. When a person is standing in the rain and somebody tells him that it is raining, the newsworthiness of this information is zero (t = 0), although it is topical and relevant.

4. Accessibility a (subjective concept, mainly concerns the recipient): The most important information is worthless if it cannot be accessed; then a = 0 (no access). On the other hand, a = 1 when the recipient has full access to the information transmitted by the sender. With the increasing flood of information the "know-where" is becoming steadily more important, and aids like catch-word registers, lexicons, card systems, and data banks are available. Associative storage would be a great help, but only the brain can provide this ideal access principle. In many countries there are computer centers with online facilities which provide direct access to information (Internet). These data banks contain information on such diverse topics as technology, physics, materials, books, and the social sciences, etc.

Even if information is accessible, a rating may still be zero when:

– the information cannot be seen by the recipient (e.g., I am dying of thirst in the desert close to a spring but I do not know that it is there.)
– the information is coded in a language that the recipient does not understand (e.g., an English tourist in China who cannot read Chinese)
– the information is coached in technical terms which can only be understood by adepts (e.g., legal texts that laymen cannot follow, or a mathematical book which is "Greek" to the uninitiated)
– the sender deliberately excludes some potential recipients (e.g., secret encrypted information, data protection in EDP systems, and sealing a letter)

5. **Existence e** (objective concept, mainly concerns the sender): Whereas accessibility involves the possibility that an individual can lay his hand on information which is in principle available, existence concerns the basic question of whether the information exists at all. Accessibility involves the recipient only, but existence depends solely on the sender. The value of e lies between 0 and 1, and it indicates how much of the available or desired information about the present case can be obtained (e.g., what fraction has already been researched). The existence e is zero for questions which are completely open, and if something is fully known, e = 1. The previously open question of whether there is life on the moon (e = 0) has now been answered completely (e = 1). For information to cure cancer of the liver, e = 0; in the case of stomach cancer it lies somewhere between 0 and 1, depending

on the stage of development. It is quite difficult to make an estimate of the value of e, since the totality of relevant information is in general not known at a given moment. The great physicist Isaac Newton (1642–1727) estimated his contribution to scientific research as a very small e value in spite of his many valuable findings. He said [M3], "I do not know what the world thinks of me; but to myself I appear as a little boy playing on the beach and who finds joy in discovering a smoother pebble or a prettier seashell than the ordinary, while the great ocean of truth lay undiscovered before me."

6. Comprehensibility c (subjective concept, concerns both the sender and the recipient): This factor describes the intelligibility of information; when the information cannot be understood at all, $c = 0$, and $c = 1$ when it is completely understood. Both sides may be at fault if all of the transmitted information does not reach the recipient. The sender might not have expressed himself clearly enough, so that the recipient grasps the intended semantics only partially in spite of being highly intelligent, or the recipient may not be intelligent enough to understand everything correctly. The mental alertness of the recipient is also important for another reason: Verbally formulated information (the explicit part) often contains implicit information which has to be read "between the lines." The recipient only receives this latter part by contemplation and having the required background knowledge.

Note: Many of the above-mentioned factors cannot be distinguished sharply and might overlap. The question of interlinking between the six parameters is not discussed further at this stage; it might be investigated in the future.

CHAPTER 11 Questions Often Asked about the Information Concept

My talks at universities and technical institutes are usually followed by lively discussions. A small selection of the frequently asked questions are now listed and answered briefly.

Q1: Have you now proved the existence of God?

A1: Conclusions must always be based on scientific results and these may give rise to further ideas. It is, however, scientifically impossible to prove the existence of God, but many aspects of this world cannot be understood at all if God is excluded.

Q2: Do your assertions refute evolution?

A2: The information theorems are natural laws and many fallacies have been revealed by means of natural laws. The basic flaw of all evolutionary views is the origin of the information in living beings. It has never been shown that a coding system and semantic information could originate by itself in a material medium, and the information theorems predict that this will never be possible. A purely material origin of life is thus precluded.

Q3: Does the definition of information not depend on the individual? In contrast to matter and energy, information does not exist as such of itself.

A3: Yes, of course. Consider three persons, Albert, Ben, and Charles who want to inform Dan which one of them was in the room.

They decided that colors would be used to distinguish between them: Albert = yellow, Ben = blue, and Charles = red. When Dan arrives later, he finds a blue note, and concludes that Ben is there. Any other person would not regard this piece of paper as information. This code agreement exists only between Albert, Ben, Charles, and Dan (see Theorems 6, 7, and 9). It is obvious that information can only be created by a cognitive mental process.

Q4: Please give a brief definition of information.

A4: That is not possible, because information is by nature a very complex entity. The five-level model indicates that a simple formulation for information will probably never be found.

Q5: Is it information when I am both sender and recipient at the same time? For example, when I shout in a valley and hear the echo.

A5: This is not a planned case of information transfer, but there are situations like writing a note to oneself or entries in a diary.

Q6: Is a photograph information according to your definition?

A6: No! Although the substitutionary function (chapter 5) is present, there is no agreed-upon code.

Q7: Does information originate when lottery numbers are drawn? If so, then that could be regarded as information arising from chance.

A7: The information resides in the rules of the game; they are composed of a fixed strategy which includes apobetics, namely to win. The actual drawing of numbers is a random process involving direct observation of reality, and, according to the theorems in chapter 5, we are thus outside the domain of the definition of information, but we do have information when the results of the draw are communicated orally or in writing.

Q8: Is there a conservation law for information similar to the conservation of energy?

A8: No! Information written with chalk on a blackboard, may be erased. A manuscript for a book with many new ideas written painstakingly over several years, will be irrevocably lost when someone throws it in the fire. When a computer disk containing a voluminous text is formatted, all the information is also lost. On the other hand, new information can be created continuously by means of mental processes (Theorem 30).

Q9: Does information have anything to do with entropy as stated in the second law of thermodynamics?

A9: No! The second law of thermodynamics is only valid for the world of matter (the lower level in Figure 14), but information is a mental entity (Theorem 15). There is, however, a concept on the statistical level of Shannon's information, which is called entropy (see appendix A1.1). This is something completely different from what is known as entropy in physics. It is unfortunate that two such different phenomena have the same name.

Q10: Natural languages are changing dynamically all the time. Doesn't this contradict your theorem that coding conventions should be conserved?

A10: New words arise continuously, like skateboards, rollerblades, wind surfing, paragliding, etc., but all of them meet a very specific need and perform a real function. There is consensus about their meaning, and nobody would confuse a rollerblade with a switchblade or paragliding with paramedical. If random strings of letters are written on a blackboard, nobody would be able to do anything with them. In this case there will be no agreed-upon convention.

Q11: Can the randomness of a result be proven?

A11: In a work of Gregory J. Chaitin (Argentina) [C2] he showed that there is no algorithm for determining whether a sequence of symbols is random or not. One must be informed of the fact if a random process has been involved (e.g., that a sequence was produced by a random number generator).

Q12: Is the criteria for information mostly subjective?

A12: Subjective aspects play a significant role when the sender decides which type of code he wants to use. He decides whether to write a letter or make a phone call. Even the way the message is transmitted is colored by his personality and by the circumstances. The transmission may be joyful, stupid, agitated, boring, or may have a special emphasis.

Q13: Does the synergy of the German physicist Hermann Haken not mean that order can arise from disorder, and that evolution could thus be possible?

A13: Haken always quotes the same examples for the origin of ordered structures. I once asked him after a lecture whether he could store these ordered structures; his answer was negative. A code is required for storing an achieved state. No codes are found in physical systems and every structure collapses when the causing gradient is suspended (e.g., a specific temperature difference).

Q14: What is your opinion of the Miller experiments which appear in school texts as "proof" of chemical evolution?

A14: No protein has ever been synthesized in such an experiment; they refer to proteinoids and not proteins as such. Even if they succeed in obtaining a true protein with a long amino acid chain and the correct optical rotation, it would still not be the start of evolution. There must be a coding system to store information about this protein so that it can be replicated at a later stage. A coding system can never originate in matter as precluded by Theorem 11. The Miller experiments thus do not contribute to an explanation of the origin of life.

Q15: SOS signals are periodic; does this not contradict your necessary condition NC2 (paragraph 4.2)?

A15: OTTO is also periodic, but it still is information. It is possible that brief sequences of symbols can contain periodic repetitions, but nobody would regard the decimal number 12.12 as a periodic fraction just because of the repetition of the digits.

Q16: Can new information originate through mutations?

A16: This idea is central in representations of evolution, but mutations can only cause changes in existing information. There can be no increase in information, and in general the results are injurious. New blueprints for new functions or new organs cannot arise; mutations cannot be the source of new (creative) information.

Q17: When the structure of a crystal is studied by means of a microscope, much information may be gained. Where and who is the sender in this case?

A17: No coding system is involved in this example and reality is observed directly. This case lies outside the domain of definition of information as discussed in chapter 5. The substitutionary function is absent, so that the theorems cannot be applied.

Q18: Has your definition of information been selected arbitrarily (see chapter 4 and 5)? Could there not be other possibilities?

A18: Of course, one could select other definitions, as often happens. My purpose was to demarcate a region where assertions of the nature of natural laws can be made. It is only in this way possible to formulate definitive assertions for unknown cases by means of known empirical theorems. The domain of definition is thus not as arbitrary as it might appear, but it has been dictated in the last instance by empirical realities.

Q19: Biological systems are more complicated than technical systems. So shouldn't an individual definition be introduced for biological information?

A19: Biological systems are indeed more complicated than all our technical inventions. However, we do not require a special principle for the conservation of energy, for example, for biological systems. The reason for this is that the principle of conservation of energy which applies in all physical systems is not only applicable in the limited area of inanimate matter but is universally valid and is thus also valid for all living systems. This is noted in the principles N2 and N3 (see chapter 2.3). If the stated theorems about information are laws of nature then they are valid for animate as well as inanimate systems. A different definition and different principles are therefore not necessary for biological systems.

Q20: Are laws of nature always quantifiable? Don't the statements only achieve this status when the observations have been successfully expressed in mathematical equations?

A20: In 1604, Galileo Galilei (1564–1642) discovered the law of falling bodies. He expressed the regularities he discovered in the form of verbal sentences in Italian (in *La nuova scienza*) which can be translated into other languages. Later, these sentences were translated with the help of a meta-language, that is the mathematical language. The mathematical language has the advantage that it allows an unambiguous and especially short presentation. Equations are an expression of quantitative details; however they only represent a part of the mathematical equipment. The phraseology of mathematical logic uses a formula apparatus but does not deal with quantitative dimensions. They represent a different and indispensable form of expression. With relation to question 20, we have to consider two aspects:

1. Not all observations in nature which can be formulated in mathematical terms are necessarily laws of nature. These must fulfill two important criteria: laws of nature must be universally valid and absolute. They must not be dependent on anything, especially not on place or time. It is therefore irrelevant who is observing nature, when and where and in what stage nature is. The circumstances are affected by the laws and not vice versa.

2. In order to be a law of nature, the facts under observation need not be formulated mathematically, although this does not exclude the possibility that a formal expression may one day be found (see examples a, b). It must also be noted that a number of correctly observed laws

of nature could later be included in a more general principle. A law of nature need not necessarily be represented by quantitative values. The description of an observation in qualitative and verbal terms suffices, if the observation is generally valid, i.e., can be reproduced as often as you like. It is only important to remember that laws of nature know no exceptions. These aspects should be made clearer in the following examples:

a) Rotary direction of a whirlpool: In the northern hemisphere of the earth, the whirlpool caused by water flowing out of a receptacle rotates in a counterclockwise direction, in the southern hemisphere in a clockwise direction. If this test should be carried out on other planets, a connection between the sense of rotation of the planet and the location of the test site above or below the equator could be established as well.

b) The right hand rule: According to the discovery made by the English physicist Michael Faraday (1791–1867) in 1831, electricity is induced in a metal conductor if it is moved into a magnetic field. The direction of the electrical flow is described in the law of nature which the English physicist John Ambrose Fleming (1849–1945) described by means of the "right hand rule" in 1884: "If one creates a right angle with the first three fingers of the right hand, and the thumb indicates the direction in which the conductor is moving and the forefinger indicates the direction of the lines of force, then the middle finger indicates the direction of the flow of electricity."

c) The Pauli principle: In 1925, the Austrian physicist and Nobel Prize winner Wolfgang Pauli (1900–1958) put forward the principle which carries his name (the exclusion principle). It maintains, among other things, that only electrons which are different from each other at least in one of the quantum numbers can be involved in forming atoms and molecules. That is, no identical electrons can exist next to one another. This principle is a law of nature which was not mathematically formulated but which is of greatest importance for the understanding of the periodic table of elements.

d) Le Chatelier's principle of least restraint: The principle formulated in 1887 by the French chemist Henry-Louis Le Chatelier (1850–1936) and the German Nobel Prize winner in Physics

(1909) Karl Ferdinand Braun (1850–1918) qualitatively describes the dependence of the chemical equilibrium on external conditions. According to the principle, the equilibrium continually shifts in order to avoid external forces (e.g., temperature, pressure, concentration of the reactionary partner). Example: In the case of a reaction linked with a change in volume (e.g., the decomposition of ammonia: $2\ NH_3 \leftrightarrow N_2 + 3\ H_2$), an increase in pressure must lead to a reduction in turnover. Accordingly, the turnover of a reaction involving a reduction in volume is increased through an increase in pressure: in the case of ammonia synthesis $N_2 + 3\ H_2 \leftrightarrow 2NH_3$, the equilibrium is shifted under the high pressure toward NH_3. Taking this result into account, the Haber-Bosch procedure of ammonia synthesis is carried out under high pressure. The principle also says that under additional heat influx, in exothermic reactions the equilibrium shifts toward the original substances and in endothermic reactions toward the produced substances. The Le Chatelier principle applies not only to reversible chemical reactions, but equally to reversible physical processes, such as evaporation or crystallization.

e) The principle of least motion: Hine recognized a law of nature which helps us to predict chemical reactions. The principle maintains that the reactions which involve the least changes to atom compositions and electron configurations are more likely to happen. Thus, using this principle, it is possible to predict why, in the Birch reduction of aromatic connections 1,4 dienes and not 1,3 dienes are produced. Dienes or diolefines are unsaturated aliphatic and cycloaliphatic hydrocarbons which contain molecules with double bonds. Note: In the first two examples (a and b) it was possible to express the verbal statements in mathematical equations. a) The rotary direction of a whirlpool can be derived from mechanics (Coriolis force). b) In 1873, the English physicist James Clerk Maxwell (1831–1879) found a mathematical description ("A Treatise on Electricity and Magnetism") which the German physicist Heinrich Hertz (1857–1894) in 1890 expressed in the first and second Maxwell equations which are still used today. c) As a result of the observations in conjunction with the Pauli principle, later a mathematical deduction of the principle using the wave function of an electron became possible. These reasons are based on the validity of the wave function. However, the law itself is still usually formulated verbally.

These examples confirm that laws of nature do not necessarily have to be quantifiable. If preferred reactions, rotary directions, or other general principles are being described, then mathematical formulas are not always effective. In some cases, the observations of the laws of nature can be deduced from more general laws. Thus, for example, the law of induction is already contained in the Maxwell equations. All the aspects of the laws of nature discussed here are equally valid in relation to theorems about information. According to their nature, the generally valid facts about information can be observed, but they are not quantifiable. Thus, the statements are described verbally. This type of description is no criterion as to whether a fact is a law of nature or not.

Q21: Can the laws of nature change in time?
A21: The laws of nature are valid everywhere in the universe and at all times without exception. There can be absolutely no exceptions. It would be tragic if the laws of nature did change as time went on. Every technical construction and measuring apparatus is a practical application of the laws of nature. If the laws of nature changed, bridges and tower blocks, calculated correctly taking the laws of nature into account, could collapse. As all physiological processes are also dependent on the laws of nature, then a change in these laws would have catastrophic consequences.

Q22: Is the sender already included in your definition of information? If a sender is already included in the definition, then the conclusion that there must be a sender is self-evident.
A22: Of course, the sender is included in neither the definition nor the prerequisite. That would be a circular argument. The laws of nature are deduced completely from experience. Thus, the existence of a sender when there is a code, has been observed a million times over. In the work in hand, the difference between theorems and definitions is clearly made. Theorems should be viewed as laws of nature. They are observed. In Theorems 1, 9, and 11, we talked about a sender. I would like to stress that this is neither a definition nor a prerequisite. The statements are much more the result of countless observations.

Q23: Can a law of nature be toppled? Or, to phrase it differently, are the laws of nature confirmatory?

A23: If we are talking about true laws of nature (true in the sense that they are not merely what we assume to be laws of nature), then they are universally valid and unchangeable and they can never be toppled. Their main feature is that they are fixed. In their practical implementation, the laws of nature cannot be proven in a mathematical sense, but they are founded and refuting in character. With their help, we are able to make accurate predictions about the possible and the impossible. For this reason, no invention which offends a law of nature is accepted by a patent office (e.g., perpetua mobilia offend the principle of the conservation of energy). Assumed law of nature: A law which is often assumed to be a law of nature but which in reality is no such thing, may be held as such for a period of time. However, it can be toppled by an example showing the opposite (falsification). True law of nature: These are true laws of nature which can never be toppled because examples of the opposite cannot exist. The validity of a law of nature cannot be proven mathematically; however it is proven in continual observations.

Q24: How many laws of nature are there?

A24: The total number of laws of nature cannot be stated exactly for two reasons: We can never be sure whether we have recognized all phenomena reliant on the laws of nature. Sometimes a number of laws can be summed up in the framework of one superordinate standpoint. There is then no point in listing each individual law. The quest for the world formula which is often mentioned assumes that there is one formula which can express all our laws of nature. However, this seems to be a utopian goal.

Q25: Have you lectured on your concept of information as a law of nature in front of specialists?

A25: I have lectured on this topic in countless national and international universities. In June 1996, I also presented my concept at an international congress which was especially concerned with the discussion on information [G18]. There was always a lively discussion, and the specialists tried to find an example of the opposite (one example would be enough to topple an assumed law of nature). A true law of nature cannot be toppled.

PART 3:

Application of the Concept of Information to the Bible

The information concept was discussed in Part 2, and many theorems having general validity were formulated. This concept figures prominently in practically all scientific disciplines. We will now consider the essential and distinctive properties of information, taking the Bible as example. Certain aspects will be clarified, and we will obtain a new way of looking at the message of the Bible. An important conclusion will be that the natural laws about information fit completely in the biblical message of the creation of life.

CHAPTER 12 Life Requires a Source of Information

The common factor present in all living organisms, from bacteria to man, is the information contained in all their cells. It has been discovered that nowhere else can a higher statistical packing density of information (see appendix A1.2.3) be found. The information present in living systems falls in the category of "operational information" as discussed in chapter 7. This information is exactly tuned in to the infinitude of life processes and situations, and its origin can be ascribed to creative constructional information (chapter 7). The different information aspects are depicted in Figure 26, where the statistical level has been omitted for the sake of simplicity. This diagram is of a general nature and can therefore be applied to any piece of information (see chapter 5 for domain of definition); it is in every case under consideration only necessary to identify the sender, the recipient, and the specifics of the various levels, syntax, semantics, pragmatics, and apobetics. The properties characteristic of life are indicated next to each level in Figure 26. In the case of the recipient, these levels can in principle be investigated scientifically, although we have to admit that our present knowledge only scratches the surface.

According to the information laws, every piece of information requires a sender. The demarcated region in Figure 26 is in principle not accessible for scientific research, namely the person of the sender. Since the sender cannot be investigated by human means, many people erroneously conclude that He does not exist, and thus they contra-

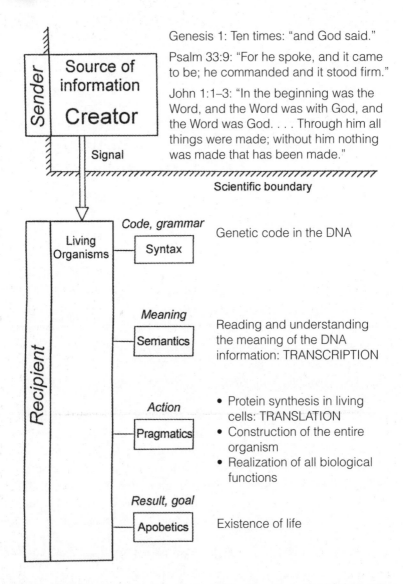

Figure 26: Concerning the origin of life. The biological information in living beings is obviously "operational information" which can be specified and investigated scientifically for the recipient on the known levels — syntax, semantics, pragmatics, and apobetics. Its origin and nature is "creative information." Scientific analysis requires the existence of a sender, but we can only find Him in the revelation of the Bible.

vene the information theorems. The requirement that there must be a personal sender exercising his own free will, cannot be relinquished. This sender, the Creator, has revealed himself so that we do have information about Him. He, Jesus, was in the world and the world was made through Him (John 1:10). Everything in the entire universe, without exception, was created by Him, as is stated in the first verses of John's Gospel and in Colossians 1:16: "For by him all things were created: things in heaven and on earth, visible and invisible, whether thrones or powers or rulers or authorities; all things were created by him and for him."

The close link between information and will was discussed in paragraph 3.3, and this idea is also clearly emphasized many times in the Bible. We read in Revelation 4:11, "You created all things, and by your will they were created and have their being." The intentional prerequisite of information is expressed in Genesis 1:26: "Let us make man in our image, in our likeness."

In the light of the information theorems, all materialistic evolution models are useless and are thus rejected.[17]

The British evolution theoreticist Richard Dawkins expresses the following expectation in his book *The Blind Watchmaker:* "The purpose of this book is to provide a non-supernatural explanation for the existence of complex living organisms" [D2]. As a consequence, we cannot expect to find a scientifically based answer in his discussion (e.g., because of Theorem 17).

---

17. Evolution models: This sentence refers to all those evolution concepts which assume the possibility that matter can be self-organizing. This view is found in the publications by supporters of evolution, to mention just a few: Manfred Eigen, Bernd-Olaf Küppers, Carsten Bresch, Franz Wuketits, and David Attenborough. In addition, there is the idea of theistic evolution where God just set the evolution ball rolling and supposedly guided it during millions of years. This latter view cannot be refuted by means of the information theorems, but it contradicts biblical revelation. In my book *Did God Use Evolution?* [G14] theistic evolution is discussed in detail and is rejected.

CHAPTER **13** The Quality and
Usefulness of Biblical
Information

The semantic value of information versus usability is graphed in Figure 25 (page 117), resulting in four different areas (quadrants). According to biblical assertions all information given out by humans is evaluated by God.

Useless information: We have subdivided useless information into two parts, namely indifferent and injurious information, and we find a permanent criterion in God's commandments: "You shall not give false testimony against your neighbor" (Exod. 20:16), because "The LORD detests lying lips" (Prov. 12:22). Such people are described in Jeremiah 8:6: "I have listened attentively, but they do not say what is right. No one repents of his wickedness, saying, 'What have I done?' Each pursues his own course like a horse charging into battle." The tongue is a small part of the body, but it can have enormous effects: "Consider what a great forest is set on fire by a small spark. The tongue also is a fire . . ." (James 3:5–6). These quotations are restricted to cases where we, as senders, transmit injurious information. God also wants to protect us from being recipients of such information, and He warns us emphatically against association with such senders:

> Proverbs 1:10: "My son, if sinners entice you, do not give in to them."

Proverbs 14:7: "Stay away from a foolish man, for you will not find knowledge on his lips."

Psalm 1:1: "Blessed is the man who does not walk in the counsel of the wicked or stand in the way of sinners or sit in the seat of mockers."

In this connection, we want to point out that Adam and Eve's sin was introduced by the evil information: "Did God really say . . . ?" (Gen. 3:1). The response of the first people to this information which threw doubt upon God's word, had inconceivable consequences. It resulted in death and suffering, pain and illness, war and wailing, and all of us are still suffering from the disastrous effects of sin. Man can both send and receive injurious information (lies, provocation, slander, mockery, and cursing) by listening and responding to it. God detests both, and every evil word is recorded in God's information registers. These books will be opened one day (Rev. 20:12) and we will be judged accordingly, as Jesus prophesied: "But I tell you that men will have to give account on the day of judgment for every careless word they have spoken. For by your words you will be acquitted, and by your words you will be condemned" (Matt. 12:36–37).

Valuable information: The most valuable information that has ever been sent is the Word of God. No other message is better and no other words ever brought more joy. There is no useless or false information in the Bible, since God's Word is absolutely true: "God is not a man, that he should lie, nor a son of man, that he should change his mind. Does he speak and then not act? Does he promise and not fulfil?" (Num. 23:19). The Bible contains certainty and truth, as well as eternal and divine words. No other information can even approach being equal to this. The Psalmist testifies from his personal experience when he cries out, "I rejoice in your promise like one who finds great spoil" (Ps. 119:162). Paul also refers to the treasure he has found: "But we have this treasure in jars of clay" (2 Cor. 4:7). God wants us always to be receivers and transmitters of this information which He values exceedingly.

1. As recipient: Many people follow various courses and take pains for the purpose of being successful in their private lives and in their careers. Already in the Old Testament God has given simple advice which can easily be followed and can have great effects: "Do not let this Book of the Law depart from your mouth; meditate on it day and night, so that you may be careful to do everything written in it. Then you will be prosperous and successful" (Josh. 1:8). Contemplation of and obedience to the Word of the living God is extremely important: "Obey me, and I will be your God and you will be my people. Walk in all the ways I command you, that it may go well with you" (Jer. 7:23).

The Word brings understanding and wisdom and it keeps us from going astray (Ps. 119:104). It renews (Ps. 119:154), enlightens and brings joy (Ps. 119:130) and shows us the way of salvation (James 1:21). Since we are dealing with the most valuable information — extremely important information, Figure 25 — we are unambiguously instructed to "Let the word of Christ dwell in you richly" (Col. 3:16). According to Helmut Matthies, director of information services of the Evangelical Alliance of Germany, the average German works 38.5 hours per week and watches television for 17.5 hours per week [M1]. The latter figure is increasing, and the watchers are exposed to an inconceivable amount of influencing, but they neglect the one necessary influence. God's will is that we should let ourselves be impregnated with His eternal message.

2. As sender: In our role as senders we will only pass on information which has impressed us. Jesus expresses this general situation in the words: "For out of the overflow of the heart the mouth speaks" (Matt. 12:34). The Psalmist always concerned himself with the Word, so that he could and would draw from this supply: "May my tongue sing of your word" (Ps. 119:172). Christians should be recognized from the well they drink. This does not mean that no negative information should proceed from them, but that they should be bearers of good news. God's evaluation is obvious from Isaiah 52:7: "How beautiful . . . are the feet of those who bring good news, who proclaim peace, who bring good tidings, who proclaim salvation."

This good news is the gospel of Jesus Christ which saves everyone who believes and accepts it. Jesus often emphasized that we should be senders of this message (Matt. 28:19–20; Mark 16:15; Luke 10:3; and Luke 12:8–9). When the Samaritan woman met Jesus at Jacob's well and recognized Him as the Christ, she put her jar down and immediately went back to the town to proclaim the message of salvation (John 4:25–30). Paul also tried any possible way of winning over different people of all backgrounds (1 Cor. 9:19–22), and he even tells himself, "Woe to me if I do not preach the gospel!" (1 Cor. 9:16). He combines assignment and contents in the following words: "We implore you on Christ's behalf: Be reconciled to God" (2 Cor. 5:20). This message is not only the most important and the most urgent, it is also the most certain message. The well-known evangelist C.H. Spurgeon (1834–1892) calls out [S9]: "If you don't have an eternal gospel to proclaim, then your message is only worth 20 pennies. You can get uncertainties elsewhere and everywhere, but matters of eternal life are only found in the Bible."

14 Aspects of Information as Found in the Bible

14.1 GOD AS SENDER — MAN AS RECIPIENT

The five aspects of information — statistics, syntax, semantics, pragmatics, and apobetics — were discussed in chapter 4, and it was stated that all five are indispensable for both the sender and the recipient. It is highly instructive to view the Bible in this way.

Sender: In Figure 27, God is shown as the source or sender of biblical information. His Word is available to us today in completed (Rev. 22:18) and written form (e.g., Exod. 17:14; Ezek. 37:16; 1 Cor. 9:10; and Rev. 1:11), after He has spoken to us in many different ways (Heb. 1:1–2). The following list indicates the wide spectrum of methods God used to speak to us:

> audibly (Exod. 19:19, Matt. 3:17)
> in His own handwriting (Exod. 31:18)
> through angels (Luke 2:10–12, Heb. 2:2)
> through prophets (Jeremiah 1:5, Hebrews 1:1)
> through dreams (Dan. 2, Matt. 1:20)
> through visions (Ezek. 1:1)
> through apostles (Acts 1:2)
> through inspiration (2 Tim. 3:16)
> through revelation (Gal. 1:12, Eph. 3:3, Rev. 1:1)
> through Jesus Christ, the Son of God (Heb. 1:2)

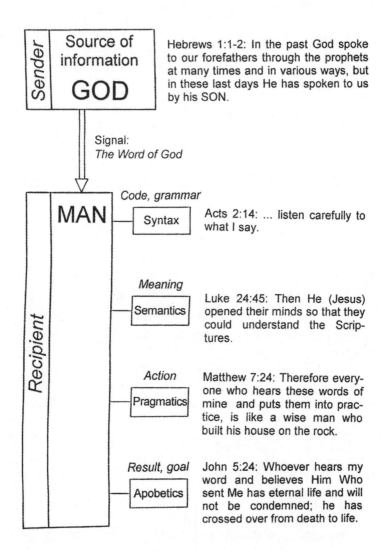

Figure 27: God as sender; man as recipient. When God speaks in the Bible, He is the Sender of information. The message of the Bible, transmitted to us as recipients, can be analyzed according to the aspects of information, namely syntax, semantics, pragmatics, and apobetics. Only when we cover all the levels, will we achieve the purpose intended by God.

God mostly used and uses people as bearers of information, but He was and is the actual sender, while we fulfill the function of recipient. All views about the origin of the Bible based on purely human sources miss the real point, even if these are couched in highly theological terms. This question about who the sender is becomes the touchstone for belief and unbelief, and thus for life and death. For Spurgeon, the question of who the sender is also asserts itself in its power [S10]: "Our own words are mere paper darts compared to the heavy artillery of God's Word." Although the Bible speaks about heavenly, spiritual, and divine matters, it is encoded in reasonable words (Acts 26:25) in human language, and not in inexpressible heavenly terms (2 Cor. 12:4). We will now consider the various aspects of information with respect to the Bible.

1. Statistics: The only value of statistical analyses of the Bible is for storage purposes (see appendix A1.2.1 and Figure 35). In addition, word counts may be of use in certain investigations.

2. Syntax: God's thoughts are available to us, encoded in human language, originally mostly in Hebrew and Greek. This message can in principle be translated into any other natural language. All over the world, many missionaries perform the blessed service of translation, so that the gospel can be proclaimed in all living languages. They thus fulfill Christ's prophetic promise that all nations will have heard the gospel message before His second coming (Matt. 24:14).

3. Semantics: The contents of the Bible make it a unique book which cannot be compared with any other book. The Bible provides answers to all vital questions on earth, and it is also the only sure compass able to guide us to eternity. In thousands of books, philosophers, founders of religions, and all kinds of scientists have tried to solve the great puzzles like: What is the origin of the earth and of life? What is man? Who is God? Is there life after death? Nobody is able to make final and true statements about these questions; only the Bible can do this on the authority and by the truth of the living God. For the purpose of understanding the semantics of the Bible, some fundamental differences which distinguish it from other books are now considered:

Scientific results: It is useful to employ linguistic findings as well as historical background information for a better understanding of the text. Even with the best erudition it might still happen that the essence of the message remains hidden. We wish to emphasize that the so-called "historical-critical method" is not a suitable approach for understanding the Bible.

Spiritual understanding: The Bible is a spiritual book which was formulated under the supervision of the Holy Spirit. In the same way, its understanding is also a spiritual process requiring the collaboration of the Holy Spirit.

Personal attitude: The Lord opens the Scriptures for those who seek (Matt. 7:7; Luke 24:25) and who obey (2 Cor. 10:5). Access is denied to those who regard themselves as wise; those who are haughty and hard of heart exclude themselves (Exod. 4:21; Isa. 6:9–10; Ezek. 2:4; Matt. 13:15; John 7:17).

Biblical concepts: The overall conception of the Bible is that it is easy to understand (2 Cor. 1:13). Jesus used many parables[18] to illustrate difficult spiritual relationships.

When one reads philosophical treatises, legal expositions, or political declarations, one too often gains the impression that more things are obscured than are explained. The Bible is composed in such a way that a child can understand the fundamental assertions and be blessed through the Word. The only condition is that the heart must be open, then the following is applicable: "Blessed are your eyes because they see, and your ears because they hear" (Matt. 13:16).

There are also difficult passages in the Bible. When God said, "My thoughts are not your thoughts, neither are your ways my ways. . . . As the heavens are higher than the earth, so are my ways higher than your ways and my thoughts than your thoughts" (Isa. 55:8–9), then this also applies to His Word. Many passages cannot be understood now, but their meaning will be revealed when, for example, the prophetically designated time has arrived.

Fullness of ideas: The English Bible (KJV) contains 783,173 words, a number which is fairly limited, but the scope of its ideas is unbounded. In exceptional cases one might read a secular book two or three times, and then its contents will be fully known, but the Bible is inex-

---

18. Parables: It should be mentioned that the parables also have an exactly opposite function. There are people for whom the parables become a judgment: "This people's heart has become calloused; they hardly hear with their ears" (Matt. 13:15). The effect the parables have depends on one's attitude: "The knowledge of the secrets of the kingdom of God has been given to you, but to others I speak in parables" (Luke 8:10). "For everyone who has will be given more, and he will have an abundance. Whoever does not have, even what he has will be taken from him" (Matt. 25:29).

haustible, and even at a hundredth reading, new ideas and relation-ships are revealed. After many years of intensive Bible study, Spurgeon testified [S10]: "The copiousness of God's Word is just as unbounded as its comprehensiveness. During the forty years of my own ministry I have merely touched the hem of the garment of divine truth, but what power flowed out from it! The Word resembles its Originator: boundless, immeasurable and infinite. If it were your task to preach throughout eternity, you would always find a theme on whatever topic may be required."

Inexhaustible: The semantic wealth of the Bible is so great that no human life is long enough to deplete it. There is, however, a unifying thread which keeps everything together.

4. Pragmatics: If the recipient (man) breaks off the message received from the sender (God) at the semantic level, then the purpose intended by God will be missed. The goal of the information in the Bible is that man should be moved to action. Jesus placed an extreme-ly high premium on this aspect of information: "Therefore everyone who hears these words of mine and puts them into practice is like a wise man who built his house on the rock" (Matt. 7:24). When deeds are not forthcoming, the Word becomes a judgment. This aspect is expounded in the parable of the ten "minas" (talents), where Jesus gave the unambiguous command: "Put this money to work . . . until I come back "(Luke 19:13). The obedient servants were amply rewarded; He said to the first one, "Well done, my good servant! . . . Because you have been trustworthy in a very small matter, take charge of ten cit-ies" (Luke 19:17). The one who did nothing, was condemned: "I will judge you by your own words, you wicked servant! You knew, did you, that I am a hard man, taking out what I did not put in, and reaping what I did not sow?" (Luke 19:22). Our deeds are judged by God (Rev. 20:12), and according to Matthew 25:31–46, Jesus will distinguish between two groups of people only: those who acted, and those who did nothing. The first group was invited into heaven: "Come, you who are blessed by my Father; take your inheritance, the kingdom prepared for you since the creation of the world" (Matt. 25:34). The reason is given in verse 40: "Whatever you did for one of the least of these brothers of mine, you did for me."

The second group is sent into the eternal fire because "Whatever you did not do for one of the least of these, you did not do for me." The message of James 1:22 becomes clear in this regard: "Do not merely listen to the word, and so deceive yourselves. Do what it says." Heinrich Kemner said justly that in the last judgment we will mostly be found guilty for what we did not do. "Anyone, then, who knows the good he ought to do and doesn't do it, sins" (James 4:17). Also in the Old Testament Moses, as instructed by God, identifies the pragmatic requirement on which life depends: "Take to heart all the words I have solemnly declared to you this day, so that you may command your children to obey carefully all the words of this law. They are not just idle words for you — they are your life" (Deut. 32:46–47).

We now use two illustrative examples to explain a false and a correct pragmatic attitude toward the Bible.

Example 1: There is an East Prussian story[19] about a teacher who discussed Matthew 5:39: "If someone strikes you on the right cheek, turn to him the other also" during a religious instruction class. One farmer was rather indignant when his son told him this, and when he met the teacher in a meadow he put this command to the test. He asked the teacher whether he practiced that which he taught the children. The reply was, "But of course, it stands in the Bible." The farmer then lashed out and struck the teacher down with a powerful blow to his face. When he struggled to his feet, the farmer quoted, "Turn to him the other also," and dealt him another heavy blow on his left cheek. Being a Bible student, the teacher countered with, "With the measure you use, it will be measured to you — and even more" (Mark 4:24), and in his turn struck the farmer. This resulted in an exchange of blows where every blow was accompanied by a biblical quotation. At that moment, the landowner traveled past and saw the fight. He stopped and sent his servant to investigate. The servant ran to the combatants, watched them for a while, and then walked back at a leisurely pace. He reported that nothing much was the matter, they were only explaining Holy Scriptures to each other.

Example 2: A blind septuagenarian African woman had a French Bible which she loved very much. She took it to the local missionary requesting him to highlight John 3:16 in red. This he did, without knowing her purpose. The blind woman then sat at the school gate and asked the emerging pupils whether any of them knew French. Being proud of their knowledge of the language, they answered in

---

19. The German poet Johann Peter Hebel (1760–1826) told a similar story with the title "Good Word, Evil Deed" in the *Little Treasure Chest of the Rhenish Home Friend*.

the affirmative. The woman then showed them the underlined verse, requesting them to read it for her. They complied eagerly. When she asked them whether they understood these words, the answer was "no." The woman then explained the meaning of this central biblical assertion: "For God so loved the world that he gave his one and only Son, that whoever believes in him shall not perish but have eternal life." It is known that 24 men became evangelists through the ministry of this woman [J2].

5. Apobetics: From the point of view of the sender, a process of information transfer has only been successful when the purpose intended for the recipient has been achieved. All aspects of information are inextricably interlinked. It is thus insufficient when everything runs smoothly up to a certain level, but the final level — the purpose — is not attained. Strictly speaking, any information level is only a stepping stone to the next higher level: Language is solely a means for achieving the semantics purpose. In its turn, semantics leads to the pragmatics level, and, in the last instance, pragmatics is only a preparatory stage for the apobetics. In chapter 4, this purposefulness of information is described as the most important aspect. This is especially true of God's message in the Bible. He has certain objectives with the Bible, of which we mention some special ones.

a) Perception: Who is God? Without the Bible, we would have known very little about God. We could deduce His existence and His power from His works of creation (Rom. 1:20), but nothing would be known about His person and His nature. The Bible thus has the purpose of making God known to us. It is obvious that all polytheistic representations are false: "I am the LORD, and there is no other; apart from me there is no God" (Isa. 45:5). God is love (1 John 4:16), life (1 John 5:20), and light (1 John 1:5). He is holy (Isa. 6:3) and hates sin so much that it carries the death penalty (Rom. 6:23). We are abundantly informed about God's Son and His function as Savior, and also about the Holy Spirit who leads us in all truth. Jesus is the only way to God. In the words of Martin Luther, "If you do not find God through Christ, you will never find Him, even if you search everywhere else."

b) Perception: Creation was purposeful. When we read the first two chapters of the Bible, it becomes clear that creation was systematically planned and made purposefully. Man is the crowning glory at the pinnacle of creation. Seen in the light of the Bible, Nietzsche's anti-apobetics is empty and not based on reality: "Man is a thread tied between animal and superman, a thread stretching above an abyss" (Zarathustra). According to the New Testament, however, everything was created by and for Christ (Col. 1:16).

c) Perception: Who is man? Alexis Carrel, a Nobel laureate, wrote a book with the title *Man the Unknown.* Apart from the Bible, we cannot fathom who we really are; our true nature would remain a mystery. The well-known German author Manfred Hausmann (1898–1986) testified as follows: "Every time I open the Bible, I am astounded anew by its depth and many-sidedness. The picture drawn of man is found nowhere else. Man is encompassed in his entirety, his greatness and his pitiableness, his tenderness and brutality, his glory and his darkness. No other book reveals such appalling and such splendid things about human nature than does the Bible. The background meanings of the stories told in it are inexhaustible." We learn from the Bible that we were separated from God through sin and are now on our way to hell. Everybody needs to be saved, and the religions encourage us to pull ourselves up by our own bootstraps — self-salvation. On the way to judgment, we are met by the One who is the "antidote" to sin: Jesus! If we understand ourselves in this light, then we know who we are.

d) Manual of instructions for life: God has prepared the best purposes and greatest blessings conceivable for our earthly life. He is concerned about our happiness in marriage, in our family, our career, and our nation, and desires to bless us with success in everything, so that the words of the Psalmist are applicable: "Whatever he does prospers" (Ps. 1:3). God's will for us is the best, as indicated in uncountable ways. The upright will be prosperous (Prov. 2:7), those who hope in Him will be strengthened (Isa. 40:31), and all who are weary and burdened will find rest (Matt. 11:28). There is only one answer to the question why God does this, namely "I have loved you with an everlasting love" (Jer. 31:3).

A machine will not operate properly in the fashion envisaged by the inventor, unless the instruction manual is obeyed. How much more then do our lives become a mess when we disregard the instructions for our life as provided by the Creator? This type of information can be regarded as operational information, as discussed in chapter 7. The Bible is the only instruction manual for a blessed and full life; the condition is briefly and simply formulated: "By living according to your word" (Ps. 119:9).

e) Signpost pointing to heaven: The highest purpose ever formulated is that God desires eternal communion with each one of us. Earthly blessings are only a minute foretaste compared to the richness of eternity. We are invited to enter heaven. The suffering and death of Jesus was the price paid for sin, so that we will not be lost. When Jesus rose up from the grave, this sacrifice was honored by God. Now anybody can get into the lifeboat which will reach the other coast, because God does not want sinners to be lost, "but rather that they turn from their ways and live" (Ezek. 33:11). God sent the Lord Jesus "as a sacrifice of atonement, through faith in his blood" (Rom. 3:25). Everyone who calls on His name (Rom. 10:13) and who receives Him (John 1:12), has crossed over from the death penalty of sin, to eternal life (John 5:24). The way to heaven is just as simple as it is sure: The Bible is the *only compass,* and Jesus is the *only way.* Anybody who turns to Jesus is saved. He then becomes a child of God and at the same time heir to heaven (Titus 3:7). This decision cannot be postponed. Bezzel once said, "The pardoning power of grace is unlimited, but it still depends on the moment."

Missionary and native: After every sermon, a missionary called on the congregation to choose Jesus. When urged to repent, someone who attended regularly for several years always responded with, "Next year." One day he became seriously ill, and the missionary brought him the required medicine with the instruction that it should be taken a year later. The native then said that he might be dead before that time and needed the medicine right now. The missionary replied, "You care for your body, but what about your soul?"

Many people, when seeking a goal for their life, are worried that it might be a failure. Our life has attained its highest purpose when we bind it to God; then all searching becomes unnecessary because of this consummation. Spurgeon once uttered the striking words [S9]: "Man's heart has only enough life to pursue one goal fully. Nobody can serve both God and mammon, because there is not enough life in one's heart to serve both."

There is a striking example in the Bible of the way somebody comes to faith; this is depicted in Figure 28. All aspects of information are covered one after the other in such a way that they can easily be followed. This Ethiopian is a good example of someone finding Christ and salvation through Scripture.

The parable of the sower: Another easily understood example of the information levels is found in the parable of the sower (Matt. 13:3–23). In this parable, Jesus uses a common occurrence of everyday life to illus-

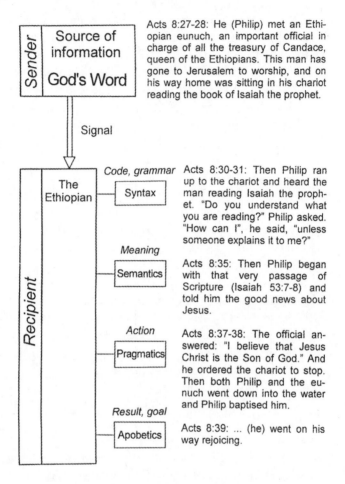

| Sender | Source of information

God's Word | Acts 8:27-28: He (Philip) met an Ethiopian eunuch, an important official in charge of all the treasury of Candace, queen of the Ethiopians. This man has gone to Jerusalem to worship, and on his way home was sitting in his chariot reading the book of Isaiah the prophet. |

Signal

	The Ethiopian	Code, grammar Syntax	Acts 8:30-31: Then Philip ran up to the chariot and heard the man reading Isaiah the prophet. "Do you understand what you are reading?" Philip asked. "How can I", he said, "unless someone explains it to me?"
Recipient		Meaning Semantics	Acts 8:35: Then Philip began with that very passage of Scripture (Isaiah 53:7-8) and told him the good news about Jesus.
		Action Pragmatics	Acts 8:37-38: The official answered: "I believe that Jesus Christ is the Son of God." And he ordered the chariot to stop. Then both Philip and the eunuch went down into the water and Philip baptised him.
		Result, goal Apobetics	Acts 8:39: ... (he) went on his way rejoicing.

Figure 28: God's Word as sender; a seeking man as recipient. A special case of the general view in Figure 27 is shown here. The example of the minister of finance of Ethiopia provides a striking overview of the successive levels of information transfer (Acts 8:26–39). The message of the Bible reached him and touched him; he came to believe in Jesus Christ and thus received eternal life. This Ethiopian is a good example for us. The functions could be interchanged, so that man is the sender and God the recipient. Seen technologically, the information transmission system from man to God is the very best available one. Any and every message from the sender reaches the recipient without distortion or loss. No meanings are misunderstood, and the pragmatics and the apobetics are guaranteed by divine promises.

trate and explain aspects of the kingdom of God. At the semantic level, the information is complete and clear. The effect of God's words (the seeds) results in four different kinds of conduct (pragmatics on the side of the recipient). The purpose intended by the sender (Jesus) is achieved in only one group of recipients (their apobetics).

14.2 MAN AS SENDER — GOD AS RECIPIENT

The case where God is the sender and man the recipient is illustrated in Figures 26 (page 136) and 27 (page 144). The question arises whether these are the recipients of the information transmitted by man. That is exactly the case, as shown in Figure 29; not only is it conceivable, but it is God's desire and purpose. We may approach God the Father or His Son, Jesus, with various conceptual goals in mind. The message is transmitted through prayer, and this transmission is vastly superior to any technological communications system:

- It is the surest connection possible, because nobody and no process can break this link. It is always and immediately operational.

- This "wireless telegraphy" cannot be blocked or shielded by anything. When the astronauts circled the moon, no radio contact with earth was possible when they were behind the moon on the far side, but we can pray anywhere; distance and separation is no obstacle. It does not matter whether one is 100 feet underground, 1,000 feet under the sea, or behind the moon. The message reaches the recipient with absolute certainty.

- Interference is encountered in all technological transmission systems, so that the original message may be distorted by external influences. Code symbols may be lost or changed, but prayer messages cannot at all be distorted; they reach the recipient unchanged.

The information transmission system from man to God is thus the very best available one. A better communication link is found only in heaven when faith is replaced by direct communion. We now discuss the separate levels from God's side.

1. Statistics: The matter of statistics does not arise here.

2. Syntax: At this level, there is no restriction of codes, because God understands all languages. No language poses any problems. Every conceivable method of expression may be used, even if it is only

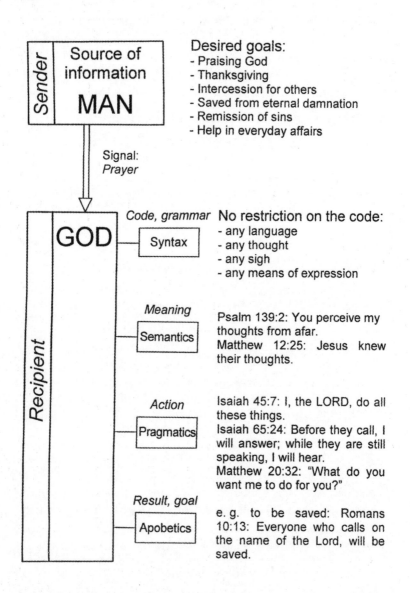

Figure 29: Man as sender, God as recipient. Seen technologically, the information transmission system from man to God is the very best available one: Any and every message from the sender reaches the recipient without distortion or loss. No meanings are misunderstood, and the pragmatics and the apobetics are guaranteed by divine promises.

a deep sigh. He can even read unformulated thoughts.

3. **Semantics:** The Psalmist said to God: "You perceive my thoughts from afar" (Ps. 139:2), so that comprehension is absolutely guaranteed. There can be no misunderstandings. Even if our verbal formulations are off the mark, our actual perceptions do reach God (1 Sam. 16:7: "The Lord looks at the heart"). There is a further positive aspect: The Holy Spirit compensates for the weaknesses and defects of the information sent by us: "The Spirit helps us in our weakness. We do not know what we ought to pray for, but the Spirit himself intercedes for us with groans that words cannot express" (Rom. 8:26).

4. **Pragmatics:** God is described as a doer in the Bible: "I, the LORD, do all these things" (Isa. 45:7). It is clear from the creation account that His words immediately become deeds, and the Bible could have the subtitle "The Great Deeds of God." Jesus' life on earth was a unique life of witnessing through deeds. He did not only preach with authority, He also acted at every conceivable opportunity: He healed those who were ill, He raised people from the dead, He forgave sins, He exorcised demons, He fed large crowds, and He controlled the weather. Eyewitnesses cried out in amazement, "Who is this? Even the wind and the waves obey him!" (Mark 4:41).

His greatest deed was the salvation He wrought on Calvary. This was already prophesied by God through Isaiah: "The LORD has laid on him the iniquity of us all" (Isa. 53:6). Today, the power of forgiveness reaches out to all sinners. Nobody need be lost. We only have to turn to the One who has the required authority, Jesus Christ. He has never ever rejected anybody who prayed to Him in earnest. God always answers our prayers in the way that is best for us, because He knows the correct time much better than we, as well as the action which will benefit us most. There is one prayer which is always answered immediately; there is no delay and no alternative when a sinner prays for salvation. If you call on the name of Jesus for this purpose, you are immediately accepted (Rom. 10:13). There is no delay between call and answer, not even one millisecond: "Before they call I will answer; while they are still speaking I will hear" (Isa. 65:24). When the one criminal on the cross next to the Son of God made the plea, "Jesus, remember me when you come into your kingdom," he was immediately given the unconditional and instantaneously effective promise: "I tell you the truth, today you will be with me in paradise" (Luke 23:42–43).

5. **Apobetics:** In the "Our Father" prayer, God gives us goals

which correspond to His purposes: "Your will be done" (Matt. 6:10). It is God's will to bring everybody to the goal of salvation: He "wants all men to be saved" (1 Tim. 2:4). God identifies himself with our desired goals when they correspond to His Word. Dietrich Bonhoeffer (1906–1945) once said that although God does not fulfill all our wishes, He does fulfill all of His countless promises. There are about 1,260 direct promises in the Bible, and thousands of aids for our daily life situations (Ps. 50:15), but His main concern is our eternal life: "His eternal purpose which He accomplished in Christ Jesus our Lord" (Eph. 3:11). He has achieved His purpose for us when Jesus becomes Lord and Master of all areas of our life. Then we "are no longer foreigners and aliens, but fellow citizens with God's people and members of God's household, built on the foundation of the apostles and prophets, with Christ Jesus himself as the chief cornerstone" (Eph. 2:19–20). Without Jesus, we will miss the purpose of our life, as the Bible warns emphatically (Col. 2:18; Heb. 2:1).

14.3 THE HIGHEST PACKING DENSITY OF INFORMATION

The statistical density of information is discussed in the appendix, chapter A1. It is clear that the highest possible packing density is attained in the DNA molecules of living cells. It also makes sense to determine information density at the other levels of information. Without recourse to actual numerical calculations, we now discuss some estimates for the Bible:

1. The semantic density of information: This can be defined as the plenitude of ideas or the "weight of the meanings" per sentence or per paragraph. The origin of man and of this world has been discussed in many scientific and popular publications. Nobody knows how many books have been written on these topics. However, most publications treat the subject from an evolutionary viewpoint, and nobody can provide genuine answers. Having said this, it is noteworthy that the Bible describes man's origin completely in one single verse: "The LORD God formed the man from the dust of the ground and breathed into his nostrils the breath of life, and the man became a living being" (Gen. 2:7). These few words comprise a remarkable information content, since they provide answers to many questions:

- Man did not develop through a chance process of evolution, but he was formed by a personal Creator.
- Contrary to all statements to this effect, man did not descend

from some animal; he was created separately.
- One single man was created originally.
- Man does not consist of matter only, but he received a vital non-material component, a spirit, through God's breath.
- He became a living being through the union of the material and the nonmaterial parts.

The saying "Truth does not require many words, but a lie cannot use enough words," now becomes meaningful. In spite of its semantic fullness, the verse quoted above requires amazingly few code symbols. No other description of man's origin is so true and at the same time formulated so concisely. We may deduce that what we have here represents the highest possible semantic information density. Other passages in the Bible also exhibit superlative semantic densities (e.g., John 3:16 contains all the information necessary for man's salvation).

2. The pragmatic density of information: This can be measured in terms of the effect E produced by input I prompted by some transmitted information. It usually requires extremely strenuous efforts to be accorded one single line entry in the *Guinness Book of Records* [G13], for example. This kind of "fame" is very short-lived, since the record for eating fried sausages, for example, 96 pieces in 4 minutes and 29 seconds [G13], may soon be broken. Many human deeds only served selfish honor, and have long since been forgotten and become meaningless. The Bible directs our thoughts in an entirely different direction. Everything we do in the name of Jesus (Col. 3:17) is eternally meaningful (Matt. 10:42). Even a cup of cold water given to "a little one" will be rewarded (Matt. 10:42). Where on earth will you get such a stupendous reward for such a simple deed? Such results are only found in the Bible. Paul compares the acts of a Christian working in the name of Jesus, with an athlete. Athletes compete for "a crown that will not last; but we do it to get a crown that will last for ever" (1 Cor. 9:25). We thus have another superlative, namely the highest possible pragmatic information density.

3. Apobetic information density: This is a measure of the height of the purpose attained after information has been received. The following episode which occurred during the time of the Spartans describes various apobetic information densities.

Example: When there was famine in one of the regions ruled by the Spartans, the local residents dispatched an eloquent messenger to Sparta. He addressed them at length and — in his own opinion — convincingly, to ask for a gift of wheat. The Spartans, however, dismissed him, because they had forgotten his introduction and thus did not understand the conclusion. Another messenger was sent soon afterward. His modus operandi was quite different: He brought an empty bag which he opened for everybody to see, and said concisely: "This bag is empty, please put something in it." This messenger obtained the required wheat, but the Spartans commented that he was too verbose. It was obvious that the bag was empty and needed to be filled; he should use fewer words when he came again.

This episode illustrates that the first messenger did not attain his purpose in spite of the meaningful contents of his speech, while the second one was immediately successful with his concise but striking information input. We thus have two distinct densities of apobetic information, and the suggestion of the Spartans to the second speaker would have resulted in an even higher value.

When considering ourselves as recipients of the message of the Bible, we can arrive at the highest possible apobetic density of information. We refer to the one verse, namely John 3:36: "Whoever believes in the Son has eternal life, but whoever rejects the Son will not see life, for God's wrath remains on him." This concise piece of information with its overwhelming depth of meaning could only appear in the Bible where high semantic information densities are expected. Just as overwhelming is the stated purpose: eternal life! Nothing has a greater value — in the words of Jesus, the whole world is worthless in this respect (Matt. 16:26) — so that anybody who has entrusted himself in faith to Jesus has achieved the *highest possible apobetic information* density.

CHAPTER 15 The Quantities Used for Evaluating Information and Their Application to the Bible

In chapter 10, six measures for quantitatively evaluating information (especially its semantics) were identified, namely semantic quality, relevance, timeliness, accessibility, existence, and comprehensibility. Let us now investigate the role of these parameters in the Bible.

1. Semantic quality q: The special semantic quality of the Bible is characterized as follows:

– It is divine: "This is the word that came to Jeremiah from the LORD" (Jer. 7:1). "I want you to know, brothers, that the gospel I preached is not something that man made up. I did not receive it from any man, nor was I taught it; rather, I received it by revelation from Jesus Christ" (Gal. 1:11–12).

– It is true: "O Sovereign LORD, you are God! Your words are trustworthy" (2 Sam. 7:28). "Your word is truth" (John 17:17).

– It comprises the message of man's salvation: "And you also were included in Christ when you heard the word of truth, the gospel of your salvation" (Eph. 1:13).

2. Relevance r: The message of the Bible is important for each and every person, because God's judgment is the same for everybody: "For no one living is righteous" (Ps. 143:2); "all have sinned and fall short of the glory of God" (Rom. 3:23). Even so, God has provided one way of salvation for everybody through His Son Jesus: "Salvation is found in no one else, for there is no other name under heaven given to men by which we must be saved" (Acts 4:12). Numerous other passages point in the same direction, for example, John 3:16, John 3:18, John 14:6, 1 John 5:12. Our profit is maximized when we correctly estimate the relevance. The attitude of the Thessalonians (1 Thess. 1:4–9) and the Philadelphians (Rev. 3:7–11) is highly commended in this respect.

The Bible very explicitly warns against an erroneous evaluation of its relevance, because then one will suffer the greatest possible loss. Paul and Barnabas told the people of Jerusalem, "We had to speak the word of God to you first. Since you reject it and do not consider yourselves worthy of eternal life, we now turn to the Gentiles" (Acts 13:46). The rich wheat farmer made plans for his life without considering God, and was told, "You fool! This very night your life will be demanded from you" (Luke 12:20). The rich man in hell (Luke 16:19–31) was not lost because of his wealth — Abraham and Job had been richer — but because he misjudged the relevance of the information at his disposal.

3. Timeliness t: Certain passages of the Bible represent some of the most ancient extant writings known to man. All the authors (excluding Luke) belonged to an insignificant, small nation of the Middle East. In the light of these facts, one might conclude that such a book could now only be of historical interest, and its contents would have been outdated long ago. One may expect that people belonging to the same nation as the authors might regard it as being of cultural interest. In spite of all such considerations, millions of people all over the world concern themselves with this Book. It is read and loved, irrespective of age, language, and level of education. No other book in history is so timely and relevant. What is the reason? Martin Luther commented, "The Bible is not an antique, neither is it modern; it is eternal."

The message of the Bible is relevant for all times. It is always up-to-date and topical because of its eternal dimension. In Matthew 24:35 Jesus expresses it thus: "Heaven and earth will pass away, but my words will never pass away." In this world, everything is perishable, except the Word: "The grass withers and the flowers fall, but the word of our God stands for ever" (Isa. 40:8). God's Word is thus always up-to-date because of its exceptional nature. The word "today" is often mentioned in the Bible, but its applicability has never been lost over thousands of years.

Joshua entreated the Israelites: "Choose for yourselves this day whom you will serve" (Joshua 24:15a), and even now God calls us in the same way. What a great blessing is entailed when we give the same reply as Joshua: "But as for me and my household, we will serve the LORD" (Josh. 24:15). When Zacchaeus experienced a complete change in his life after meeting Jesus, Christ told him, "Today salvation has come to this house" (Luke 19:9). This blessing is ours also, today, when we turn to Jesus. When you have done this, you will continuously be nourished by the up-to-date Word of God: "Man does not live on bread alone, but on every word that comes from the mouth of God" (Matt. 4:4).

4. Accessibility a: At present, the total volume of knowledge is doubled every seven years. For electrical technology, this period is five years, and it is even less in the case of information technology. If a scientist really wants to keep abreast, he will have to spend 100 hours every day just reading, which is impossible. It becomes very difficult, and sometimes impossible, to find relevant information in the present knowledge explosion. Access has become problem number one. In the case of the Bible, the situation is quite different: The wisdom it contains is complete and permanent, and there is thus an essential distinction between it and human knowledge. God's information is contained in one book so that we can have easy and complete access to it. This access, through continuous use, has been commanded by God:

"Do not let this Book of the Law depart from your mouth; meditate on it day and night" (Josh 1:8).

"O land, land, land, hear the word of the LORD!"(Jer. 22:29).

"Let the word of Christ dwell in you richly" (Col. 3:16).

"Like newborn babies, crave pure spiritual milk, so that by it you may grow up in your salvation" (1 Pet. 2:2).

In addition, we are encouraged to read the Bible through the exemplary witness of others. "Now the Bereans . . . received the message with great eagerness and examined the Scriptures every day" (Acts 17:11). The Psalmist longs for the word (Ps. 119:81), because he finds renewal (Ps. 119:25), strength (Ps. 119:28), hope, and salvation (Ps. 119:81).

5. Existence e: There is one further important question: Does the Bible really contain all the information required for knowing God and ourselves, to live according to God's standards, and to achieve His eternal purpose? All important questions are answered clearly and unambiguously, but critics and doubters introduce uncertainties and vagueness. Spurgeon rightly concluded that "Nothing is easier than doubting. A poorly educated person with mediocre abilities can raise more doubts than can be resolved by the cleverest men of science from all over the world."

Because of the completeness of the biblical message, we may not delete anything from this message nor add anything (Rev. 22:18–19), and for every interpretation the fundamental rule holds: "Do not go beyond what is written" (1 Cor. 4:6).

6. Comprehensibility c: This has already been discussed in paragraph 14.1 under "biblical concepts."

We can now formulate the following highly significant conclusions:

- The Bible contains the most important information conceivable. It is divine in essence, and indicates the way to our Father's house.

- The relevance value of the information of the Bible for every person is $r = 1$, the highest possible value. It comprises the best advice for this life, and is the only compass that guides us to heaven.

- The information of the Bible is always up-to-date ($t = 1$). Whereas most scientific publications become outdated after ten years,[20] the Bible can never become outdated.

- We can readily access the information of the Bible ($a = 1$). It can be obtained all over the world, and the contents are easy to understand.

- The information of the Bible is comprehensive and complete ($e = 1$).

- No false information is contained in the Bible; it is the only Book of truth (John 17:17).

- We find the highest semantic density of information in the Bible, as well as the best pragmatic information (commandments, rules of living, and our relationship with God and other people). It comprises the highest possible apobetics, namely an invitation to enter heaven!

---

20. A well-known physicist, nearing retirement, recently told me that science is like a bog. Only the surface is useful, but ten centimeters down everything is dead and outdated; nothing can be used.

16 A Biblical Analogy of the Four Fundamental Entities — Mass, Energy, Information, and Will

The four basic quantities in creation: These four entities, namely mass (or matter), energy, information, and volition, were discussed in paragraph 3.3. The latter two were described as being nonmaterial. Both material quantities, mass and energy, are subject to conservation laws, being linked by the equivalence formula $E = m \times c^2$. This means that they cannot be created by any natural process, neither can they be destroyed. Does this now mean that mass and energy are by nature eternal? No, it should be noted that none of the natural laws has existed forever, neither will any of them always be valid in the future. They were created together with everything else (see Theorem N10b in paragraph 2.3) and perform their wisely allocated functions only since creation week. "By the seventh day God had finished the work he had been doing" (Gen. 2:2).

The question about the origin of matter and the energies we observe in action is already answered in the first verse of the Bible: God created them! Everything came into being through His inconceivable power (Jer. 10:12 and Rom. 1:20). The active person at creation was Jesus, "through whom he made the universe" (Heb. 1:2). Jesus is also the sustainer of the entire creation, "sustaining all things by his powerful word" (Heb. 1:3). His creative and His sustaining acts are not restricted to matter and energy, but also hold for the information contained in biological systems. We can now conclude (John 1:1–3; Col. 1:16; Heb. 1:2):

– Jesus is the source of all energy,
– Jesus is the source of all matter, and
– Jesus is the source of all biological information.

The totality of the information present in living organisms, designated I, represents a value characterized by high quality as well as a large volume. In the beginning, information was established through volition. The Bible tells us about the link between will and wisdom:

– "You created all things, and by your will they were created and have their being" (Rev. 4:11).
– "How many are your works, O LORD! In wisdom you made them all; the earth is full of your creatures" (Ps. 104:24).
– "Christ, in whom are hidden all the treasures of wisdom and knowledge" (Col. 2:2–3).

In the light of Colossians 1:17 and Hebrews 1:3, we can say that Jesus sustains all energy, all matter, and all biological information (i.e., He sustains all life). Everything that exists does so through Christ; He is the First Cause of all things. However, supporters of the doctrine of evolution deny each and every purposeful cause for this world and deny any possibility of a personal sustaining will. They thus mislead themselves and are forced to regard information as a material quantity which originated in matter. We have scientifically shown that this view is erroneous.

According to His will, God gave us many creative gifts. For example: Our free will enables us to act creatively. The gift of language is the instrument through which we can produce new information (creative information!). There are two things which we cannot do: we cannot create mass (or energy), neither can we destroy it.

The spiritual meaning of the four basic entities: It should be noted that the above-mentioned four fundamental quantities have a spiritual dimension in the Bible where man is concerned. For example, in 1 Corinthians 2:14–15 a distinction is made between the natural man and the spiritual man. The former is exclusively concerned with this world, and is not bothered with the message of the Bible. His philosophy ignores God, and he thus does not consider Jesus Christ, neither is he concerned about God's purpose, salvation. He will be eternally lost without the Savior of sinners. Paul describes this situation in the following words: "For the message of the cross is foolishness to those who are perishing, but to us who are being saved it is the power of God" (1 Cor. 1:18).

On the other hand, a spiritual person lives in close communion with God (Eph. 5:18–20). The phrase "in Christ" occurs 196 times in the New Testament (e.g., John 15:4; Rom. 6:1; 1 Cor. 1:30; Gal. 3:28), referring to somebody who has tied his life to Jesus and who is sure of his eternal life (1 John 5:13). Such a person eagerly hears and reads God's Word (Rev. 1:3) and has access to the spiritual dimension of the Bible.

The four basic entities — mass, energy, information, and will — are illustrated in Figure 30, each time with the appellation "spiritual" in analogy to the biblical description of a spiritual person. It is now clear that these four created entities originated from God, the Creator. When a natural man is changed into a spiritual person, it is also a creative act of God, working through Jesus: "Therefore, if anyone is in Christ, he is a new creation; the old has gone, the new has come!" (2 Cor. 5:17). This creative transformation from old to new, from the natural to the spiritual, and from lost to saved, is called both repentance in the Bible (Luke 22:32; Acts 3:19) and being born again (John 3:3 and 1 Pet. 1:23). This act can only be accomplished through our own will (e.g., Matt. 23:37; Luke 19:14). Our willingness or our rejection is decisive for life and death, comprising the choice between heaven and hell. The four spiritual foundations take a central place for a born-again, a believing, or a spiritual person:

1. Spiritual information: In the Old Testament, God said parabolically that He has a fixed purpose when sending His Word to a recipient: "As the rain and the snow come down from heaven, and do not return to it without watering the earth and making it bud and flourish, so that it yields seed for the sower and bread for the eater, so is my word that goes out from my mouth: It will not return to me empty, but will accomplish what I desire and achieve the purpose for which I sent it" (Isa. 55:10–11). This clearly illustrates the purpose-achieving and the human-assisting way of divine information.

By means of several technological and biological examples we will illustrate (see appendix A3) that in such systems, in each case:

— energy is *saved,*
— waste of energy is *prevented,*
— energy is *utilized,* and
— the consumption of energy is *optimized.*

The divine (or spiritual) information affects us in a similar way, because it

— *saves* us from being led astray,
— *prevents* us from wasting our lives,

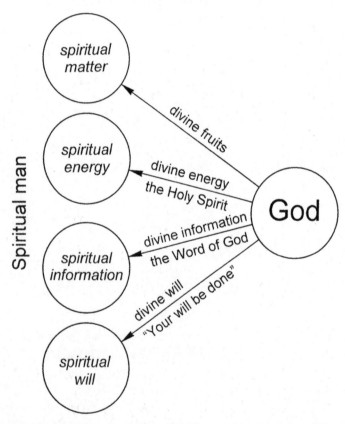

Figure 30: Basic units in the life of a spiritual person. The four fundamental entities — mass, energy, information, and will — as depicted in Figure 8, have been created by God. In the case of believers, we find a spiritual analogy for these entities, described by the Bible as divine in essence.

- *uses* our gifts in life (natural talents, time, and money),
- *optimizes* our life situations (marriage, occupation, and pastimes), and
- *saves* our life from perdition, giving us eternal life.

2. Spiritual will: There is a saying which goes like this: "Whoever does what he desires, often does what he should not do." Martin Luther stated, "Whenever our free will does what is inherent, then we commit a deadly sin." Even the Apostle sent to many nations, Paul, confessed, "I know that nothing good lives in me, that is, in my sinful nature. For I have the desire to do what is good, but I cannot carry it out. For what I do is not the good I want to do; no, the evil I do not want to do — this I keep on doing" (Rom. 7:18–19). Our best ethical intentions for doing good will not be successful if we rely on our own strength. Egoism is the most certain human characteristic.

Jesus described our will and nature much more strikingly than all philosophers, humanists, and psychologists: "The spirit is willing, but the body is weak" (Matt. 26:41). The deadly poison of sin is so deeply infused in us since Adam's fall, that we are "sold as a slave to sin" (Rom. 7:14) in the truest sense of the word. "Good" intentions will not deliver us from this condition, but we require redemption through Him who conquered sin. The command "Be transformed by the renewing of your mind" (Rom. 12:2) cannot be obeyed in our own power, but only through close ties with Jesus and by the constant influence of God's Word on our mind.

The principle mentioned by Goethe in his poem ("Erlkönig": King of the Elves) "And if you are unwilling, I will use force," does not hold for us. We gladly submit ourselves to God's will as Jesus taught us in the Lord's Prayer and as He lived daily right up to the Cross: "Yet not my will, but yours be done" (Luke 22:42). When your will is bound to God's Word through your conscience, then you are no longer egocentric (e.g., Isa. 53:6: "each of us has turned to his own way") but Christ-centered (e.g., Col. 3:23: "Whatever you do, work at it with all your heart, as working for the Lord, not for men").

3. Spiritual energy: There is no machine which can run continuously without input of energy. Similarly, a spiritual person is not a perpetual mobile. His source of spiritual energy is the Holy Spirit, without whom nobody can call Jesus Lord of his life (1 Cor. 12:3). The ministry of the disciples was not based in themselves, but in the divine energy given to them: "You will receive power when the Holy Spirit comes on you; and you will be my witnesses" (Acts 1:8). Paul expresses the immense source of available energy when he refers to "his incomparably great power for us who believe. That power is like the working [Greek energeia] of his mighty strength, which he exerted in Christ" (Eph. 1:19–20). Although Paul was weak of body (2 Cor. 12:9), his spiritual achievements were incomparable: "To this end I labour, struggling with all his energy, which so powerfully works in me" (Col. 1:29). God commands us to "be strong in the Lord and in his mighty power" (Eph. 6:10).

4. *Spiritual matter:* Except for mass deficits occurring in nuclear processes, there is also a conservation law for matter. If, by way of analogy, we search for something permanent in our spiritual life, it will be found in the fruits of our labors for God according to the Bible. Heinrich Kemner always emphasized the difference between success and fruit. Natural man seeks success in life, but a spiritual person finds it in fruit. Success depends mainly on our efforts, but fruit stems from grace and it only grows when our life is linked with Jesus. He unlocked this secret in the parable of the vine: "No branch can bear fruit by itself; it must remain in the vine. Neither can you bear fruit unless you remain in me. I am the vine; you are the branches. If a man remains in me and I in him, he will bear much fruit; apart from me you can do nothing" (John 15:4–5). All our works will be revealed when God judges the world. Whatever we may regard as great successes in our life will be consumed in God's testing fire; only fruit in Jesus will be conserved and earn rewards (1 Cor. 3:11–14). It is God's declared will that we should build our life on the fruit (John 15:2; Rom. 1:13; Gal. 5:22; Phil. 4:17; Col. 1:10), for Jesus said, "I chose you . . . to go and bear fruit — fruit that will last" (John 15:16).

> Only one life, it will soon be past;
> Only what's done for Christ, will last!

Appendix

APPENDIX A1 The Statistical View of Information

A1.1 SHANNON'S THEORY OF INFORMATION

Claude E. Shannon (born 1916), in his well-known book *A Mathematical Theory of Communications* [S7, 1948], was the first person to formulate a mathematical definition of information. His measure of information, the "bit" (binary digit), had the advantage that quantitative properties of strings of symbols could be formulated. The disadvantage is just as plain: Shannon's definition of information entails only one minor aspect of the nature of information, as we will discuss at length. The only value of this special aspect is for purposes of transmission and storage. The questions of meaning, comprehensibility, correctness, and worth or worthlessness are not considered at all. The important questions about the origin (sender) and for whom it is intended (recipient) are also ignored. For Shannon's concept of information, it is completely immaterial whether a sequence of symbols represents an extremely important and meaningful text, or whether it was produced by a random process. It may sound paradoxical, but in this theory, a random sequence of symbols represents the maximum value of information content — the corresponding value or number for a meaningful text of the same length is smaller.

Shannon's concept: His definition of information is based on a communications problem, namely to determine the optimal transmission speed. For technical purposes, the meaning and import of a message are of no concern, so that these aspects were not considered.

Shannon restricted himself to information that expressed something new, so that, briefly, information content = measure of newness, where "newness" does not refer to a new idea, a new thought, or fresh news — which would have encompassed an aspect of meaning. It only concerns the surprise effect produced by a rarely occurring symbol. Shannon regards a message as information only if it cannot be completely ascertained beforehand, so that information is a measure of the unlikeliness of an event. An extremely unlikely message is thus accorded a high information content. The news that a certain person out of two million participants has drawn the winning ticket, is for him more "meaningful" than if every tenth person stood a chance, because the first event is much more improbable.

Before a discrete source of symbols (NB: not an information source!) delivers one symbol (Figure 31), there is a certain doubt as to which one symbol ai of the available set of symbols (e.g., an alphabet with N letters $a1, a2, a3, \ldots , a_N$) it will be. After it has been delivered,

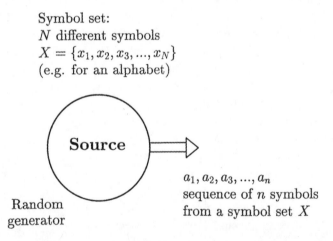

Symbol set:
N different symbols
$X = \{x_1, x_2, x_3, ..., x_N\}$
(e.g. for an alphabet)

Source

Random generator

$a_1, a_2, a_3, ..., a_n$
sequence of n symbols
from a symbol set X

Figure 31: Model of a discrete source for generating sequences of symbols. The source has a supply of N different symbols (e.g., an alphabet with 26 letters), of which a long sequence of n symbols is transmitted one after another at a certain time. The source could be a symbol generator which releases random sequences of symbols according to a given probability distribution, or it could be an unknown text stored on magnetic tape which is transmitted sequentially (i. e. one symbol at a time).

the previous uncertainty is resolved. Shannon's method can thus be formulated as the degree of uncertainty which will be resolved when the next symbol arrives. When the next symbol is a "surprise," it is accorded a greater information value than when it is expected with a definite "certainty." The reader who is mathematically inclined may be interested in the derivation of some of Shannon's basic formulas; this may contribute to a better understanding of his line of reasoning.

1. **The information content of a sequence of symbols:** Shannon was only interested in the probability of the appearance of the various symbols, as should now become clearer. He thus only concerned himself with the statistical dimension of information, and reduces the information concept to something without any meaning. If one assumes that the probability of the appearance of the various symbols is independent of one another (e.g., "q" is not necessarily followed by "u") and that all N symbols have an equal probability of appearing, then we have: The probability of any chosen symbol x_i arriving is given by $p_i = 1/N$. Information content is then defined by Shannon in such a way that three conditions have to be met:

i) If there are k independent messages[21] (symbols or sequences of symbols), then the total information content is given by $I_{tot} = I_1 + I_2 + ... + I_k$. This summation condition regards information as quantifiable.

ii) The information content ascribed to a message increases when the element of surprise is greater. The surprise effect of the seldom-used "z" (low probability) is greater than for "e" which appears more frequently (high probability). It follows that the information value of a symbol x_i increases when its probability p_i decreases. This is expressed mathematically as an inverse proportion: $I \sim 1/p_i$.

iii) In the simplest symmetrical case where there are only two different symbols (e.g., "0" and "1") which occur equally frequently

---

21. Message: In Shannon's theory, a message is not necessarily meaningful, but it refers to a symbol (e.g., a letter) or a sequence of symbols (e.g., a word). In this sense, the concept of a "message" is even included in the DIN standards system, where it is encoded as 44 300: "Symbols and continuous functions employed for the purpose of transmission, which represent information according to known or supposed conventions."

(p_1 = 0.5 and p_2 = 0.5), the information content I of such a symbol will be exactly one bit.

According to the laws of probability, the probability of two independent events (e.g., throwing two dice) is equal to the product of the single probabilities:

$$p = p_1 \times p_2 \qquad\qquad (1)$$

The first requirement (i) $I(p) = I(p_1 \times p_2) = I(p_1) + I(p_2)$ is met mathematically when the logarithm of equation (1) is taken. The second requirement (ii) is satisfied when p_1 and p_2 are replaced by their reciprocals $1/p_1$ and $1/p_2$:

$$I\,(p_1 \times p_2) = \log(1/p_1) + \log(1/p_2). \qquad\qquad (2)$$

As yet, the base b of the logarithms in equation (2) entails the question of measure and is established by the third requirement (iii):

$$I = \log_b (1/p) = \log_b (1/0.5) = \log_b 2 = 1 \text{ bit} \qquad\qquad (3)$$

It follows from $\log_b 2 = 1$ that the base $b = 2$ (so we may regard it as a binary logarithm, as notation we use log2 = lb; giving lb x = $(\log x)/(\log 2)$; log x means the common logarithm that employs the base 10: log x = log10 x). We can now deduce that the definition of the information content I of one **single** symbol with probability p of appearing, is

$$I(p) = \text{lb}(1/p) = -\text{ lb } p \geq 0. \qquad\qquad (4)$$

According to Shannon's definition, the information content of a single message (whether it is one symbol, one syllable, or one word) is a measure of the uncertainty of its reception. Probabilities can only have values ranging from 0 to 1 ($0 \leq p \leq 1$), and it thus follows from equation (4) that $I(p) \geq 0$, meaning that the numerical value of information content is always positive. The information content of a number of messages (e.g., symbols) is then given by requirement (i) in terms of the sum of the values for single messages

$$I_{\text{tot}} = \text{lb}(1/p_1) + \text{lb}(1/p_2) +...+ \text{lb}(1/p_n) = \sum_{i=1}^{n} \text{lb}(1/pi) \qquad (5)$$

As shown in [G7], equation (5) can be reduced to the following mathematically equivalent relationship:

$$I_{tot} = n \times \sum_{i=1}^{N} p(x_i) \times lb(1/(p(x_i))) = n \times H \qquad (6)$$

Note the difference between n and N used with the summation sign $\sum$. In equation (5) the summation is taken over all n members of the received sequence of signs, but in (6) it is summed for the number of symbols N in the set of available symbols.

Explanation of the variables used in the formulas:

n = the number of symbols in a given (long) sequence (e.g., the total number of letters in a book)

N = number of different symbols available

(e.g.: $N = 2$ for the binary symbols 0 and 1, and for the Morse code symbols and –

$N = 26$ for the Latin alphabet: A, B, C, . . . , Z

$N = 26 \times 26 = 676$ for bigrams using the Latin alphabet: AA, AB, AC, . . . , ZZ

$N = 4$ for the genetic code: A, C, G, T

x_i; $i = 1$ to N, sequence of the N different symbols

I_{tot} = information content of an entire sequence of symbols

H = the average information content of one symbol (or of a bigram, or trigram; see Table 4); the average value of the information content of one single symbol taken over a long sequence or even over the entire language (counted for many books from various types of literature).

Shannon's equations (6) and (8) used to find the total (statistical!) information content of a sequence of symbols (e.g., a sentence, a chapter, or a book), consist of two essentially different parts:

a) the factor n, which indicates that the information content is directly proportional to the number of symbols used. This is totally inadequate for describing real information. If, for example, somebody uses a spate of words without really saying anything, then Shannon would rate the information content as very large, because of the great number of letters employed. On the other hand, if someone who is an expert, expresses the actual meanings concisely, his "message" is accorded a very small information content.

b) *the variable H*, expressed in equation (6) as a summation over the available set of elementary symbols. *H* refers to the different frequency distributions of the letters and thus describes a general characteristic of the language being used. If two languages A and B use the same alphabet (e.g., the Latin alphabet), then *H* will be larger for A when the letters are more evenly distributed, i.e., are closer to an equal distribution. When all symbols occur with exactly the same frequency, then $H = \mathrm{lb}\, N$ will be a maximum.

An equal distribution is an exceptional case: We consider the case where all symbols can occur with equal probability, e.g., when zeros and ones appear with the same frequency as for random binary signals. The probability that two given symbols (e.g., G, G) appear directly one after the other, is p_2; but the information content *I* is doubled because of the logarithmic relationship. The information content of an arbitrary long sequence of symbols (n symbols) from an available supply (e.g., the alphabet) when the probability of all symbols is identical, i.e.:

$p_1 = p_2 = \ldots = p_N = p$, is found from equation (5) to be:

$$I_{\text{tot}} = \sum_{i=1}^{n} \mathrm{lb}(1/p_i) = n \times \mathrm{lb}(1/p) = -n \times \mathrm{lb}\, p. \qquad (7)$$

If all *N* symbols may occur with the same frequency, then the probability is $p = 1/N$. If this value is substituted in equation (7), we have the important equation:

$$I_{\text{tot}} = n \times \mathrm{lb}\, N = n \times H. \qquad (8)$$

2. The average information content of one single symbol in a sequence: If the symbols of a long sequence occur with differing probabilities (e.g., the sequence of letters in an English text), then we are interested in the average information content of each symbol in this sequence, or the average in the case of the language itself. In other words: What is the average information content in this case with relation to the average uncertainty of a single symbol?

To compute the average information content per symbol I_{ave}, we have to divide the number given by equation (6) by the number of symbols concerned:

$$I_{ave} = I_{tot}/n = \sum_{i=1}^{N} p(x_i) \times \text{lb}(1/p(x_i)). \qquad (9)$$

When equation (9) is evaluated for the frequencies of the letters occurring in English, the values shown in Table 1 are obtained. The average information content of one letter is I_{ave} = 4.045 77. The corresponding value for German is I_{ave} = 4.112 95.

The average I_{ave} (x) which can be computed from equation (9) thus is the arithmetic mean of the all the single values $I(x)$. The average information content of every symbol is given in Table 1 for two different symbol systems (the English and German alphabets); for the sake of simplicity i is used instead of I_{ave}. The average information content for each symbol I_{ave} $(x) \equiv i$ is the same as the expectation value[22] of the information content of one symbol in a long sequence. This quantity is also known as the entropy[23] H of the source of the message or of the employed language ($I_{ave} \equiv i \equiv H$). Equation (9) is a fundamental expression in Shannon's theory. It can be interpreted in various ways:

a) Information content of each symbol: H is the average information content I_{ave} (x) of a symbol x_i in a long sequence of n symbols. H thus

---

22. Expectation value: The expectation value E is a concept which is defined for random quantities in probability calculus. The sum $\sum p_k \times g(x_k)$ taken over all k single values, is called the expectation value E of the probability distribution, where $g(x)$ is a given discrete distribution with x_k as abscissae and p_k as ordinates (= the probability of appearance of the values x_k). This value is also known as the mean value or the mathematical hope.

23. Entropy: This concept was first introduced in thermodynamics by Rudolf Clausius about 1850. Later, in 1877, Ludwig Boltzmann (1844–1906) showed that entropy is proportional to the logarithm of the probability of a system being in a certain state. Because the formal derivation of the mathematical formulas for physical entropy is similar to equation (9), Shannon (1948) also called this quantity entropy. Unfortunately, the use of the same term for such fundamentally different phenomena has resulted in many erroneous conclusions. When the second law of thermodynamics, which is also known as the entropy theorem, is flippantly applied to Shannon's information concept, it only causes confusion. In thermodynamics, entropy depends on the temperature, which cannot at all be said of informational entropy.

No.	English Letter	p_i	$p_i \times \text{lb}\dfrac{1}{p_i}$	German Letter	p_j	$p_j \times \text{lb}\dfrac{1}{p_j}$
1	-	0.2000	0.46439	-	0.1515	0.41248
2	E	0.1050	0.34141	E	0.1470	0.40662
3	T	0.0720	0.27330	N	0.0884	0.30938
4	O	0.0654	0.25732	R	0.0686	0.26518
5	A	0.0630	0.25128	I	0.0638	0.25331
6	N	0.0590	0.24091	S	0.0539	0.22711
7	I	0.0550	0.23014	T	0.0473	0.20822
8	R	0.0540	0.22739	D	0.0439	0.19797
9	S	0.0520	0.22180	H	0.0436	0.19705
10	H	0.0470	0.20733	A	0.0433	0.19613
11	D	0.0350	0.16928	U	0.0319	0.15855
12	L	0.0290	0.14813	L	0.0293	0.14922
13	C	0.0230	0.12517	C	0.0267	0.13956
14	F	0.0225	0.12316	G	0.0267	0.13956
15	U	0.0225	0.12316	M	0.0213	0.11828
I6	M	0.0210	0.11704	O	0.0177	0.10302
17	P	0.0175	0.10214	B	0.0160	0.09545
18	Y	0.0120	0.07657	Z	0.0142	0.08716
19	W	0.0120	0.07657	W	0.0142	0.08716
20	G	0.0110	0.07157	F	0.0136	0.08432
21	B	0.0105	0.06902	K	0.0096	0.06435
22	V	0.0080	0.05573	V	0.0074	0.05238
23	K	0.0030	0.02514	Ü	0.0058	0.04309
24	X	0.0020	0.01793	P	0.0050	0.03822
25	J	0.0010	0.00997	Ä	0.0049	0.03760
26	Q	0.0010	0.00997	Ö	0.0025	0.02161
27	Z	0.0010	0.00997	J	0.0016	0.01486
28				Y	0.0002	0.00246
29				Q	0.0001	0.00133
30				X	0.0001	0.00133
		$\displaystyle\sum_{i=1}^{27} p_i = 1$			$\displaystyle\sum_{j=1}^{30} p_j = 1$	

Table 1: The probabilities p_i of the appearance of the letters in English and German, as well as their entropy. The letters are arranged according to frequency of use, and not alphabetically. ($\text{lb}\,x = \log_2 x$)

$$H_{1E} = \sum_{i=1}^{27} p_i \times \text{lb}\frac{1}{p_i} = 4.04577 \quad \text{Letter entropy (English)}$$

$$H_{1G} = \sum_{j=1}^{30} p_j \times \text{lb}\frac{1}{p_j} = 4.11295 \quad \text{Letter entropy (German)}$$

is a characteristic of a language when n is large enough. Because of the different letter frequencies in various languages, H has a specific value for every language (e.g., $H_1 = 4.045\ 77$ for English and for German it is $4.112\ 95$).

b) Expectation value of the information content of a symbol: H can also be regarded as the expectation value of the information content of a symbol arriving from a continuously transmitting source.

c) The mean decision content per symbol: H can also be regarded as the mean decision content of a symbol. It is always possible to encode the symbols transmitted by a source of messages into a sequence of binary symbols (0 and 1). If we regard the binary code of one symbol as a binary word, then H can also be interpreted as follows (note that binary words do not necessarily have the same length): It is the average word length of the code required for the source of the messages. If, for instance, we want to encode the four letters of the genetic code for a computer investigation and the storage requirements have to be minimized, then H will be lb 4 = 2 binary positions (e.g., 00 = A, 01 = C, 10 = G, and 11 = T).

d) The exceptional case of symbols having equal probabilities: This is an important case, namely that all N symbols of the alphabet or some other set of elements occur with the same probability $p(x_i) = 1/N$. To find the mean information content of a single symbol, we have to divide the right side of equation (8) by n:

$$H \equiv I_{ave}(x) \equiv i = \text{lb } N \qquad (10)$$

We now formulate this statement as a special theorem:

Theorem A1: In the case of symbol sequences of equal probability (e.g., the digits generated by a random number generator) the average information content of a symbol is equal to the information content of each and every individual symbol.

A1.2 MATHEMATICAL DESCRIPTION OF STATISTICAL INFORMATION
A1.2.1 The Bit: Statistical Unit of Information
One of the chief concerns in science and technology is to express results as far as possible in a numerical form or in a formula.

Quantitative measures play an important part in these endeavors. They comprise two parts: the relevant number or magnitude, and the unit of measure. The latter is a predetermined unit of comparison (e.g., meter, second, watt) which can be used to express other similarly measurable quantities.

The **bit** (abbreviated from *binary digit*) is the unit for measuring information content. The number of bits is the same as the number of binary symbols. In data processing systems, information is represented and processed in the form of electrical, optical, or mechanical signals. For this purpose, it is technically extremely advantageous, and therefore customary, to employ only two defined (binary) states and signals. Binary states have the property that only one of the two binary symbols can be involved at a certain moment. One state is designated as binary one (1), and the other as binary nought (0). It is also possible to have different pairs of binary symbols like 0 and L, YES and NO, TRUE and FALSE, and 12 V and 2 V. In computer technology, a bit also refers to the binary position in a machine word. The bit is also the smallest unit of information that can be represented in a digital computer. When text is entered in a computer, it is transformed into a predetermined binary code and also stored in this form. One letter usually requires 8 binary storage positions, known as a byte. The information content (= storage requirement) of a text is then described in terms of the number of bits required. Different pieces of text are thus accorded the same information content, regardless of sense and meaning. The number of bits only measures the statistical quantity of the information, with no regard to meaningfulness.

Two computer examples will now illustrate the advantages (e.g., to help determine the amount of storage space) and the disadvantages (e.g., ignoring the semantic aspects) of Shannon's definition of information:

Example 1: Storage of biological information: The human DNA molecule (body cell) is about 79 inches (2 m) long when fully stretched and it contains approximately 6×10^9 nucleotides (the chemical letters: adenin, cytosin, guanin, and thymin). How much statistical information is this according to Shannon's defintion? The N = 4 chemical letters, A, C, G, and T occur nearly equally frequently; their mean information content is $H = \text{lb } 4 = (\log 4)/(\log 2) = 2$ bits. The entire DNA thus has an information content of $I_{tot} = 6 \times 10^9$ nucleotides x 2 bits/nucleotide $= 1.2 \times 10^{10}$ bits according to equation (10). This is equal to the information contained in 750,000 typed A4 pages each containing 2,000 characters.

Example 2: The statistical information content of the Bible: The King James Version of the English Bible consists of 3,566,480 letters and 783,137 words [D1]. When the spaces between words are also counted, then n = 3,566,480 + 783,137 - 1 = 4,349,616 symbols. The average information content of a single letter (also known as entropy) thus amounts to H = 4.046 bits (see Table 1). The total information content of the Bible is then given by I_{tot} = 4,349,616 x 4.046 = 17.6 million bits. Since the German Bible contains more letters than the English one, its information content is then larger in terms of Shannon's theory, although the actual contents are the same as regards their meaning. This difference is carried to extremes when we consider the Shipipo language of Peru which is made up of 147 letters (see Figure 32 and Table 2). The Shipipo Bible then contains about 5.2 (= 994/191) times as much information as the English Bible. It is clear that Shannon's definition of information is inadequate and problematic. Even when the meaning of the contents is exactly the same (as in the case of the Bible), Shannon's theory results in appreciable differences. Its inadequacy resides in the fact that the quantity of information only depends on the number of letters, apart from the language-specific factor H in equation (6). If meaning is considered, the unit of information should result in equal numbers in the above case, independent of the language.

The first four verses of the Gospel of John is rendered in three African and four American languages in Table 2. In my book *So steht's geschrieben* [*It Is Written*, G12, p. 95–98] the same verses are given in 47 different European languages for purposes of comparison. The annotation "86 W, 325 L" means that 86 words and 325 letters are used. The seventh language in Table 2 (Mazateco) is a tonal language. The various values of B and L for John 1:1–4 are plotted for 54 languages in Figure 32. These 54 languages include 47 European languages (italics) and seven African and American languages. It is remarkable that the coordinates of nearly all European languages fall inside the given ellipse. Of these, the Maltese language uses the least number of words and letters, while the Shipipo Indians use the largest number of letters for expressing the same information.

The storage requirements of a sequence of symbols should be distinguished from its information content as defined by Shannon.

Storage space is not concerned with the probability of the appearance of a symbol, but only with the total number of characters. In general, 8 bits (= 1 byte) are required for representing one symbol in a data processing system. It follows that the 4,349,616 letters and spaces (excluding punctuation marks) of the English Bible require eight times as many bits, namely 34.8 million.

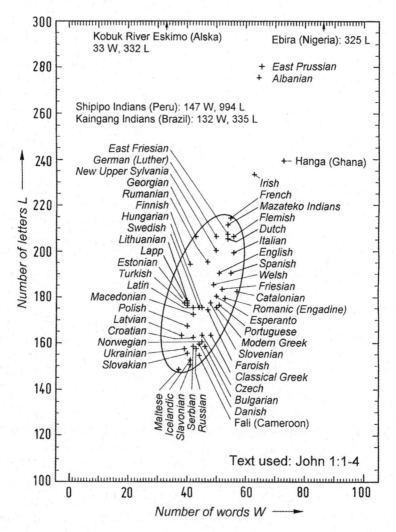

Figure 32: The number of letters L and words W illustrating statistical properties of various languages.

No.	African and American languages
1	1 Hụrẹ ụmọrụmọ, d'a va yẹ ka aa mẹ ẹhẹ, Ịrẹyị Ohomorihi hụrẹ yà ịzọọ nị. Ịrẹyị ọnọọ vị ana yà ịda Ohomorihi, Ịrẹyị ọnọọ gẹdẹ-gẹdẹ vị Ohomorihi. 2 Hụrẹ ụmọrụmọ ọnọọ, Ịrẹyị ọnọọ hụrẹ yà ịda Ohomorihi nị. 3 Ini oze Ịrẹyị ọnọọ Ohomorihi zị mẹ avaba ịsa nị. Ịnị avaba ịsa on'Ohomorihi tụ́ saka-saka, ayị nyị ikonya ẹnẹ ẹ̀yị vị ini oze Ịrẹyị ọnọọ ọ yà tụ́ọọ. 4 Ịrẹyị ọnọọ ọ mẹ ka ịsavị-savị ẹ̀ yàra nị. Ọyịyàra ọnọọ aa sị etohueyii zụ̀ aza nị. (EBIRA, Nigeria; 86 W, 325 L)
2	1 Bunso zaa piiligu, so ba n boona Yelibii n daa n na, o ba Naawun saani, ka o ni Naawunni niɲi lunko, 2 ka o ni Naawunni daa n ba niɲi piiligu maa. 3 O zu n na, bunso zaa daa n maali, ka pa o zu, bunso zaa daa n ki maali. 4 A kpali o zu, bunso zaa n daa n maali la marini nyevuri, ka nyevuri maa mi ti nisaaldima paaligu, ba nyaara. (HANGA, Ghana; 73 W, 240 L)
3	1 A ɗaarra jày pî yèy tâaye nà, tâanjirre nà ni Fay. Yèy gi tâage Fay. 2 A ɗaarra tâanji ni Fay. 3 Jày pî mbangsi ni erra. Cen jày mbangsi, to naa ni erra gi ba. 4 E hîige gûyrra. Gûyrra maan tâage kayang da nit ây. (FALI, Cameroon; 44 W, 155 L)
4	1 Aullaǧniisaqqaaǧataqman ittuq uqałiq, uqałiq iqataupluni Agaayutmi, suli uqałiq Agaayutapluni. 2 Ilaa piqatauniqsuq Agaayutmi aullaǧnii-saqqaaǧatałiǧmi. 3 Ilaa piqatigiplugu Agaayun iñiqtaqaqtuq supayaamik. Atausriq-unniiñ iluqaaniñ iñiqtaǧikkaɲaniñ iñiqtauṅǧitchuq piilaaǧlugu. 4 Uqałiq iñugutiqaqhuni iɲmiñi, taavruma iñuułhum iñuich qaggutigai, kaɲiqsiłiksraɲatnun Agaayutmik. (KOBUK RIVER ESKIMO, Alaska; 33 W, 332 L)
5	1 Ja Joi Ibo yoiquinra, en mato yoiai. Jabichoressiqui, jahuequescarin Dios iśhon, jan jato quiquinshamanhaquin onanmai; noa yoyo icatoninbi huetsabaon non icábo onancanai quescáaquin. Ja Joi Ibora, Diosen nato nete joniaamatianbi jaa iqui. Jara jatíbitian Dios betanbishaman jaconhirai jaque. Jainoaśh jaribi iqui, Dios betan senenribi. 2 Jascara iquenra, en mato banebainquin yoiai. Ja Joi Ibora, Diosen nete joniaamatianbi jaa iqui. Jascara icaśhśha, jaribi iqui Dios, jainoaśh ja betanbishamanribi jatíbitian jaque. 3 Ja Joi Ibo betan rabéanan jatíbi jahuéquibo jonianośhonra, Diosen shinana iqui. Jascara icaśh'śhiqui, jatíbi non oinai jahuéquiboyabi nato neten jaa jahuéquibo, ja Joi Ibon joniaabires; jascáanon iśhon Diosenbi imaa icaśh. Jatíbi jan joniayamaquetianra, jahuebi yamaqueanque. 4 Jascati jatíbitian jaa iśhonra, joniboribi jan joniaa iqui. Jascara iśhonra, jatíbitianbiressibi noa jatíbi jatíbitian jan jamai. Jascáaquin noa jatíbitian jan jamai iśhonra, jatíbi noabo jan acai noa aconquin onanmaquin; jahuequescarin Dios iśhon. Nato netemea jahuéquibo joecan tenaquetian non oinai quescáaquinra, jan noa Dios onanmai. (SHIPIPO-CONIBO, Indian, Peru; 147 W, 944 L)
6	1 Topẽ tỹ nén ũ kar han ja tũg ki tóg nĩ ja nĩ, ẽg tỹ ũ to: "Topẽ vĩ," he mũ ẽn ti, hã to ẽg: Jesus, he mũ. Topẽ mré tóg nĩ nĩ. Topẽ vỹ tỹ ti nĩ gé. 2 Topẽ tỹ nén ũ kar han tũg ki tóg Topẽ mré nĩ nĩ. 3 Ti hã tugrĩn tóg nén ũ kar han, Topẽ ti, ẽg tỹ ũ to: "Topẽ vĩ," he mũ ẽn tugnĩn. Ã pir mỹ Topẽ tóg nén ũ han tũ nĩ, ti hã mre tóg nén kar han kãn. 4 Ẽg tỹ ũ to: "Topẽ vĩ," he mũ ẽn vỹ rĩr nĩ, hã kỹ tóg ẽg rĩnrĩr han mũ gé. Jẽngrẽ ri ke ti nĩ, ũ tỹ ẽg rĩnrĩr han mũ ẽn ti. Ti tỹ ẽg kanhrãn to ken hã vẽ. (KAINGANG, Indian, Brazil; 132 W, 335 L)
7	1 C²ia⁴ nca³ to²ts²in³-le⁴ cjoa⁴ to⁴c²oa⁴ ti¹jna³ je² en¹. Je² en¹ ti¹-jna³t²a³ Ni³na¹. Je² en¹ ña³qui³ Ni³na¹ ni¹. 2 Je²-vi⁴ xi³ ti¹jna³t²a³ Ni³na¹ c²ia⁴ nca³ to²ts²in³-le⁴ cjoa⁴. 3 Je² tsa²c²e¹nta³ nca³yi³je³ tso³jmi². Tsa² tsin² je², ni⁴to⁴jme³-jin² xi³ tjin¹ xi³ qui³s²e¹nta³. 4 Je² xi³ tjin¹-le⁴ cjoa⁴vi³jna³chon³. Je² cjoa⁴vi³jna³chon³ je² 1²i¹ xi³ si¹²i³ sen³-le⁴ cho⁴ta⁴. (MAZATECO, Indian, Mexico; 54 W, 212 L)

Table 2: John 1:1–4 in different languages. (The author is sincerely grateful for the Bible texts made available by Mr. A. Holzhausen, Wycliffe Bible translator, Burbach/Germany.)

A1.2.2 The Information Spiral

The quantities of information of a large number of examples from languages, everyday events, electronic data processing, and biological life, are given in Table 3 in terms of bits. A graphical representation of the full range of values requires more than 24 orders of magnitude (powers of ten), so that a logarithmic spiral has been chosen here. A selection of values from Table 3 is represented in Figure 33 (page 191) where each scale division indicates a tenfold increase from the previous one.

Two different information ranges are illustrated in Figure 34, namely biological information as stored in DNA molecules — represented by the ant — and a microchip as used in the latest computers.

1. Computer technology: Konrad Zuse (1910–1996), a German inventor, pioneered the concept of a program-driven computer when he built the first operational electrical computing machine Z3 in 1941. It utilized 600 telephone relays for calculations, and 2,000 relays for storage. It could store 64 numbers in every group of 22 binary positions, could perform between 15 and 20 arithmetic operations per second, and one multiplication required 4 to 5 seconds. The next advance was the introduction of vacuum tubes (first generation electronic computers), and the ENIAC computer became operational in 1946. It had more than 18,000 vacuum tubes and other components wired together by means of more than half a million soldered connections. One addition operation required 0.2 thousandths of a second and a multiplication could be performed in 2.8 thousandths of a second. This installation utilized a word length[24] of 10 decimal places, it weighed 30 tons, and consumed 150 kW of electrical power. After several years of research, transistors were invented in 1947. They were much smaller and faster than vacuum tubes, and their introduction as switching elements initiated the second computer generation in 1955. The next milestone on the way leading to the powerful computers of today was the idea of integrated circuits (ICs). Different components are incorporated and interconnected in similar-looking units made of the same materials. The first IC was made in 1958,

---

24. Word length: A set of bits which is processed as a unit is called a word. The range of numbers which can be handled, as well as the number of data storage locations which can be addressed, depends on the length and the structure of the word (see also Table 3).

Bits	Comparison of different quantities of information
	I = statistical information content i = statistical information content of one symbol S = storage space v = transfer speed $\qquad$ (lb $x = \log_2 x$)
	Units of information
1	1 bit
1024	1 Kbit = 2^{10} bits = 1024 bits
1.049×10^6	1 Mbit = 2^{20} bits = 1024^2 bits = 1,048,576 bits
1.074×10^9	1 Gbit = 2^{30} bits = 1024^3 bits = 1,073,741,824 bits
1.100×10^{12}	1 Tbit = 2^{40} bits = 1024^4 bits = 1,099,511,627,776 bits
8	1 Byte = 8 bits
8192	1 Kbyte = 1024 Bytes = 8192 bits
8.389×10^6	1 Mbyte = 1,048,576 Byte = 8,388,608 bits
8.590×10^9	1 Gbyte = 1.073742×10^9 Bytes = 8.5899×10^9 bits
8.796×10^{12}	1 Tbyte = 1.099512×10^{12} Bytes = 8.796×10^{12} bits
	Information content of a single letter: in an alphabet with 27 symbols (26 letters + 1 space):
4.755	a) all letters appearing with the same frequency: $\quad i$ = lb 27 = log 27/log 2 = 4.755 bits/letter
4.133	b) considering the actual frequency distribution $\quad$ in German (see *Table 1*): i = 4.113 bits/letter
4.05	c) considering the actual frequency distribution $\quad$ in English (see *Table 1*): i = 4.05 bits/letter d) considering groups of two letters in German $\quad$ (bigrams as in *Table 4*): i = 3.32 bits/letter
3.1	e) considering groups of three letters in German $\quad$ (trigrams as in *Table 4*): i = 3.1 bits/letter.
1 to 2	f) considering redundancy of a language [B5] $\quad i$ = 1 to 2 bits per letter
	Information content of a numeral in different numbering systems:
1	a) Binary system: 2 different symbols (0 and 1) $\quad i$ = lb 2 = 1 bit/numeral
3.32	b) Decimal system: 10 different digits (0,1,2, ..., 9) $\quad i$ = lb 10 = log 10/log 2 = 3.32 bits/numeral

Table 3: Examples of quantities of information in terms of bits. This table continues over the next five pages.

Bits	Comparison of different quantities of information
4	c) Hexadecimal system: 16 different symbols (0,1,2,3,4,5,6,7,8,9,A,B,C,D,E,F) i = lb 16 = 4 bits/numeral
	Genetic code: DNA molecules contain four chemical letters (nucleotides): A, C, G, T where a triplet of 3 nucleotides codes for a single amino acid.
2	a) Information content of one letter (equal frequency) i = lb 4 = 2 bits/nucleotide
6	b) Information content of a triplet in a DNA molecule: i = (3 letters/triplet) × (2 bits/letter) = 6 bits/triplet
4.32	c) Information content of one amino acid when there are 20 possibilities (for the sake of simplicity equal frequencies are assumed): i = lb 20 = 4.32 bits/amino acid
1.44	d) Information content of one letter when the actual amino acids are considered: i = 4.32 bits/amino acid = 4.32 bits/triplet = = 1.44 bits/letter
	Some everyday examples:
198	Counting numbers for one minute: v = 3.3 bits/second = 198 bits/minute
960	Typing for one minute: v = 16 bits/s = 960 bits/min
1320	Playing the piano for one minute: v = 22 bits/s = 1320 bits/minute
35,000	Information collected by the human ear in one second: v = 3.5 × 10^4 bits/s
16,000	One typed A4 page with 2,000 characters: S = (2,000 symbols) × (8 bits) = 1.6 × 10^4 bits
12,800	Computer screen: S = (20 lines) × (80 characters) = = 1,600 bytes = 1.28 × 10^4 bits
3.1 × 10^5	TV screen: 300 Kbit in 1/30 second: v = 300 × 1,024 = 307,200 bits in 1/30 second
3.1 × 10^5	Telephone conversation 300 Kbit/minute: v = 300 × 1,024 = 307,200 bits/minute

Bits	Comparison of different quantities of information
	Satellite communications:
1.843×10^7	a) First communications satellite Telstar (1962): 60 phone conversations per minute $I = 60 \times 307,200$ bits/minute $= 1.843 \times 10^7$ bits/min
7.373×10^7	b) First commercial satellite (Early Bird = Intelsat I; 1965): 240 simultaneous telephone conversations $I = 240 \times 307,200$ bits/minute $= 7.373 \times 10^7$ bits/min
1.014×10^{10}	c) Intelsat VI (1986): 33,000 simultaneous phone calls $I = 33,000 \times 307,200$ bits/minute $= 1.014 \times 10^{10}$ bits/min
2×10^6	Hi Fi music record: 2 Mbits per minute
1.5×10^{10}	Compact disk (CD) : 1.5×10^{10} bits
40×10^{12}	Special Connection with fiber optics Technical University of Zürich/Switzerland (test 1996) 600,000 simultaneous telephone conversations; 40×10^{12} bit per second
	In the field of computing:
16 000	Internal storage of a first generation EDSAC computer: 2,000 Bytes = 16,000 bits
1.007×10^7	Floppy diskette: 1.2 Mbytes $= 10.066 \times 10^6$ bits
1.174×10^7	Stiffy diskette: 1.4 Mbytes $= 11.74 \times 10^6$ bits
1.258×10^7	Internal storage of an early mainframe computer (e. g. TR440, 1970): 256 Kilo words with 48 bits = $= 12,582,912$ bits
4.54×10^7	Storage capacity of a magnetic tape, length 720 m, 1,600 bits per inch: $S = 1,600$ bpi $\times 720,000$ mm/2.54 mm/inch = $= 4.54 \times 10^7$ bits
9.6×10^7	A fast printer can print 1,250 lines containing at most 160 characters each, per minute, so that the number of bits printed in an hour is: $v = 1,250 \times 160 \times 60 \times 8 = 9.6 \times 10^7$ bits/h
1.34×10^8	Internal memory of a PC: 16 Mbytes $= 16 \times 1,048,567$ bytes = $= 16,777,216$ bytes $= 1.34 \times 10^8$ bits
1.72×10^{10}	Hard disk of a PC: between 500 Mbytes and 2 Gbytes 2 Gbytes $= 2 \times 8.5899 \times 10^9$ bits $= 17.1798 \times 10^9$ bits

Bits	Comparison of different quantities of information
1.678×10^{10}	Internal memory of a mainframe computer: 2,000 MByte = 2,000 x 8,388,508 bits = 1.678×10^{10} bits
10^{12}	Theoretical capacity of holographic storage in bits per cubic cm
10^{12}	The fastest computer in the world (Sandia National Laboratories in Albuquerque, New Mexico, 1996) Intel Computer with 7,264 pentium chips $v = 1.06 \times 10^{12}$ operations per second
	Examples from science and literature:
4.8×10^6	Electrotechnical terms: 60,000 words with approximately 10 letters per word; $S = 4.8 \times 10^8$ bits
1.28×10^7	Great universal lexicon, Meyers, 15 volumes: 200,000 catchwords = 200,000 x 8 x 8 = 1.28×10^7 bits
2×10^7	Medical terms: 250,000, $S = 250,000 \times 10 \times 8 = 2 \times 10^7$ bits
4.2×10^8	Organic chemistry nomenclature: 3.5 million, assuming 15 letters per name; $S = 3.5 \times 10^6 \times 15 \times 8 = 4.2 \times 10^8$ bits
3.47×10^7	King James Version of the Bible: 783,137 words; 3,566,480 letters $I = (3,566,480 + 783,137 -1)$ characters x 4.05 bits/symbol $= 17.6 \times 10^6$ bits $S = (3,566,480 + 783,137 -1) \times 8 = 34.72$ million bits
8×10^8	100 draft law bills = 50,000 typed pages $I = 50,000 \times 2,000 = 10^8$ characters = 8×10^8 bits
5.76×10^{12}	The present number of scientific journals: 100,000 [B1]. Assumptions: 100 pages per journal, 6,000 characters per page, published monthly. Annual increase in information: $S = 100,000 \times 100 \times 6,000 \times 12 \times 8 = 5.76 \times 10^{12}$ bits

Bits	Comparison of different quantities of information
3.5×10^{11}	Books at the 44th Frankfurt Book Exhibition, 1992; a total of 350,000 books, of which 101,000 were new editions. $I = 350{,}000$ books $\times 10^6$ bits/book $= 3.5 \times 10^{11}$ bits
6.2×10^{11}	At present, 620,000 books are available in Germany: $I = 620{,}000$ books $\times 10^6$ bits/book $= 6.2 \times 10^{11}$ bits. Every year more than 60,000 new titles are published.
10^{13}	Library of Congress (Washington, USA): 10^7 volumes [S3]. $I = 10^7$ volumes $\times 10^6$ bits/book $= 10^{13}$ bits
10^{18}	The sum total of all human knowledge in books: 10^{18} bits. Consider 1 book of 100 typed pages $= 200{,}000$ characters $= 1.6 \times 10^6$ bits. This means that 10^{18} bits are spread over 625 thousand million books. If we take the average thickness of a book to be 15 mm, the total shelf space B is given by $B = 625 \times 10^9$ books $\times 1.5$ cm/book $= 937.5 \times 10^9$ cm $= 9.5$ million km $= 235$ times the length of the equator $=$ approximately 100 books for every person in the world!
9.06×10^{12}	The daily volume of image data transmitted by satellites: transfer rate: 100 Mbit/s $I = 100 \times 1.048 \times 10^6 \times 86{,}400 = 9.055 \times 10^{12}$ bits per day.
	Examples from life:
3.9×10^6	The number of mother tongue words known by one person is 100,000, according to Küpfmüller [S3]: (the German "Volksbrockhaus" contains 250,000 words). With an average of 6 letters per word, speaking requires 1.5 bits per letter, and writing 5 bits ($=$ lb 32): $S = 100{,}000 \times 6 \times (5 + 1.5) = 3.9 \times 10^6$ bits
10^{14}	The memory capacity of the human brain regarded purely physically, is, according to [S3]: a) *McCullach:* between 10^{13} and 10^{15} bits b) *Küpfmüller:* 3.9×10^6 bits (only memorized words) c) *Müller:* (1,500 bits/complex) $\times$ (1,000 cognitive complexes) $= 1.5 \times 10^6$ bits

Bits	Comparison of different quantities of information
	d) *Von Neumann:* 10^{10} nerve cells in the brain, 14 bits/s for a standard receptor, after 60 years: $S_{max} = 10^{10} \times 14$ bits/s $\times$ (60 years) $\times$ (365 days/year) $\times$ (24h/day) $\times$ (3600 s/h) $= 2.65 \times 10^{20}$ bits As expounded fully in [G10], the information storage capacity of the human brain cannot be explained in terms of neuron switching only.
10^{21}	The storage capacity of 1 cubic cm of DNA: 10^{21} bits (DNA = deoxyribonucleic acid)
3.4×10^{24}	The daily involuntary flow of data in the human body [S3] as for example the enormous production of macromolecules: $v = 3.9 \times 10^{19}$ bits/s $= 3.37 \times 10^{24}$ bits per day
7.9×10^{8}	Images received by the human eye taken as 14 images per second [S3]: $v = 10^{10}$ bits/s $I = (10^{10}$ bits/s$)/(14$ images/s$) = 7.86 \times 10^{8}$ bits/image
1.2×10^{10}	Human body cell: 6×10^{9} nucleotides in the DNA $I = (6 \times 10^{9}$ nucleotides$) \times (2$ bits/nucleotide$) = 1.2 \times 10^{10}$ bits The human body cell contains a double set of hereditary information (one set each from the father and from the mother)
8×10^{6}	DNA molecule of *Escherichia coli.* This bacterial cell weighs 10^{-13} g and is only 2 μm long. Its DNA molecule is 1 mm long when stretched and it contains 4 million letters (nucleotides). $I = (4 \times 10^{6}$ nucleotides$) \times (2$ bits/nucleotide$) = 8 \times 10^{6}$ bits Cell division lasts about 20 minutes and the rate of recognition of the letters is 1,000 times faster. This means that the reading speed is $(8 \times 10^{6}$ bits$) \times 1,000/(20 \times 60) = 6.6 \times 10^{6}$ bits/s

Table 3: Comparison of various statistical information quantities.

This table comprises a variety of information quantities selected from the following fields: The letters of natural languages and the genetic code, computer technology, science and literature, and biological life. All the values appearing in the leftmost column are numbers of bits, the statistical unit of information. In some cases a brief derivation is given for ease of understanding.

based on the novel integration idea proposed by Kilby and Hoerni. Further development of this concept, and the steady increase in the number of circuit elements per silicon chip, saw the advent of the third computer generation. ICs have undergone a rapid development since the first simple ones introduced in 1958. Today, 64-Megabit chips are commonplace.

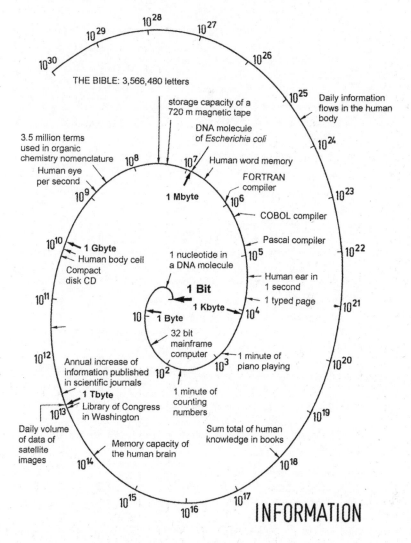

Figure 33: The information spiral.

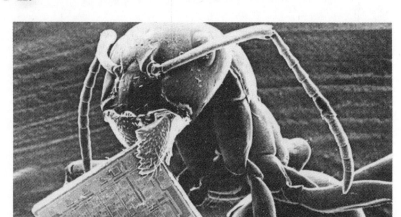

Figure 34: The ant and the microchip. Microchips are the storage elements of present-day computers. Their details are practically invisible, since structure widths are about one millionth of a meter. What a 30-ton computer of the University of Pennsylvania (USA) could do in 1946 can now be accomplished by a chip less than 6 square mm in size. Only a few years ago, chips which could store the text of four typed pages were regarded as revolutionary. Today, all the telephone numbers of a city like Canberra, Australia, can be stored on one chip, and their speed of operation is so fast that the Bible could be read 200 times in one second, but there is one thing that all the chips in the world will never be able to do, namely to copy an ant and all it can do. (Source: "Werkbild Philips"; with the kind permission of "Valvo Unternehmens-bereichs Bauelemente" of Philips GmbH, Hamburg.)

Five degrees of integration can be distinguished according to the number of components per structural unit:

SSI	(Small Scale Integration)	1 to 10
MSI	(Medium Scale Integration)	10 to 10^3
LSI	(Large Scale Integration)	10^3 to 10^4
VLSI	(Very Large Scale Integration)	10^4 to 10^6
GSI	(Grand Scale Integration)	10^6 and upward

High levels of integration, where between 500 and 150,000 transistors are accommodated on one silicon chip having an area of between 5 and 30 mm^2, led to the development of microprocessors. This technology made it possible to have complete processing or storage units on a single chip. The number of circuits that can be integrated on one chip doubled approximately every second year. The first experimental chip capable of storing more than one million bits (1 Megabit = 2^{20} bits = 1,048,576 bits), was developed in 1984 by IBM. The silicon wafer used measured 10.5 mm x 7.7 mm = 80.85 mm^2, so that the storage density was 13,025 bits per square mm. The time required to access data on this chip was 150 nanoseconds (1 ns = 10^{-9} s). The degree of integration increased steadily in subsequent years.

The question arises whether the density of integration could be increased indefinitely. In an article in *Elektronische Rechenanlagen (Electronic Computers)* [F4], O.G. Folberth pointed out the obstacles that would have to be overcome in future developments. Such hurdles in manufacturing technology, complexity of design, and testing problems, are, however, not fundamental, but there are hard physical boundaries of a final nature which would be impossible to overcome (geometric, thermic, and electrical limits). The maximum integration density which can be achieved with present-day silicon technology, can be calculated; it is found to be 2.5 x 10^5 lattice units per mm^2.

The improvement of hardware elements made it possible for computer terminals and personal computers to be as powerful as earlier mainframe computers. One of the fastest computers made is the CRAY C916/16, one of the C-90 series. The processing speed of this 16 processor computer is about 10 GFLOPS (= 10 Giga-FLOPS). One FLOPS (floating point operations per second) means that one computation involving real numbers with floating decimal signs, can be executed in one second; 10 GFLOPS is thus equal to 10 thousand million arithmetic calculations like addition and multiplication performed in one second.

2. Degree of integration in living cells: We have now been represented with an astounding development involving the increasing degree of integration (number of circuit elements in one chip) and the integration density (degree of miniaturization; circuit elements per area unit) as seen in computer technology. There is no precedent for such a rapid and unique development in any other field of technology.

The information stored in the DNA molecules of all living cells is indispensable for the numerous guided processes involving complex and unique functions. The human DNA molecule (body cells) is about

79 inches (2 m) long when stretched, and it contains 6×10^9 chemical letters. We may well ask what the packing density of this information could be, and it is fairly easy to calculate. According to Table 3, the information content of one nucleotide is two bits, giving a total of 12×10^9 bits for one DNA molecule. Divide this by the number of bits in one Kbit (1024); this results in a degree of integration of 11.72 million Kbits, which is 180 times as much as the above-mentioned 64 Megabit chip. The density of integration is discussed more fully in the next section.

This comparison makes it patently clear that the evolutionary view requires us to believe things which are totally unreasonable. Thousands of man-years of research as well as unprecedented technological developments were required to produce a Megabit chip, but we are expected to believe that the storage principles embodied in DNA, with their much higher degree of integration, developed spontaneously in matter which was left to itself. Such a "theory" is, to say the least, absurd in the highest degree!

A1.2.3 The Highest Packing Density of Information

The greatest known density of information is that in the DNA of living cells. The diameter of this chemical storage medium, illustrated in Figure 35, is 2 nm = 2×10^{-9} m, and the spiral increment of the helix is 3.4 nm (Greek *hélix* = winding, spiral). The volume of this cylinder is $V = h \times d^2 \times \pi /4$:

$$V = 3.4 \times 10^{-7} \text{ cm} \times (2 \times 10^{-7} \text{ cm})^2 \times \pi/4 = 10.68 \times 10^{-21} \text{ cm}^3 \text{ per winding}$$

There are 10 chemical letters (nucleotides) in each winding of the double spiral, giving a statistical information density of:

$$\acute{U} = 10 \text{ letters}/(10.68 \times 10^{-21} \text{ cm}^3) = 0.94 \times 10^{21} \text{ letters per cm}^3$$

If we limit the average information content of 4.32 bits for an amino acid (see chapter 6) to one letter (nucleotide) of the genetic code, then we find it to be 4.32:3 = 1.44 bits per letter. We can now express the statistical information density of DNA as follows, where 2 bits are taken as the information content of one letter (also see Table 3, genetic code, case a):

$$\acute{U} = (0.94 \times 10^{21} \text{ letters/cm}^3) \times (2 \text{ bits/letter}) = 1.88 \times 10^{21} \text{ bits/cm}^3$$

This packing density is so inconceivably great that we need an illustrative comparison. The photographic slide A in Figure 35

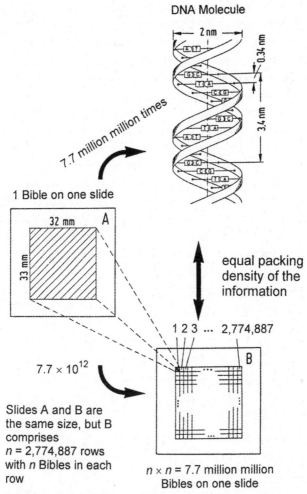

Figure 35: Comparison of statistical information densities. DNA molecules contain the highest known packing density of information. This exceedingly brilliant storage method reaches the limit of the physically possible, namely down to the level of single molecules. At this level the information density is more than 10^{21} bits per cm^3. This is 7.7 million million times the density obtained when the entire Bible is reproduced on one photographic slide A. Only if 7.7 million million Bibles could be represented on one slide B (this is only theoretically possible!), having 2.77 million rows and 2.77 million columns with the entire Bible reproduced in each miniscule rectangle, would we obtain an information packing density equal to that present in all living cells.

contains the entire Bible from Genesis to Revelation on its 33 mm x 32 mm surface, reproduced by means of special microfilm processes [M5]. From the computation given in [G11, p. 78–81], it follows that the DNA molecule entails a storage density 7.7 million million times as great as that of slide A which contains the entire Bible. If we want to obtain the DNA packing density on a photographic slide B, we would have to divide its surface into 2.77 million rows and 2.77 million columns and copy an entire Bible in a readable form in each of the tiny rectangles formed in this way. If this were possible, we would have reached the density of the information carried in each and every living cell. In any case, we should remember that it is technologically impossible to produce slide B, because all photographic techniques are limited to macroscopic reproductions and are unable to employ single molecules as units of storage. Even if it were possible to achieve such a photographic reduction, then we would still only have a static storage system, which differs fundamentally from that of DNA. The storage principle of DNA molecules is dynamic, since the contained information can be transferred unchanged to other cells by means of complex mechanisms.

These comparisons illustrate in a breathtaking way the brilliant storage concepts we are dealing with here, as well as the economic use of material and miniaturization. The highest known (statistical) information density is obtained in living cells, exceeding by far the best achievements of highly integrated storage densities in computer systems.

A1.3 Evaluation of Communication Systems

Technical communication systems: After the discussion of Shannon's definition of information in paragraph A1.1, the relevant question is: What is the use of a method which ignores the main principles of a phenomenon? The original and the most important application of Shannon's information theory is given by the two so-called encoding theorems [S7]. These theorems state, *inter alia*, that in spite of the uncertainty caused by a perturbed communication link, the reception of a message could be certain. In other words, there exists an error-correcting method of encoding which assures greater message security with a given block (message) length.

Furthermore, the unit of measure, the bit, derived from Shannon's definition of information, is fundamental to a quantitative assessment of information storage. It is also possible, at the statistical level, to compare directly given volumes of information which are encoded in various ways. This problem has been discussed fully in the previous paragraph A1.2.

Communication systems in living organisms: Bernhard Hassenstein, a German biologist and cyberneticist, gave an impressive example illustrating both the brilliant concept of information transfer in living organisms, and its evaluation in terms of Shannon's theory:

> It is difficult, even frightening, to believe that the incomparable multiplicity of our experiences, the plethora of nuances — lights, colors, and forms, as well as the sounds of voices and noises . . . all the presentations of these in our sense receptor cells, are translated into a signaling language which is more monotonous than Morse code. Furthermore, this signaling language is the only basis through which the profusion of inputs is made alive in our subjective perception again — or for the first time. All our actions and activities are also expressed in this signaling language, from the fine body control of athletes to the hand movements of a pianist or the mood expressions of a concert hall performer.
>
> Whatever we experience or do, all the impulses coursing through our nervous system from the environment to our consciousness and those traveling from our brain to the motor muscles, do so in the form of the most monotonous message system imaginable. The following novel question was only formulated when a scientific information concept had been developed, namely, what is the functional meaning of selecting a signaling language using the smallest number of symbols for the transmission of such a vast volume of information? This question could be answered practically immediately by means of the information concept of information theory.
>
> The British physiologist W.H. Rushton was the first person to provide the answer which greatly surprised biologists, namely: There exists a result in information theory for determining the capacity of a communication system in such a way that its susceptibility to perturbating interference is minimized. This is known as the method of standardization of the properties of the impulses. The technique of pulse code

modulation was discovered in the 1930s, but its theoretical principles were only established later. The symbolic language employed in living nervous systems corresponds exactly to the theoretical ideal of interference-free communication. It is impossible to improve on this final refinement of pulse code modulation, and the disadvantage of a diminished transmission capacity is more than offset by the increase in security. The monotonousness of the symbolic language of the nervous system thus convincingly establishes itself as expressing the highest possible freedom from interference. In this way, a very exciting basic phenomenon of physiology could be understood by means of the new concepts of information theory.

It should now be clear that Shannon's information theory is very important for evaluating transmission processes of messages, but, as far as the message itself is concerned, it can only say something about its statistical properties, and nothing about the essential nature of information. This is its real weakness as well as its inherent propensity for leading to misunderstandings. The German cyberneticist Bernhard Hassenstein rightly criticizes it in the following words: "It would have been better to devise an artificial term, rather than taking a common word and giving it a completely new meaning." If we restrict Shannon's information to one of the five aspects of information, then we do obtain a scientifically sound solution [G5]. Without the extension to the other four levels of information, we are stuck with the properties of a transmission channel. No science, apart from communication technology, should limit itself to just the statistical level of information.

Natural languages may be analyzed and compared statistically by means of Shannon's theory, as we will now proceed to do.

A1.4 STATISTICAL ANALYSIS OF LANGUAGE

It is possible to calculate certain quantitative characteristics of languages by means of Shannon's information theory. One example of such a property is the average information content of a letter, a syllable, or a word. In equation (9), this numerical value is denoted by *H*, the entropy.

1. Letters: If, for the sake of simplicity, we assume that all 26 letters plus the space between words occur with the same frequency, then we have:

H_0 = lb 27 = log 27/log 2 = 4.755 bits/letter   (11)

It is known that the frequency of occurrence of the different letters is characteristic of the language we are investigating [B2 p 4]. The probability p_i of occurrence of single letters and the space are given for English and German in Table 1, as well as the average information content per letter, H. On applying equation (9) to the various letter frequencies P_i in German, the average information content (= entropy) of a symbol is given by:

$$H_1 = \sum_{i=1}^{30} p_i \times \text{lb}(1/p_i) = 4.112\ 95 \text{ bits/letter} \qquad (12)$$

The corresponding value for English is H_1 = 4.04577 bits per letter. We know that the probability of a single letter is not independent of the adjacent letters. Q is usually followed by u, and, in German, n follows e much more frequently than does c or z. If we also consider the frequency of pairs of letters (bigrams) and triplets (trigrams), etc., as given in Table 4, then the information content as defined by Shannon, decreases statistically because of the relationships between letters, and we have:

$$H_0 > H_1 > H_2 > H_3 > H_4 > \ldots > H_{oo} \qquad (13)$$

With 26 letters, the number of possible bigrams is 26^2 = 676, and there could be 26^3 - 26 = 17,550 trigrams, since three similar letters are never consecutive. Taking all statistical conditions into consideration, Küpfmüller [K4] obtained the following value for the German language:

$$H_{oo} = 1.6 \text{ bits/letter} \qquad (14)$$

For a given language, the actual value of H_0 is far below the maximum value of the entropy. The difference between the maximum possible value H_{max} and the actual entropy H, is called the redundance R. The relative redundance is calculated as follows:

$$r = (H_{max} - H)/H_{max} \qquad (15)$$

For written German, r is given by (4.755 – 1.6)/4.755 = 66%. Brillouin obtained the following entropy values for English [B5]:

No.	Bi-gram	p_i	$p_i \times lb\dfrac{1}{p_i}$	Tri-gram	p_j	$p_j \times lb\dfrac{1}{p_j}$
1	EN	0.0447	0.20042	EIN	0.0122	0.07756
2	ER	0.0340	0.16586	ICH	0.0111	0.07208
3	CH	0.0280	0.14444	NDE	0.0089	0.06063
4	ND	0.0258	0.13613	DIE	0.0087	0.05955
5	EI	0.0226	0.12357	UND	0.0087	0.05955
6	DE	0.0214	0.11869	DER	0.0086	0.05901
7	IN	0.0204	0.11455	CHE	0.0075	0.05294
8	ES	0.0181	0.10476	END	0.0075	0.05294
9	TE	0.0178	0.10345	GEN	0.0071	0.05068
10	IE	0.0176	0.10258	SCH	0.0066	0.04781
11	UN	0.0173	0.10126	CHT	0.0061	0.04488
12	GE	0.0168	0.09904	DEN	0.0057	0.04249
13	ST	0.0124	0.07854	INE	0.0053	0.04007
14	IC	0.0119	0.07608	NGE	0.0052	0.03945
15	HE	0.0117	0.07508	NUN	0.0048	0.03697
16	NE	0.0117	0.07508	UNG	0.0048	0.03697
17	SE	0.0117	0.07508	DAS	0.0047	0.03635
18	NG	0.0107	0.07004	HEN	0.0047	0.03635
19	RE	0.0107	0.07004	IND	0.0046	0.03572
20	AU	0.0104	0.06851	ENW	0.0045	0.03508
21	DI	0.0102	0.06748	ENS	0.0044	0.03444
22	BE	0.0096	0.06435	IES	0.0044	0.03444
23	SS	0.0094	0.06329	STE	0.0044	0.03444
24	NS	0.0093	0.06276	TEN	0.0044	0.03444
25	AN	0.0092	0.06223	ERE	0.0043	0.03380
26	SI	0.0083	0.05738	LIC	0.0042	0.03316
27	UE	0.0082	0.05683	ACH	0.0041	0.03251
28	DA	0.0081	0.05628	NDI	0.0041	0.03251
29	AS	0.0078	0.05462	SSE	0.0039	0.03121
30	NI	0.0070	0.05011	AUS	0.0036	0.02922
⋮	⋮	⋮	⋮	⋮	⋮	⋮
		$\displaystyle\sum_{i=1}^{676} p_i = 1$			$\displaystyle\sum_{j=1}^{17550} p_j = 1$	

Table 4: Probability of occurrence p_i of the 30 most common bi-grams/trigrams in German, and their entropy values (derived from 10,000 letters used in ordinary German texts by Bauer/Goos). With 26 letters involved, it means that there are $N^2 = 676$ bigrams and $N^3 - N = 17,550$ trigrams. These numbers thus appear as the upper limits of summation for calculating the entropy for bigrams, H_{Bi}, and trigrams, H_{Tri} ($lb\,x = \log_2 x$):

$$H_{Bi} = \sum_{i=1}^{676} p_i \times lb\frac{1}{p_i} \; ; \quad H_{Tri} = \sum_{j=1}^{17550} p_j \times lb\frac{1}{p_j}$$

H_1 = 4.03 bits/letter
H_2 = 3.32 bits/letter
H_3 = 3.10 bits/letter
H_{oo} = 2.14 bits/letter

We find that the relative redundance for English, r = (4.755 - 2.14)/4.755 = 55% is less than for German. In Figure 32 the redundancy of a language is indicated by the positions of the different points.

Languages usually employ more words than are really required for full comprehensibility. In the case of interference, certainty of reception is improved because messages usually contain some redundancy (e.g., illegibly written words, loss of signals in the case of a telegraphic message, or when words are not pronounced properly).

2. Syllables: Statistical analyses of the frequencies of German syllables have resulted in the following value for the entropy when their frequency of occurrence is taken into account [K4]:

$$H_{syll} = 8.6 \text{ bits/syllable} \qquad (16)$$

The average number of letters per syllable is 3.03, so that

$$H_3 = 8.6/3.03 = 2.84 \text{ bits/letter.} \quad (17)$$

W. Fucks [F9] investigated the number of syllables per word, and found interesting frequency distributions which determine characteristic values for different languages.

The average number of syllables per word is illustrated in Figure 36 for some languages. These frequency distributions were obtained from fiction texts. We may find small differences in various books, but the overall result does not change. In English, 71.5% of all words are monosyllabic, 19.4% are bisyllabic, 6.8% consist of three syllables, 1.6% have four, etc. The respective values for German are 55.6%, 30.8%, 9.38%, 3.35%, 0.71%, 0.14%, 0.2%, and 0.01%.

For English, German, and Greek, the frequency distribution peaks at one syllable, but the modus for Arabic, Latin, and Turkish is two syllables (Figure 36). In Figure 37, the entropy $H_S \equiv H_{syllable}$ is plotted against the average number of syllables per word for various languages. Of the investigated languages, English has the smallest number of syllables per word, namely 1.4064, followed by German (1.634), Esperanto (1.895), Arabic (2.1036), Greek (2.1053), etc. The average ordinate values for syllable entropy $H_{syllable}$ of the different languages

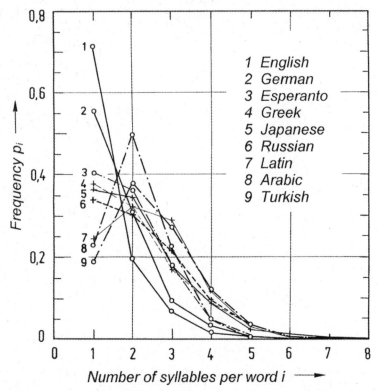

Figure 36: Frequency distributions $p_{(i)}$ for various languages, from which the average number of syllables per word can be derived. When a long enough text in a language is investigated, a characteristic frequency of the number of syllables per word is found. For many languages, monosyllabic words occur most frequently (e.g., English, German, and Greek), but for other languages, bisyllabic words are most common (e.g., Latin, Arabic, and Turkish).(p_i = relative frequency of occurrence of words consisting of i syllables; i = average number of syllables per word.)

have been found by means of equation (9), but it should be noted that the probabilities of occurrence of monosyllabic, bisyllabic, etc. words were used for p_i. The value of $H_{syllable}$ = 1.51 found for German, should not be compared with the value derived from equation (16), because a different method of computation is used.

3. Words: Statistical investigations of German showed that half of

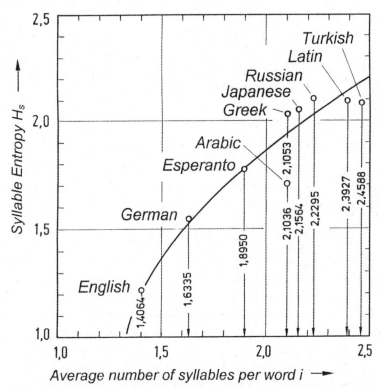

Figure 37: Statistical characteristics of various languages. Using equation 9, we may calculate the average information content per syllable, H_s, for a given language. This value is peculiar to the language, and when the various values are plotted, we obtain the distribution shown in this diagram.

all written text comprises only 322 words [K4]. Using these words, it follows from equation (9) that the word entropy, H_{word} = 4.5 bits/word. When only the 16 most frequently used words, which already make up 20% of a text, are considered, H_{word} is found to be 1.237 bits per word. When all words are considered, we obtain the estimated 1.6 bits per letter, as indicated in equation (14). The average length of German words is 5.53 letters, so that the average information content is 5.53 x 1.6 = 8.85 bits per word.

It should now be clear that certain characteristics of a language may be described in terms of values derived from Shannon's theory of information. These values are purely of a statistical nature, and do not tell us anything about the grammar of the language or the contents of a text. Just as the effective current I_{eff} of a continually changing electrical input (e.g., as a control parameter in a complex technological experiment) could be calculated as a statistical characteristic, it is also possible to establish analogous linguistic properties for languages. Just as I_{eff} can say nothing about the underlying control concepts, so such linguistic characteristics have no semantic relevance.

A1.5 STATISTICAL SYNTHESIS OF LANGUAGE

After having considered statistical analyses of languages in the previous section, the question now arises whether it would be possible to generate, by purely random combinations of symbols:

    a) correct sentences in a given language
    b) information (in the fullest sense of the concept)

Our point of departure is Figure 38. Random sequences of symbols can be obtained by means of computer program (1). When the letters may occur with equal frequency, then sequences of letters (output A in Figure 38) are obtained which do not at all reflect the simplest statistical characteristics of German or English or any other language. Seen statistically, we would never obtain a text which would even approximately resemble the morphological properties of a given language.

One can go a step further by writing a program (2), which takes the actual frequency of letter combinations of a language into consideration (German in this case). It may happen that the statistical links between successive letters are ignored, so that we would have a first order approximation. Karl Küpfmüller's [K4] example of such a sequence is given as output B, but no known word is generated. If we now ensure that the probabilities of links between successive letters are also accounted for, outputs C, D, and E are obtained. Such sequences can be found by means of stochastic Markov processes, and are called Markov chains.

Program (2) requires extensive inputs which take all the groups of letters (bigrams, trigrams, etc.) appearing in Table 4 into account, as well as their probability of occurrence in German. With increased ordering, synthetic words arise, some of which can be recognized as German words, but structures like "gelijkwaardig," "ryljetek," and "fortuitousness" are increasingly precluded by the programming.

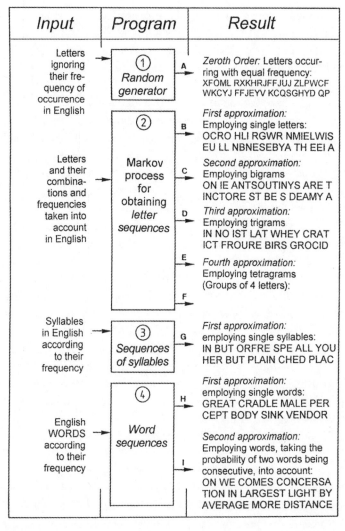

Input	Program	Result
Letters ignoring their frequency of occurrence in English	① Random generator A	*Zeroth Order:* Letters occurring with equal frequency: XFOML RXKHRJFFJUJ ZLPWCF WKCYJ FFJEYV KCQSGHYD QP
Letters and their combinations and frequencies taken into account in English	② Markov process for obtaining letter sequences B C D E F	*First approximation:* Employing single letters: OCRO HLI RGWR NMIELWIS EU LL NBNESEBYA TH EEI A *Second approximation:* Employing bigrams ON IE ANTSOUTINYS ARE T INCTORE ST BE S DEAMY A *Third approximation:* Employing trigrams IN NO IST LAT WHEY CRAT ICT FROURE BIRS GROCID *Fourth approximation:* Employing tetragrams (Groups of 4 letters):
Syllables in English according to their frequency	③ Sequences of syllables G	*First approximation:* employing single syllables: IN BUT ORFRE SPE ALL YOU HER BUT PLAIN CHED PLAC
English WORDS according to their frequency	④ Word sequences H I	*First approximation:* employing single words: GREAT CRADLE MALE PER CEPT BODY SINK VENDOR *Second approximation:* Employing words, taking the probability of two words being consecutive, into account: ON WE COMES CONCERSA TION IN LARGEST LIGHT BY AVERAGE MORE DISTANCE

Figure 38: "Language synthesis" experiments for determining whether information can arise by chance. Sequences of letters, syllables, and words (including spaces) are obtained by means of computer programs. The letters, all combinations of letters, syllables, and words (a complete German lexicon) were used as inputs. Their known frequencies of occurrence in German texts are fully taken into account in this "language synthesis." The resulting random sequences A to I do not comprise information, in spite of the major programming efforts required. These sequences are semantic nonsense, and do not correspond with any aspect of reality.

What is more, only a subset of the morphologically typical German sounding groups like WONDINGLIN, ISAR, ANORER, GAN, STEHEN, and DISPONIN are actual German words. Even in the case of the higher degree approximations one cannot prevent the generation of words which do not exist at all in speech usage.

A next step would be program (3) where *only actual German syllables* and their frequency of occurrence are employed. Then, in conclusion, program (4) prevents the generation of groups of letters which do not occur in German. Such a program requires a complete dictionary to be stored, and word frequencies are also taken into account (first approximation). As a second approximation, the probability of one word following another is also considered. It should be noted that the programs involved, as well as the voluminous data requirements, comprise many ideas, but even so, the results are just as meager as they are unambiguous: In all these cases we obtain "texts" which may be morphologically correct, but are semantic nonsense.

A word is not merely a sequence of letters, but it has a nomenclatorial function which refers to a specific object (e.g., Richard the Lion Heart, Matterhorn, or London) or a class of objects (animal, car, or church) according to the conventions of the language. Every language has its own naming conventions for the same object, as for example "HOUSE," German "HAUS," Spanish "CASA," French "MAISON," and Finnish "TALON." In addition, a single word also has a meaning in the narrow sense of the word.

On the other hand, a sentence describes a situation, a condition, or an event, i.e., a sentence has an overall meaning. It consists of various single words, but the meaning of a sentence comprises more than just a sequential chain of the meanings of the words. The relationships between the sense of a sentence and the meanings of the words it contains are a semantic problem which can only be investigated in the framework of the delicately shaded meanings of the language conventions existing between the sender and the recipient of the message.

Conclusion: Even though complete sets of letter groups, syllables, and words are used, together with their previously established frequency distributions, the statistically produced texts generated by various programming systems lack the decisive criteria which would ensure that a sequence of letters comprises a real message. The following criteria have to be met before a sequence of symbols can be accorded the status of information (a message):

1. *Meaning accorded by the sender:* A set of symbols must have been transmitted by a sender and must be directed at a recipient. (If the described process did generate a letter sequence like "I LOVE YOU," I would be able to understand the text, but it still is not information as far as I am concerned, because it was not transmitted by somebody who loves me.)

2. *Truth based in reality:* The set of symbols must contain actual truth pertaining to the real world. (If a statistical process might produce a sentence like "PARIS IS THE CAPITAL OF FRANCE," this is correct and true, but it has no practical significance, because it is not rooted in a real experience.)

3. *Recognizable intention:* A sequence of symbols must be purposefully intentional, i.e., it must have been conceptualized by a sender.

4. *Oriented toward a recipient:* The sequence of symbols must be addressed to or directed at somebody. (When a letter or a telegram is dispatched, the sender has a very definite recipient in mind; a book has a certain specific readership; when a bee performs a food dance, important information is conveyed to the other bees in the hive; DNA information is transferred to RNA which then leads to protein synthesis.) Recipient orientation is also involved even when there is a captive audience in addition to the intended recipient (e.g., unintentional listening in to a conversation in a train compartment).

> **Theorem A2:** Random letter sequences or sequences produced by statistical processes do not comprise information. Even if the information content could be calculated according to Shannon's theory, the real nature of information is still ignored.

In the historical debate in Oxford in 1860 between Samuel Wilberforce (1805–1873) and the Darwinist Thomas H. Huxley (1825–1895), the latter stated that if monkeys should strum typewriters randomly for a long enough time, then Psalm 23 would emerge sooner or later. Huxley used this argument to demonstrate that life could have originated by chance, but this question is easily resolved by means of the information theorems. It follows from the theorems mentioned in chapter 4 and from Theorem A2 that information is not at all involved. The comparison invoked by Huxley has no bearing on information nor on life. The properties of information discussed in chapter 5, show that Huxley spoke about random sequences, but information was not involved in this argument about monkeys typing. It is impossible for information to originate in matter by random processes (see Theorem 1).

Questions a) and b) raised above, can now be answered unambiguously:

– It is only possible to synthesize, by means of a statistical process, correct sentences obeying the conventions of a given language, if the required know-how is included beforehand in the data (valid morphemes, syllables, and words) and in the programs. These programs require enormous efforts, and it is then even possible to generate sentences which obey the syntactical rules of the language. Even if some meaning could be ascribed to a sequence of words obtained in this way, it can still not be regarded as having "message quality," because it originated in a random process.

– Statistical processes cannot generate real information or real messages.

A2 Language: The Medium
for Creating,
Communicating, and
Storing Information

A2.1 NATURAL LANGUAGES

Man's natural language is the most comprehensive as well as the most differentiated means of expression. This special gift has been given to human beings only, allowing us to express all our feelings and our deepest beliefs, as well as to describe the interrelationships prevailing in nature, in life, and in the field of technology. Language is the calculus required for formulating all kinds of thoughts; it is also essential for conveying information. We will now investigate this uniquely human phenomenon. First of all, some definitions of language are given, and it should be clear that a brief definition is not possible as is the case for information [L3, p. 13–17]:

> **Definition L1:** Language is an exclusively human method for communicating thoughts, feelings, and wishes; it is not rooted in instinct, and it employs a system of freely structured symbols (Spair).

> **Definition L2:** A language is a system of arbitrary sound symbols by means of which a social group interacts (Bloch and Trager).

Definition L3: Language is the institution used by human beings for communication and interaction by means of conventional and voluntary oral-auditory symbols (Hall).

Definition L4: Henceforth, I will understand language to comprise a set (finite or infinite) of sentences, each of which is finite in length and consists of a finite set of elements (Chomsky).

A2.1.1 General Remarks on the Structure of Human Language

Language is the ability to express information. Apart from various secondary means of expression like mime and gesture-language, natural spoken language is the most important and most extensive vehicle for communicating information. An unlimited range of subject matter can be expressed by means of human language, achieved by a brilliantly conceived structural system, for all languages comprise a hierarchical system of lingual units. The smallest units are the sounds, and it is noteworthy that only about 600 sounds which could in principle be produced by the human speech organs, are used in the known 5,100 languages. When a child learns a language, those sounds heard most frequently are repeated, and other sounds are thus not learned. The child diminishes the range of sounds until, eventually, the frequency distribution typical of his mother tongue is obtained.

Among languages, the number of sounds employed, varies between 15 and 85. The Rotokas language spoken on Bougainville Island, New Guinea, has the shortest alphabet, namely only 11 letters — six consonants and five vowels: a, b, e, g, i, k, o, p, r, t, and u. Having said this, we still do not know how many different sounds can be produced with these letters. On the other hand, the Nepalese language employs more than 60 letters, while 72 letters including obsolete ones, are used in Kampuchean. The largest number of vowels, 55, is found in Sedang, a language used in central Vietnam; this includes the various pitches at which "similar" vowels are voiced. At the other extreme, the Caucasian language Abkhazian, has only two vowels. Another Caucasian language, Ubyxian, employs the greatest number of consonants, between 80 and 85, while the above-mentioned Rotokas uses only six, the smallest known number.

The sounds which serve as acoustic elements of a language are known in linguistics as *phonemes*. In German, most phonemes are represented by single letters, but often two or three letters are required (e.g., ei, eu, and sch). With only a few exceptions, phonemes are meaningless sounds — they carry no meaning. The most concise meaningful units are the *morphemes*, which are the simplest structures at the lowest linguistic level. At the top of the lingual hierarchy is the most complex level, namely the entire text. Being the smallest functional language unit, a morpheme is comprised of one or more phonemes, e.g., simple words without prefixes and suffixes. A morpheme is itself part of a *lexeme* or word, or identical to one. Lexemes are the basic units of the vocabulary of a language in conventional form (e.g., singular nouns or the infinitive form of a verb). Many words appearing in a text are usually inflected forms of the lexical unit. There are very many possible ways of word formation, but all languages employ only a fraction of this total. The greatest number of different sound combinations would be attained when all sounds or phonemes could be combined with all others in every possible sequence. Sequences like ktx, nxr, or bfg appear to be possible, but do not occur in English or German. The allocation of the meanings of sound combinations (words) are arbitrary and must be learned through experience, but the combination of words to form sentences is a different matter.

It is very remarkable that, although we do not know the meaning of a word which we have not yet heard, we can understand sentences that have never before been voiced, and we can produce an infinite number of new sentences which can immediately be understood by the members of our language group.

The words of a language are linked together in sentences according to fixed rules. These rules (grammar) prevent the construction of chaotic word jumbles, and provide languages with practically unlimited ways of expression. Every sentence is a sequence of morphemes, but not every sequence of morphemes makes up a sentence. The rules of grammar determine the way in which morphemes and words should be combined to express a certain meaning, and syntactical rules (syntax = construction of sentences) determine which word combinations form acceptable sentences and which combinations are unacceptable for the language involved. Language expressions have a definite meaning in the sense that the members of a given language community have allocated their meaning by common agreement (convention).

Semantics describe all possible conceptual meanings or structures which can be expressed in the form of sentences. It does not only involve general meanings and concepts of words, groups of words, and sentences, but also the relationships between these meanings and reality, the so-called referential relationships.

In spite of the large number and variety of languages, there are many remarkable common properties:

1. Wherever there are people, the gift of language is evident.

2. Linguistically seen, there are no "primitive" languages. Every language has its own complexities and its own strengths and weaknesses according to the relevant semantics.

3. Although the relationships between sounds and the meanings of language elements are arbitrary, they nevertheless are fixed by the conventions of the language.

4. The human vocal organs are able to produce about 600 different sounds, but any one language uses only a specific selection of these sounds. The number of different sounds lies somewhere between 15 and 85 for a given language, and these sounds are combined to form words (elements which convey meanings). In their turn, the words can be used to form an unlimited number of possible sentences.

5. Every language possesses its own unique grammatical structure which describes the rules for forming words and sentences within that language.

6. Every spoken language comprises a limited number of sound elements which can be classified in various ways. A universal distinction, valid for all languages, is that between consonants and vowels.

7. All languages have comparable grammatical categories, like nouns, verbs, and numerals.

8. Some semantic units like feminine, masculine, and human being are common to all languages.

9. It is in all languages possible to refer to the past, to refute assertions, to set questions, and to formulate commands.

10. The vocabulary of any language can be extended. New words are given a meaning through convention, and are subject to the relevant morphological rules, the acceptable sounds, and the prescribed symbols.

11. Any normal child can learn any selected language, independent of place of birth, geographical region, or racial or social group. It follows that the ability of articulating any arbitrary language by means of the vocal organs is inherent and, thanks to the gift of reason, any lingual systems can be learned to such an extent that arbitrary sentences in that language can be constructed and understood.

12. It is in principle possible to formulate any arbitrary idea in any language. Human languages are able to convey an unlimited number of meanings and contents, in contrast to the communication systems of animals.

A2.1.2 Complexity and Peculiarities of Languages

The German poet Friedrich Gottlieb Klopstock (1724–1803) asserted, "Every language is, as it were, the storehouse of the most unique concepts of a nation." Language characterizes a nation and it is strongly influenced by the environment. We shall now discuss some examples which illustrate the statement that "the vocabulary of a language indicates WHAT a nation thinks; the syntax indicates HOW the people think."

The Beduins have various names for a camel, each of which expresses some specific aspect of its place in their life. Some hunting tribes in East Africa use a range of words for expressing various shades of brown, but they have only one term for all other colors lumped together. In some Slavic languages the auxiliary verb "to be" plays a minor role compared to its position in the Germanic and the Latin languages. This indicates a quite different realization of the problem of "being" for the respective nations. The Eskimo languages have many different words for snow. For example, they distinguish between falling snow, snow lying on the ground, and solid snow cut into blocks. A certain language of the Philippines employs 92 different words for 92 different ways of traveling. The Tabassarian language spoken in Daquestan (in the former Soviet Union) acknowledges 35 kinds of nouns, and in a certain Eskimo language there are 63 present tense forms and up to 252 inflections for simple nouns. The North American Indian language, Chippewa (Minnesota), holds the record for the largest number of verb forms, about 6,000, and another Amerindian language, Haida, employs the greatest number of prefixes, namely 70.

In the Nepalese Kulung language there are three different words for "come," indicating whether one comes from above (yuo), from below (tongo), or from the same level (bano). In a mountainous country, these distinctions are very meaningful, but they would not be required in the Netherlands. The Nepalese have five different words for "mountain" which indicate various altitudes. This language also has an extensive vocabulary for describing family relationships; not only do they distinguish between paternal and maternal lines, but they also encompass various age groups. There are four different words for "we," indicating, for example, whether the addressed person is included or not, and they also differentiate between many persons and two only.

In Sunba sentences, a single sound is included which has no inherent meaning, but indicates how the person who is talking acquired the information. This caused problems until the Wycliffe missionary involved discovered that it meant that the person either experienced it personally, or was relating something which he had heard. This usage is important for Bible translation, since the Bible writers usually report personal experiences.

Approximately one-third of all languages on earth are tonal. This means that the same word expressed with a change of pitch (or pitch contour) carries a different meaning. With some tonal languages, when written down, the pitch contour is indicated. To do this it would conceivably be possible to employ musical notation, but this would be too cumbersome for daily use. In any case, in tonal languages it is not the absolute pitch which is important, but the correct change in pitch (pitch contour) when one pronounces individual syllables. Most tonal languages use from two to six pitch contours, which may be indicated by a superscript behind each syllable (see block 7 in Table 2), or by using accent marks as in French. Tonal languages are found in and around China, and also in Africa and America. We often find tonal and non-tonal languages in close proximity, but often there is no indication of a "family tree of languages."

Metaphysical ideas can be expressed exceptionally well in the Amerindian language Hopi, while an ephemeral state cannot be formulated abstractly in the Indo-Germanic languages. For example, the word "run" usually elicits the questions: where? whence? or whither? But to describe the essence of running, we require combinations like "running as such," or "simply running." In the Hopi language, a single suffix is appended for such a purpose.

We should not regard the Amerindian languages as primitive in the light of the following important statements about them [O4]:

As counted in 1940, there are about 150 Indian languages which have nothing in common with the European linguistic heritage. Their vocabularies are enormous and their grammar indicates that the grunting noises made by Indians in western movies are far removed from their actual lingual proficiencies. They are characterized by pleasant melodious sounds, an imaginative art of expression, fine nuances and descriptions, and methodical constructions . . . although they lack words for abstract concepts like truth, love, soul, or spirit. William Penn, the founder of Pennsylvania (= Penn's rural forest-land), who lived in a neighborly accord with the Delawares, described their way of reasoning in the following words: "I know no European language which contains more words depicting friendliness and generosity in the colorfulness of their sounds and intonation than their language."

In many languages, the nouns are classified according to grammatical gender. In the Latin languages the nouns are either masculine or feminine, and in German, Greek, and the Slavic languages there is a third gender, the neuter. There is no satisfactory explanation for this arbitrary classification of objects and concepts in different genders. It is, for example, difficult to understand why the German words "Mädchen" (girl) and "Weib" (wife or woman) are regarded as belonging to the neuter gender. Mark Twain (1835–1910) commented as follows: "In German, a young lady has no gender, while parsnips are feminine." In Hebrew, gender plays an even more important part than in most European languages. Not only nouns, pronouns, and adjectives are distinguished according to gender, but verbs also. The simple sentence "I love you" can be expressed in six different ways. It is different when it is said by a man or by a woman, or directed at a man or a woman, or directed at a group of men or a group of women. The best known "genderless" language is Chinese, which has only one word for the pronouns "he," "she," and "it."

Most noteworthy is the peculiarities of languages as far as semantic categories like parts of speech and idiomatic expressions are concerned. In many cases, special structures are required to express gradual differences. In the Igbira language of Nigeria, the sentence "He has said that he would come tomorrow," for example, is regarded as an uncertainty rather than a promise. The Wycliffe Bible translators battled with this problem when they had to translate biblical promises into this language [H3]. The assertion in Mark 14:49, "But the Scriptures must be fulfilled," describes a completely open event in this form. To make a statement definite, the Igbira language employs a double negative. The above-mentioned sentence thus had to be translated as follows: "It is not possible that God's Book would not become true."

Peter Dommel, one of the Wycliffe missionaries, reported that the Kaureh tribe in Irian Jaya uses only three different numerals, namely one, two, and many. To express "three," they say "one and two," and in the same way "four" is "two and two." Only in recent years have numerals, borrowed from Indonesian, been introduced to indicate "large" numbers.

It should be clear from these examples that no two languages correspond fully in respect to word meanings, and they do not at all correspond where grammatical and semantic structures are concerned. Every language has its own unique wealth, its own special complexity, and also its own weaknesses.

A2.1.3 The Origin of Languages

There is a practically limitless number of speculations and theories about the origin of human languages [C1]. According to the natural sounds and imitation theory, humans mimicked the sounds made by animals. Although human languages contain many imitation words, such mimicry of animal sounds cannot be employed for a systematic analysis, because imitations vary quite arbitrarily from nation to nation. When a German cock crows, it cries "kikeriki," for example, an English cock crows "cock-a-doodle-doo," while Russians reproduce this sound as "kukuriki." An Eskimo can convincingly imitate the call of a whale, but it does not occur to him to name a whale by this sound.

Other theories maintain that human languages were derived from emotional exclamations, or that the first words were sounds used to accompany or emphasize certain gesticulations. The evolutionary idea of an upward development of grunts and snorts to cultural languages through the primitive languages of aboriginal nations has been thoroughly refuted by comparative linguistics. Even the different and separated Amerindian tribes in California possessed an extremely complex and subtle language. It was practically impossible to unlock this language grammatically and translate it adequately. The most complex Amerindian language of all is Comanche [C1]. Some sounds are whispered and others have to be formed by using only the larynx. During the First World War this language was used as a secret code [U1]. Two Comanche Indians were employed for telephone messages, one at each end. At the transmitting end, one of them translated the English message into Comanche, and these messages could not be deciphered, because the grammar was too far removed from European languages, and it would have taken several years of intensive study for the opposing side to have learned the language.

Such "code talkers" were employed during the Second World War as well, having been selected from different tribes (e.g., Comanche, Chippewa, Hopi, and Navajo), and the American Marine Corps employed 375 Navajos [U1]. The first four verses of the Gospel of John might serve to convey the complexity of this language:

1 Hodeeyáadi Saad jílí, Saad éí Diyin God bil hojíló, índa Saad éí Diyin God jílí. 2 T' áá éí hodeeyáadi Diyin God bil hojíló; 3 éí t'áá'altsoní ájiilaa, índa dahólonígíí t'áálá'í ndi t'áá hádingo t'áadoo la'ályaa da. 4 Iiná hwii' hóló, áko éí iinánígíí nihokáá'dine'é bá bee adindíín.

Conclusion: All languages are unique and all perform their functions well. They comprise morphological, grammatical, and semantic complexities and structures which were not devised by any person. The members of aboriginal tribes do not even realize that they use finely shaded categories. They also do not know the structure of their grammar, so that their language could not have been devised by their forebears.

Johann Peter Sübmilch established in 1756 that man could not have invented language without having the necessary intelligence, and also that intelligent thought in its turn depends on the previous existence of speech. The only solution to this paradox is that God must have given human beings language as a gift.

V. Fromkin and R. Rodman [F8] concluded that there was no proof for or against the divine origin of language, just as nobody can scientifically prove the existence or the non-existence of God.

In actual fact: One cannot prove the existence of God, but He has revealed himself in creation in such a way that we can deduce

His greatness and His wisdom (Ps. 19; Rom. 1:19–20). The same holds for the origin of languages. An evolutionary development can be precluded immediately, and it is clear from the complexity of all languages that behind and above the brilliant concepts figuring in all of them, there must be an originator of the ideas. We thus accept the biblical report that God gifted man with this special ability when he was created. The gift of speech is apparent from the following particulars:

- creation of the necessary special speech apparatus for articulation
- the ability to create words (Gen. 2:19)
- the ability to learn a language
- creative use of the language phenomenon

Originally, there was only one language (Gen. 11:1), but at the Babel judgment (Gen. 11:7) God caused many languages to arise, preserving the ability to express all thoughts in words. Using several examples, we have illustrated the complexity, and the special strengths and weaknesses of some languages.

At the moment, some 5,100 languages and dialects are spoken on earth. Many have become extinct, up to 3,000 during the past thousand years, and only about 100 languages are spoken by more than one million people each. Two-thirds of the entire world population employ only five languages: Mandarin Chinese, Hindustani, English, Russian, and Spanish.

A2.1.4 Written Languages

The invention of writing is one of the greatest intellectual achievements of man. (Perhaps Adam could have received the gift of writing together with the gift of speech. If so, writing was not "invented" by man.) Human memory does not last long and the storage capacity of the brain is limited, but this problem is overcome over distance as well as over time. Writing is essential for a people to develop literature, recorded history, and technology. Groups without writing therefore do not go beyond a certain stage in culture (e.g., aboriginal peoples). Only a written language allows the possibility of information storage, so that inventions and discoveries (e.g., in medicine and technology) will not be lost, but can be added to and developed further. Writing can thus be defined as follows:

Definition D6: Writing is a human communication system set up by convention, which represents language as a sequence of symbols. These symbols should be able to be transmitted and received, must be mutually understood, and must represent spoken words. Writing reproduces spoken language in the form of symbols.

We can only speak of real writing when pictograms represent the spoken words of a given language through their shapes and sequences. The spoken word acquires a temporal dimension by means of writing; historical traditions usually require permanent records to be kept, and the same holds for science in most communities. Various nations invented their own writing technique — the Sumerians used pictograms about 3500 B.C., Egyptian hieroglyphics originated 3000 B.C., in the Middle East cuneiform writing was in use around 2500 B.C., and Chinese ideograms date from 1500 B.C. The latest and most important stage was however the invention of an alphabet. An alphabet consists of a predetermined number of written symbols, each of which represents one spoken sound only — at least in the ideal theoretical case. All these symbols can be used in arbitrary combinations to reproduce the different words of a language. When an alphabet is used, it means that the number of symbols is reduced to a rational minimum; its flexibility and the direct correspondence to the sounds of the spoken language has the effect that such writing makes it very much easier for anyone to learn and to use that particular language. Alphabetical writing originated around 2500 B.C. in the region of present-day Israel, Lebanon, and Syria. Today, only the following alphabets are in use: Hebrew, Latin, Greek, Cyrillic, Georgian, Arabic, Persian, and Indian.

There are three kinds of writing systems:

1. Word based: Every symbol represents a word or a morpheme (e.g., Chinese).

2. Syllabic: Every symbol represents a syllable (e.g., Korean).

3. Alphabetic: Every symbol generally represents a phoneme (e.g., English, Spanish).

If it is not necessary to represent a certain number of sounds, then the set of symbols can be reduced even more. In the case of the genetic code, the number of different symbols is a minimum because of the certainty of transmission; the same holds for binary codes and for Morse code.

A2.2 SPECIAL LANGUAGES USED IN THE ANIMAL WORLD

A language can be regarded as a system whereby certain sounds or gestures convey certain meanings. In this sense, many animals like birds, bees, crabs, wolves, and dolphins communicate with one another, but as far as fundamental characteristics are concerned, human language is vastly different from the communication systems employed by animals:

1. *Creativity:* Only human language can be creative. When speaking, one can arbitrarily link together many lingual units to form well-constructed new sentences. Man is able to produce sentences which he has never before uttered, and he also can understand sentences which he has never beforehand heard. Any arbitrary matter can be verbalized. The communication systems used by animals are fixed and limited. The history of experiments with animals, purporting to teach them some complex language, is characterized by failure.

2. *Voluntary conventions:* The vocabularies of all human languages all over the world consist predominantly of arbitrary vocal structures which correspond to the relevant concept or object purely by convention. In contrast, the sounds and gestures used in "animal languages" are inherently fixed, and can thus not be arbitrarily assigned some other meaning.

3. *Comprehensiveness:* The number of thoughts that can be expressed in a human language is unlimited, but it is fixed and bounded in the animal world. The dance performed by bees is in principle such an effective communication system that numerous different messages could be conveyed, but in practice, the system, being restricted to a few concepts only, is inflexible.

4. *Reason for transmission:* The messages sent by animals depend on certain stimuli (e g., fear, warning, desire to mate, and quest for food), but man is not limited to such strictures.

Although there are fundamental differences in quality between human languages and the communication systems of animals, the messages conveyed by the latter do qualify as "information." All five aspects of information as discussed above, are found here, as will now be illustrated by bee dancing.

Bee dances: Bee dances, although simple, afford an illustrative example of the five aspects of information on the biological plane. The well-known Austrian zoologist Karl von Frisch (1886–1982) [F7] investigated and described this phenomenon to some depth. The general situation between sender and recipient is illustrated in Figure 39, as well as the syntactic, semantic, pragmatic, and apobetic levels. The transmitting bee, which has discovered a new and plentiful source of food on its latest flight, now passes this essential information (intentional communication) on to the other bees in the hive (the recipients). The employed signals are body movements. Although only a few bees are involved simultaneously, the code convention did not originate with the sender bee, nor with the recipients. This is a typical example of the situation depicted in Figure 24.

The syntax of the message is defined by various characteristics of the dance: namely the sequence of the motions, and the number of gyrations per time unit, as well as the direction of the straight line part of the movement. The attendant bees understand the meaning (semantics) of the specifically encoded information:

Distance of the food source: If the distance is, say, 350 feet, the gyrations follow one another rapidly and the motions are fast. For greater distances, the movements become less rapid, but the straight-line part is emphasized and protracted. There is a nearly mathematical relationship between the distance of the food source in feet and the number of gyrations per minute.

The direction of the food source: The direction of the straight part communicates the position of the food source in two ways, depending on whether the dancing is performed on a vertical wall of the hive, or on a horizontal plane such as the apron at the entrance. The sun is used as a compass.

The kind of flower: Nectar-gathering bees communicate the kind of blossom by means of the odor clinging to the bee's body and to the honey container. Another indispensable source of nourishment is pollen. When pollen is gathered, no nectar having an identifiable odor is carried, but some part of the blossom is brought back.

The gestural language of wolves: A wolf is able to communicate fine shades of meaning by means of its eyes, lips, and tail. It can express 11 emotional states, including confidence, threat, uncertainty, depression, a defensive attitude, and subjugation, by different tail positions [F8]. This seems to be a complex system by means of which thousands of states could be encoded, but it lacks the decisive elements of a language, namely the ability to creatively combine single language elements to construct a sentence.

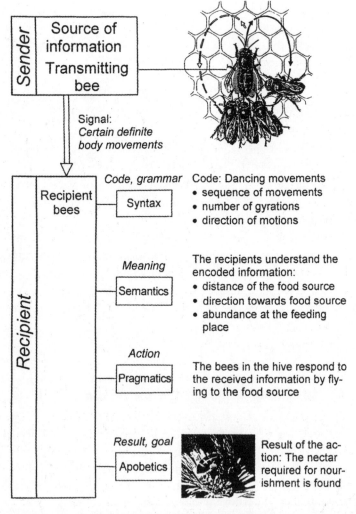

Figure 39: Bee dancing. This bee activity is a case of transmitting information; all aspects of information can be described precisely.

"Speaking birds": Parrots and budgies have the ability to faithfully imitate words and even sentences of human language. They simply reproduce what they hear. When a parrot says, "Polly wants a glass of water," this does not reflect an actual desire. Even when it says, "Good morning," it still is not a real greeting. There is no real meaning behind this "speech" of the bird; it does not speak English or German or even its own language when it makes these sounds. In contrast to the previous examples, this mimicry does not represent a communication system.

A2.3 Does "Artificial Intelligence" Exist?

The concept "artificial intelligence" — abbreviation AI — increasingly appears in catch phrases in many scientific journals as well as in popular literature [N1, S6, W1, and W7]. This falsely used catchword creates the impression that there will be no distinction between human intelligence and that of a computer in the future. The first computers were optimistically called electronic brains. Fortunately, this idea has been discarded, since there is no comparison between the human brain and a computer [G10]. Unfortunately, the American expression "artificial intelligence" was adopted uncritically, and caused more confusion than enlightenment. The question actually involves the following aspects:

- The objective is not (we hope!) to create systems which would artificially improve the intelligence of somebody with insufficient intellect, like one can employ an artificial kidney in the case of poor kidney performance.
- The word "intelligence" does not only refer to the intellect, but also includes the gathering, transmission, and evaluation of messages. An office specializing in intelligence does not deal with intellectual matters, but is concerned with information.

There is no fixed definition of AI, but the envisaged objective could be briefly described as follows: It involves a certain software technology and not, for example, the hardware of a new computer generation or some new kind of computer architecture. It does involve the development of programming systems for dealing with issues like the following:

1. **Expert systems:** This involves information systems where questions and answers in some area of specialization can be stored in the

form of if-then-else rules; new cases are incorporated as they occur. In medical diagnosis, in the search for mineral resources, and even in income tax consultations, the branching nature of the questions and the material requires special programming. An expert system essentially comprises a database containing single facts as well as the relevant rules and an inference mechanism consisting of a rule interpreter and an applicable strategy. Such systems can only be used in cases where knowledge can be formalized in rules, because programs cannot recognize semantic relationships and cannot link semantic elements.

2. Robotics: Robots are the next stage of development of partly automated machines and they play an increasingly important role in manufacturing processes. They can gather data from their surroundings by means of sensors for pressure, heat, and light, for example, and evaluate these in terms of stored program values. Then the programmed movements are carried out by manipulative mechanisms. Such systems can achieve impressive effects, as illustrated by the organ-playing robot in Figure 5 (chapter 1). It should, however, be emphasized that robots can do nothing more than that for which they have been programmed; the ingenuity and foresight of the programmer when he models the relevant knowledge is of crucial importance.

3. Image processing: This involves the construction or reconstruction of images from data. Highly suitable areas of application are tomography (Greek *tome* = cut, *graphein* = write; in conjunction with

Figure 40: "Good morning! I am the new medical director. Now please tell me how you're doing" (sketched by Carsten Gitt).

x-rays) and the preparation of satellite images. The main concern is to recognize objects by contrasting shades of grey and by applying certain algorithms to pictures. Such images can then be erased, changed, or inserted elsewhere.

Image processing includes methods for the recognition, description, and comparison of sample objects.

4. Speech processing: This includes:

- the conversion of spoken words into symbols independent of the person who speaks (the development of a "speech typewriter")
- translation from one language to another
- the ability to converse in natural language

In this area, the limitations of AI are particularly obvious, because it is in principle impossible to prepare software that can really understand and process meanings, as would be necessary for exercises requiring lingual discernment (e.g., translating, summarizing texts, and answering questions). Speech recognition and comprehension as well as the creative use of language are essential cognitive faculties of man, and is the prerogative of human intelligence.

Since the 1950s, the use of computers for natural language has been considered a challenge. The first efforts were directed to the automation of translation. For this purpose, a complete dictionary was stored, as well as the equivalents in the target language. Employing simple rules for word positioning and for the construction of sentences, the program then looked for associated concepts. However, all these

Figure 41: Speechless (sketched by Carsten Gitt).

efforts came to a dead end. The frequently quoted sentence, "The spirit is willing, but the flesh is weak," was translated into Russian and then translated back. The result was "The vodka is strong, but the steak is bad."

Joseph Weizenbaum of the Massachusetts Institute of Technology (Boston) wrote a program called ELIZA in which he ignored linguistic analyses, but employed a fixed answering schema thought to be sufficiently refined. The only result obtained was an understanding of language that was totally unrealistic. This program looked for certain words or word samples in the expressions of the input text, and selected suitable answers from a set of stored sentences or sample sentences. If, for example, a sentence containing the word "mother" is entered, then the system looks for a standard sentence in which this word occurs and responds with: "Tell me more about your mother." Most of the entered words are ignored by the program, but in spite of this, a very extensive background library is required for dealing with the large number of possible sentences that can be formulated by a person to give the impression of conversing with him.

Conclusion: The problem of enabling a computer to deal with natural language is still unsolved and will never be resolved. It is not possible to model a comprehension of semantic categories (e.g., metaphors, idioms, humor, and exaggerations), unmentioned intentions and convictions of the speaker, or emotions and motivations, for a computer. Human abilities like common sense, intelligence, and creativity cannot be simulated mechanically, because the intelligent use of language includes observation, thought, and actions. Even the best programs used for speech processing do not know what they are talking about, in the truest sense of this expression.

Computer programs which would really be able to imitate language comprehension and perform correct translations fail, as far as the following are concerned:

- Comprehension of meaning: A program cannot "understand" semantic relationships, neither can it link them with one another.

- Grammatical analysis: When translating text, a grammatical analysis is required initially. A program which analyzes some text without considering its meaning will not be able to analyze numerous sentences correctly.

- Language usage depends on its context: The meaning of a sentence cannot be found by adding the meanings of single words. What is more, the meaning of single words depends on the context in which they appear.

- Language employs background knowledge: Each and every sentence is rooted in a specific frame of reference and it can often only be understood in terms of a knowledge of this background.

- The richness of a language resides in poetic turns of speech and in its metaphors. These occur much more frequently in everyday speech than we might realize. There are countless sentences for which the meaning cannot be derived from the meanings of the component words.

- Languages are multivocal: In all languages, some words have more than one meaning (e.g., board as a noun can mean a wooden slab, or daily meals, and it also has more than one meaning as a verb), but this phenomenon is not restricted to words only. At all higher information levels (structural, semantic, pragmatic, and apobetic) there are uniquely personal components which cannot be accessed mechanically.

As we have seen, "artificial intelligence" is a misnomer, and, in addition to gradational differences, there are fundamental differences between human intelligence and AI:

- We should distinguish between data and knowledge, between algorithmically conditioned branching of a program and a deliberate decision, between sorting by comparison and associations, between an averaging of values and comprehension of meaning, between a formal decision tree and individual choice, between a sequence of computer operations and creative thought processes, and between the accumulation of data and a learning process. A computer can only do the former; herein lie its strengths, its areas of application, but also its limitations.

- AI could be regarded as a higher level of data processing, but definitely not as the beginning of independent thought on the part of computers. We err greatly when we believe that it would be possible to develop a system which will purportedly be something other than just a computing system. A chess-playing computer cannot think independently; it is no better or no worse than the strategy programmed into it by human intelligence.

– A machine cannot think independently; it can only algorithmically process information formulated and entered beforehand by one or more persons.

The AI question is discussed more fully in [G8]. Systems developed by "AI programmers" will become more meaningful in many areas, but in the light of our knowledge of the information concept, we should always keep in mind that no machine, however well programmed, will ever be able to generate creative information (see chapter 8), because this is fundamentally an intellectual process. We can now define [G8, p 41]:

Definition D7: The distinctive characteristic of creative information is its novelty, i.e., "to think what nobody else has thought." This aspect can be described with concepts like inventiveness, creativity, originality, unconventionality, innovativeness, advancement, and abundance of ideas. Every piece of creative information represents an intellectual effort and is directly linked to an originator who is a person endowed with a free will and with cognitive abilities.

APPENDIX A3 Energy

A3.1 ENERGY, A FUNDAMENTAL QUANTITY

The concept of energy (Greek *energeia* = activity) plays such a central role in all of physics as well as in the other natural sciences and in technology, that it is regarded as a fundamental entity, as information is shown to be. In contrast to information, energy belongs to the material world — the lowest level of Figure 14 (chapter 4). Energy appears in numerous forms, many of which can be converted into another form. Many physical processes fundamentally involve nothing else than the conversion of one form of energy into another. The most important forms of energy are:

- mechanical work (energy)
- potential and kinetic energy (energy of rotation and energy of translation)
- the energy of gravitational fields, and of electrical, magnetic, and electromagnetic fields
- heat energy
- electrical energy
- the energy which binds nucleons in atomic nuclei
- chemical energy
- radiation energy of particles (electrons, protons, and neutrons)
- the equivalence of mass and energy

All physical events and processes obey two fundamental principles, known in thermodynamics as the "first law" and the "second law."

The first law: This important natural law, also known as the "energy law" or the "law of conservation of energy," was first formulated in 1842 by a German physician, Robert Mayer (1814–1879). It states that energy cannot be created in the observable world, neither can it be destroyed. This law is not an axiom, but is derived from experience as are all natural laws (see Theorem N1, paragraph 2.3). In every chemical or physical process, the total energy of the system and its environment, and thus also the total quantity of energy in the universe, remains constant. It is thus impossible to destroy energy or to add to the total quantity of energy. It can only be converted into other forms. Some important consequences of the energy law are:

- Only events which do not change the total amount of energy, can occur in nature. Walter Gerlach (1889–1979), a German physicist, formulated this principle as follows [R1]: "The law of the conservation of energy plays the role of a police commissioner: it decides beforehand whether a line of thought is acceptable or forbidden."

- The impossibility of a perpetual motion machine of the first kind: No machine can be constructed which, after being set in motion, can continue working unless the supply of energy is renewed.

- The different kinds of energy correspond quantitatively, and these energy equivalents can be determined empirically.

The second law: The first law is only concerned with the conversion between heat energy and mechanical energy or vice versa, without any regard as to whether the conversion actually takes place or not. The second law, however, determines the *direction* of the process. By themselves, all processes run in only **one** direction, i.e., they are irreversible. We know from experience that if a hot block of copper is put in contact with a cold block in an isolated container, heat will be exchanged; the hot block continues to convey heat to the cold one until an average temperature occurs in both blocks. If two blocks at the same temperature are placed in the container, nothing will happen. It does not contradict the first law when one block becomes warmer and the other one cooler, as long as there is no overall loss or gain of heat.

The second law provides us with a criterion for predicting the direction of a given energy process. An abstract though quite meaningful concept — entropy S — is required for a mathematical formulation of this law. Entropy is a quantifiable value which changes whenever heat is converted. In its briefest form, the second law can be expressed as $dS \geq 0$ (for closed systems). The following conclusions can then be drawn:

— Entropy cannot be destroyed, but it can be produced.
— It is impossible to construct a periodically functioning machine which does nothing else but deliver useful work by cooling a single reservoir of heat. This means, for example, that the heat content of the sea cannot be used for propelling a ship.
— Heat cannot by itself flow from a cooler body to a warmer one (R. Clausius, 1850).
— It is impossible to build a *perpetual motion machine of the second kind:* It never happens in nature that an automatic process can let the amount of entropy decrease with no other effect.

The following formulation was first proposed by J. Meixner [M2]: "In the gigantic factory of natural processes, the function of manager is taken over by the production of entropy, because it prescribes the direction and the kinds of the events of the entire industry. The energy principle only plays the role of accountant, being responsible for the balance between what should be and what is."

The ability of a system to perform useful work: This is an important concept, since work (mechanical effort) can be completely converted into heat. The reverse process, the complete conversion of heat into useful work is theoretically impossible. This asymmetry is a primary result of the second law. In addition, the second law asserts that closed systems tend toward a state where the usable energy is a minimum, and the entropy becomes a maximum. The change in the amount of entropy indicates whether a process is reversible or not. The better a process can prevent an increase in entropy, the more useful energy can be produced. Potential and kinetic energy, as well as electrical energy, can be arbitrarily converted into one another in such a way that the process is very nearly completely reversible and can thus produce a maximum amount of useful work.

On the other hand, heat energy can only be partially converted into mechanical work or into some other form of energy. It is impossible to convert more than a certain fraction of the supplied heat energy, as given by the formula $\eta = (T_2 - T_1)/T_2$ for an ideal Carnot machine (a reversible Carnot cycle; see also paragraph 2.5). This thermodynamically possible amount of useful energy is known by a distinctive name — exergy. The fact that it is impossible to obtain more work from a heat engine than allowed by η_C follows directly from the second law.

Living organisms have a greater efficiency (= useful mechanical work obtained from a given energy input) than the maximum thermal efficiency allowed by the second law. This does not contradict this natural law, but indicates that the Creator has endowed body muscles with the capacity to convert chemical energy directly into mechanical work, and do so much more efficiently than ordinary heat engines can.

Conclusion: The law of entropy precludes all events which might lead to a decrease in entropy, even while obeying the energy law. Entropy thus reveals itself to be one of the most important and most remarkable concepts of physics.

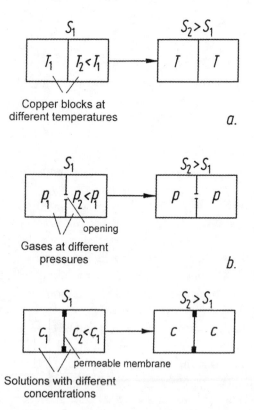

Copper blocks at different temperatures

Gases at different pressures

Solutions with different concentrations

Figure 42: Three processes in closed systems: Two blocks of copper having different temperatures eventually attain the same temperature. If two compartments contain gases at different pressures, the pressures will quickly be equalized through the opening. Two salt solutions having different concentrations exchange their salt content through a permeable membrane. In all three cases, the common aspect is that the entropy of later states is greater than for the initial conditions (S2 > S1).

Entropy and disorder? In countless publications, examples are given which illustrate that when the entropy of a system increases, the amount of disorder also increases; in other words, the orderliness is diminished. This idea has unfortunately also been extended to biological systems. The following arguments refute such a view:

- Biological processes take place in open systems, and are not closed. The second law allows a decrease in entropy as long as there is a corresponding increase in entropy in the environment. What is completely precluded is that the overall amount of entropy could be diminished.

- There can be no generally valid relationship between entropy and disorder, because entropy is a physical quantity which can be formulated exactly, but there is no exact formulation for disorder. The present author attempted a classification of the order concept in [G5], and different kinds of order are depicted in Figure 43.

- The examples selected for illustrating the apparent relationship between entropy and disorder are, without exception, systems where there is no interaction between components. Such systems are irrelevant as far as biological structures are concerned, since thousands of chemical reactions take place within minute spaces.

- Biological order is based on the information present in all cells. The quality and quantity of this information should now be obvious — see chapter 6 and paragraph A1.2.3.

The ripple patterns produced in beach sand by retreating tides represent a certain order imparted by energetic processes (Figure 44), but there is no underlying code and also no intention. Such order does not represent information and thus cannot be stored.

A3.2 STRATEGIES FOR MAXIMIZING THE UTILIZATION OF ENERGY

The utilization and consumption of energy is always a question of converting one form of energy into another. When the energy produced by a certain source is utilized, the objective is to use the energy as economically as possible. In other words, maximum efficiency is the goal, employing a strategy for maximization. The following sections are devoted to a discussion of technical and biological systems where this principle is used. When energy is consumed, the inverse strategy

SYSTEMS WHOSE COM-
PONENTS DO NOT INTER-
ACT OR DO SO ON A LIM-
ITED SCALE

An increase in entropy means
that there is an increase in
disorder:
• Temperature equalization
• Mixing of gases
• Equalization of concentration
• Equalization of pressure

TEMPORAL AND SPATIAL
STRUCTURES (Synergetics):
• Crystals (e.g., snowflakes)
• Bénard structure
• Zhabotinski reaction
• Instabilities
• Laser

ORDER
ACCORD-
ING TO
LAWS OF
NATURE

ENTROPY
Order depend-
ing on probabili-
ties (respectively
disorder)

STRUCTURE
Order achieved
through the in-
put of energy

The only linkage is on
the statistical level

"BY ITSELF"

ORDER

PLANNED

INFOR-
MATION
encoded
order

— Apobetics
— Pragmatics
— Semantics
— Syntax
— Statistics

STRUCTURE
order which
CANNOT be
encoded

INTEN-
TIONAL
ORDER

SOFTWARE

Natural and formal languages:
• Technical building plans (building
  drawings, design)
• Technical drawings (structural
  drawings, circuit diagrams)
• Prescriptions
• Genetic code
• Human languages (German,
  English, Russian)
• Computer languages
  (Fortran, BASIC, C)
• Writing, formal languages
  of chemistry and mathematics,
  musical notation, pictograms,
  flag codes, algorithms

HARDWARE

Order is based on
encoded plans:
• Architectural order
  (buildings, works of art)
• Technical order
  (machines, computers)
• Chemical products
  (artificial materials,
  medicines, food)
• Living organisms
  (plants, animals, people)

Figure 43 (page 234): The four kinds of order. The entity "order" which characterizes systems can only be described verbally and not mathematically. We can distinguish between order achieved by means of natural laws and intentional order. Structures which figure in physical systems can only be maintained as long as the gradients responsible for their existence (e.g., temperature difference), are active. Such an ordering cannot be stored and thus does not refer to a possible evolution. In the lower part of the diagram, ordered systems which are without exception based on some plan are listed. In these cases, information is either involved directly, or there are structures which originated through information.

becomes important, namely minimization of consumption: the available fuel must be used as economically as possible. The required work then has to be done with a minimal input of energy. The brilliant methods and the superlative results achieved by biological systems are discussed in paragraph A3.3.

A3.2.1 Utilization of Energy in Technological Systems

Man's inventiveness has produced numerous concepts in the field of energy production and utilization. In most cases, the conversion of energy from the primary source to the consumer entails a number of forms of energy. For example, the chemical energy of fuel is converted into heat, the heat is then utilized to produce mechanical work, which, in its turn, is converted into electrical power. In a car engine, the chemical energy of the fuel

Figure 44: Ripple marks on beach sand are an example of a structure which originated through the input of energy; this ordering is not based on information (no code is involved).

changes into heat in the combustion chambers, and the explosive expansion of the gases is converted into mechanical work. An electric light bulb converts electrical energy into heat and light. Losses occur during all these conversions, and the ratio between the input energy and the recovered energy represents the efficiency of the process. Even in present-day coal-burning steam generating plants, the efficiency is only about 40%. This means that 60% of the chemical energy of the coal is lost.

In 1993, the total amount of energy generated in Germany was 536.6 TWh [F2, p 1007]. About 5% of this total was water energy, 29.6% was obtained from nuclear reactions, and the rest was generated by the combustion of fossil and other fuels (coal and lignite 55.4%, plus natural gas, oil, and diverse other sources). With the exception of the limited hydro-electrical sources, all these processes involve heat conversion with its low efficiency.

Great technological efforts are exerted to achieve direct conversion of energy without any intermediate forms. Examples include fuel cells, magnetohydrodynamic generators, and photo-voltaic elements. The efficiency of the latter is only about 10%, and the others are not yet technologically viable.

Even in the sunny southern regions of Europe, solar power installations, employing concave mirrors to generate steam (which then drives turbines for the production of electricity), require a total mirror surface of 26,000 m^2 (2.5 football fields) to generate 1 GWh per annum [X1]. This amounts to one million kilowatt-hours per year — enough to supply 350 homes. It would require an enormous area of 42 square miles (68 square km) to generate the same quantity of electricity as that which can be produced by one 1,300 megawatt nuclear power plant. This area could accommodate 150,000 urban inhabitants.

Wind-driven power plants also require a lot of space. It would require 800 to 900 windmill towers of 492 feet (150 m) to equal the energy production of one 1,300 megawatt nuclear plant. Four chains of such windmills separated by a distance of 1,312 feet (400 m) would extend over a distance of 50 miles (80 km).

A3.2.2 Utilization of Energy in Biological Systems (Photosynthesis)

Photosynthesis is the only natural process by means of which large quantities of solar energy can be stored. Requiring only carbon dioxide (CO_2), water (H_2O), and small quantities of certain minerals, it is the fundamental process for supplying the energy which plants need for growth and reproduction. The organic substances produced by plants are the primary source of nutrition and energy for all heterotrophic[25] organisms which cannot utilize photosynthesis directly. It can truthfully be stated that photosynthesis is the primary source of energy for all life processes and it also provides most of the usable energy on earth. All fossil fuels and raw materials like coal, lignite, crude oil, and natural gas have been derived from the biomass of earlier times which was formed by photosynthesis.

This process synthesizes complex, energy-rich substances. What usually happens in oxidation/reduction reactions is that a strong oxidizing agent oxidizes a reducing substance, but photosynthesis is exceptional in this respect. It employs a weak oxidizing substance (CO_2) to oxidize a weak reducing agent (H_2O) to produce a strong oxidizing substance (O_2) and a strong reducing compound (carbohydrate). This process requires the input of external energy, namely sunlight. Such a process can only occur in the presence of a substance which can absorb light quanta, transfer the energy to other molecules, and then revert to its initial state where it can again absorb quanta of light. Chlorophyll performs this complex function. There are five types of chlorophyll (a, b, c, d, and f), which differ only slightly in chemical structure. Occurring in "higher" plants and in green algae, types a and b are the most important. The chemical equation for photosynthesis is:

$$6 \ CO_2 + 6 \ H_2O + \text{light energy} \rightarrow C_6H_{12}O_6 + 6 \ O_2 \quad (1)$$

In this process, glucose is synthesized from CO_2 and H_2O by employing the energy of sunlight. The capture of light energy and its conversion to chemical energy is only one part of the process. These initial reactions are called photochemical reactions, and all subsequent reactions where chemical energy is utilized for the synthesis of glucose do not require light energy; they are thus known as dark or umbral reactions.

The ability to absorb light varies very strongly from one substance to

---

25. Heterotrophic cells are cells which require complex nutrients like glucose and amino acids for constructing their vital macro-molecular compounds and to provide the necessary energy. On the other hand, there are the so-called phototropic cells which are photosynthetically active and can thus store chemical energy by the direct conversion of light energy.

another. Water absorbs very little light and thus appears to be colorless. The color of a substance depends on the absorption (and reflection) of certain wavelengths of light. When the degree of absorption is plotted against wavelength, we obtain an absorption spectrum. Chlorophyll only absorbs blue light (wavelength 400 to 450 nm) and red light (640–660 nm), so that the reflected light is green. The active spectrum of a process refers to its efficiency in relation to its wavelength. It is therefore noteworthy that the absorption spectrum of chlorophyll closely corresponds to the active spectrum of photosynthesis. This indicates that a finely tuned concept underlies this vital process and an efficiency calculation supports the view that a brilliant mind is involved.

The efficiency of photosynthesis: According to equation (1), exactly 1 mol^{26} of glucose is generated from 6 mol CO_2 [1] requiring an energy input of 2,872.1 kJ. For 1 mol of CO_2, this amounts to 478.7 kJ. As a loss of energy is inherent in each and every energy conversion, the actual quantity of light energy required is greater. Although red light quanta possess less energy (about 2 eV/light quantum) than blue light quanta (approximately 3 eV/quantum), due to different efficiency both types produce approximately the same amount of photochemical work. It has been determined experimentally that 8 to 10 light quanta are required for every molecule of CO_2. The energy content

---

26. One mol (1 mol) is the quantity of a substance in grams corresponding to its molecular weight (also known as relative molecular mass). The molecular weight of a compound is a dimensionless ratio obtained by adding the atomic weights of the constituent atoms. For example: The molecular weight of CO_2 = 12 + 2 x 16 = 44, so that 1 mol of CO_2 is 44 grams. It is noteworthy that the number of molecules in one mol of any substance is equal, namely (6.0221367 ± 0.0000036) x 10^{23}. This number is known as the Avogadro number NA, which is a fundamental physical constant.

27. The energy equivalence of light quanta: According to the law of Stark and Einstein (the law of the equivalence of quanta), one photon with energy h x v can excite only one molecule (h is Planck's constant and Ó is the frequency of the light waves). Since one mol of any substance consists of 6.022 x 10^{23} molecules, it means that the amount of energy required for this excitation or conversion process, is given by E = 6.022 x 10^{23} x h x Ó. This quantity of energy is called the photochemical equivalent (= 1 Einstein = 1 mol of quanta). The energy equivalence of light quanta (photons) is not constant, but depends on the wave length Ï = c/Ó so that it is usually given in molar units. The number of photons in 1 mol of light is identical to the Avogadro number NA.

of 1 mol of red light quanta (= 6.022 x 10^{23} quanta [2][27]) amounts to 171.7 kJ. Therefore, 9 mol of red light quanta (the average of 8 and 10) is found by multiplying 171.7 kJ x 9. The result is 1,545.3 kJ. The efficiency Ë can be calculated as the ratio between the theoretical amount of energy required to assimilate 1 mol CO_2 (478.7 kJ) and the actual energy content of the incident red light (1545.3 kJ):

$$\eta_{red} = 478.7/1,545.3 \times 100\% = 31\%$$

The energy content of blue light quanta is 272.1 kJ/mol, so it follows that $\eta_{blue} = 20\%$.

Volume of photosynthesis: The productivity of plants is not only qualitatively but also quantitatively highly impressive. A single beech tree which is 115 years old has 200,000 leaves which contain 180 grams of chlorophyll and have a total area of 1,200 m^2, and can synthesize 12 kg of carbohydrates on a sunny day, consuming 9,400 liters of CO_2 from a total volume of 36,000 m^3 of air [S4]. Through the simultaneous production of 9,400 liters of oxygen, 45,000 liters of air are "regenerated"! On a worldwide scale, 2 x 10^{11} tons of biomass is produced annually by means of photosynthesis [F6]. The heat value of this mass is about 10^{14} watt-years (= 3.15 x 10^{21} Ws). The entire human population annually consumes about 0.4 TWa = 1.26 x 10^{19} Ws (1 TWa = 1 Terawatt-year = 3.1536 x 10^{19} Ws), and all the animals require 0.6 TWa. Together, these add up to only one percent of the total annual biomass production.

Respiration: The result of breathing, namely the release of energy, is the opposite of photosynthesis. These two processes are in ecological equilibrium, so that the composition of the atmosphere stays constant, unless it is disturbed by human intervention like heavy industries. It should also be noted that the mechanisms for photosynthesis and respiration are astoundingly similar. The substances involved belong to the same chemical classes. For example, a chlorophyll molecule consists of four pyrrole rings arranged round a central atom, which is magnesium in the case of chlorophyll, and iron in the case of hemoglobin, the active substance on which respiration is based. Both processes occur at the interface of permeable lipid membranes. The inevitable conclusion is that a single brilliant concept underlies both processes and that both are finely tuned to each other. We can thus reject an evolutionary origin, since two such astoundingly perfect and similar processes could not possibly have originated by chance in such diverse organisms.

Conclusion: It has not yet been possible to explain the incredible complexity of the molecular mechanisms on which photosynthesis is based. The same situation holds for respiration. The fact that the chemical equations and some of the intermediate enzyme driven steps are known should not create the impression that these processes are really understood; on the contrary, what we don't yet know is incomparably more than what we do know. The American biophysicist Albert L. Lehniger [L1] regards these unresolved questions as some of the most fascinating biological problems. All solar energy engineers dream of devising a process which can convert sunlight directly into fuel. Although photosynthesis takes place in every single green leaf of all plants, having been conceived in an astoundingly brilliant way, *even the most inventive engineer is unable to imitate the process.* Every phototropic cell is supplied with the information required to undertake such an optimal energy conversion process.

A3.3 THE CONSUMPTION OF ENERGY IN BIOLOGICAL SYSTEMS: STRATEGIES FOR MINIMIZATION

Every cell requires energy continuously for its vital functions like the synthesis of new molecules, or the production of a daughter cell. In multicellular organisms there are further purposeful reactions (e.g., locomotion, and the control of body temperature). The conversion of energy in every cell, whether animal, vegetable, or microbial, is based on the same principles and mechanisms. In contrast to technological practices, living organisms avoid the inefficient use of heat as an intermediate energy form. Cellular processes are isothermic; this means that the temperature does not change.

The concept of energy: It should be emphasized that the energy-carrying nutrient molecules do not generate heat when they are oxidized. The molecular concept of biological oxidation involves numerous precisely tuned individual catalytic enzyme reactions which follow one another in exactly the required sequence, and employ just as many intermediate compounds. Adenosin triphosphate (ATP) has some special chemical properties which enable it to perform important functions. It belongs to the group of nucleotides, comprising adenine, C5-sugar, D-ribose, and phosphate groups. When nutrients are oxidized to generate energy, the more energy-rich ATP is formed from adenosin diphosphate (ADP). The energy stored in ATP can then subsequently be utilized by conversion into chemical work (e.g., biosynthesis), mechanical actions (e.g., muscular effort), or osmotic transportation. When this happens, the ATP loses one phosphate group, and reverts to ADP. In this energy transfer system, ATP is thus the charged substance, and the ADP is neutral. The numerous very complex intermediate chemical steps in this ATP/ADP energy cycle are catalyzed by a specific set of enzymes. In addition to this general flow of biological energy, there are some very clever special mechanisms for energy conversion.

Certain fishes like the electric eel can generate electrical pulses of several hundred volts directly from chemical energy. Similarly, light flashes emitted by some animals and organisms represent converted chemical energy. The bombardier beetle converts the chemical energy contained in hydrogen peroxide into explosive pressure and volume changes.

Machines constructed for the purpose of energy utilization essentially involve the generation of easily transportable electrical energy in a round-about way by first producing heat. Heat Q can only perform useful work W when there is a temperature difference T_2-T_1. The theoretical maximum amount of work that can be performed by a heat engine, is given by the Carnot formula:

$$W = Q \times (T_2-T_1)/T_2$$

T_2 can be the initial temperature of the steam entering a turbine, for example, and T_1 can be the exhaust temperature. It follows that large temperature differences are required to produce a reasonable amount of useful work. In living cells, the processes for generating energy must be fundamentally different, since all reactions have to take place at the temperature of the cell; in other words, the processes must be isothermic. The refined energy concepts realized in cells utilize substances which are unstable to heating, but still achieve exceptionally high degrees of efficiency.

The cells: A living cell can be compared with a factory comprising several departments, each of which has a certain number of machines.

The work of all the cell's departments and machines involves optimally geared interrelationships exhibiting planning down to the last detail. The end products are produced through a coordinated sequence of numerous individual processes. We can rightly state that we are dealing with the smallest fully automated production line in the world; it even has its own computer center and its own power generating plants (the mitochondria). With their diameter of 100 nm, the prokaryotes are the smallest cells, while birds' eggs are the largest. Ostrich eggs measure about 0.1 m = 10^8 nm, and the average radius of the cells of multicellular organisms lies between 2,000 nm and 20,000 nm (= 2 to 20 μm). Large living beings consist of tremendously large numbers of cells (about 10^{14} for humans), while the smallest organisms like bacteria are unicellular. Two large classes of cells are distinguished according to their structural organization, namely prokaryotic cells (Greek karyon = nucleus) and eukaryotic cells (Greek *eu* = good). Many unicellular organisms like yeast cells, protozoa, and some algae, are eukaryotic, as well as nearly all multicellular forms. Their cells contain a nucleus, mitochondria, and an endoplasmic reticulum. The prokaryotes comprise the bacteria and the blue algae. Compared to the eukaryotes, they are considerably smaller (only 1/5,000th in volume), less differentiated and less specialized, and they lack many of the structures like a nucleus or mitochondria.

Summary: We can now summarize the essential characteristics of energy utilization by organisms, which is fundamentally different from technological processes:

1. Isothermic energy conversion: Energy processes take place at a constant temperature (they are isothermic); pressures and volumes are also constant. The roundabout and inefficient technological methods which depend on the generation of heat are circumvented.

2. The greatest possible miniaturization: One of the aims of technology, the miniaturization of equipment, is realized in cells in a way that cannot be imitated. The energy generating and consuming processes in an organism are coupled at the molecular level. We can rightly speak of "molecular machines," representing the ultimate in miniaturization.

3. Optimal operation: Each and every one of the approximately ten thousand milliard (10^{13}) muscular cells in the human body possesses its own decentralized "power generating plant." These can become operational as and when required, and are extremely economical as far as the transfer of energy is concerned.

4. The indirect conversion of energy: Energy is not applied directly, but the ATP system acts as a transfer medium from the energy-generating process to the reaction consuming energy. It should be noted that ATP, a substance of high energy content, is not used for storing energy, only to transfer it. The ATP-driven, energy-consuming processes can be of a very diverse nature: mechanical work is performed in contracting muscles; electrical energy is set free in the respective organs of some animals; when substances are absorbed or transported osmotic work is done, and in many cases the result is chemical work. All of these processes are included in an extensive metabolic chain effected by an extremely complex and often incompletely understood enzyme system.

5. *High efficiency:* Compared to fermentation (from glucose to lactic acid), respiration (from glucose to CO_2 and H_2O) is an extremely efficient process, releasing all the energy stored in glucose molecules. The efficiency of the transportation of electrons in this case is 91%, a ratio which engineers can only dream of. This fascinating process occurs in a brilliantly constructed system which continuously employs the "principle of a common intermediate product for the transfer of energy." ATP is the link between reactions which supply energy and those which require energy; in other words, cells have an energy exchange unit which is readily convertible. The processes which release energy provide the "currency" which is then spent by those processes requiring energy. The ATP system channels the transfer of energy, providing the cell with excellent control over the flow of energy.

The biological energy conversion system is so brilliantly and cleverly designed that energy engineers can only watch, fascinated. Nobody has yet been able to copy this highly miniaturized and extremely efficient mechanism.

A3.4 CONSERVATION OF ENERGY IN BIOLOGICAL SYSTEMS

In regard to the relationship between physics and biology, Alfred Gierer, a physicist of Tübingen (Germany), concluded [G1]: "Physics is the most general science since it can be applied to all events in space and time, while biology is the most complex science which involves ourselves to a large extent." Some important questions now arise: Are there any processes occurring in living organisms where physical and chemical laws do not apply? Does a living organism differ fundamentally from a machine or not? Could biology be based on physics? Two aspects should be considered very carefully before we can answer such questions, namely:

1. *Course of events:* All biological processes strictly obey physical and chemical laws (see Theorems N2, N3, and N4 in paragraph 2.3).

These laws, however, only delineate the external framework within which the relevant events generally occur. The environment imposes additional constraints. Furthermore, the inherent operational information (see chapter 11 for a definition) underlies all functions of living organisms. All these mostly very complex processes are program controlled.

2. Origin: Just as each and every machine, from a simple corkscrew to a computer, cannot be explained in terms of natural laws and environmental conditions only, so also does every biological system require an inventor, a constructor, a source of ideas. Every creator of a technological invention must know the laws of physics; he employs these laws to construct a suitable mechanism. Although the laws impose constraints, they also provide conditions which can be utilized. He displays his ingenuity when, by using constructional and architectural ideas, he constructs a machine which employs the natural laws in such a way that it is obviously an optimal solution. The same holds for the Creator of biological systems. How much more is His wealth of ideas and His unfathomable wisdom reflected in living systems!

Physical laws can describe and delineate the progress of biological processes, but they fail to explain their complexity and the wealth of their structures and functions. Anybody who discusses questions of origin and of spirituality on a purely material plane removes himself completely from the realities of life by such a mechanistic reduction.

The following examples of energy conservation illustrate the immeasurable inventiveness of the Creator. In many cases, the laws of nature are employed right up to the limits of what is physically possible.

A3.4.1 Animal "Chlorophyll"

Photosynthesis has now been recognized as a brilliant invention for the conversion of the energy of the sun to produce energy donors. There are three kinds of animal [D4] which have a similar "built-in" capacity, namely the snail *Tridachia crispata*, the three-millimeter spiral worm *Convoluta roscoffensis* which lives on the coast of Normandy and Bretagne, and the microscopic green *Paramecium bursaria*.

The tridachia snails are found in the waters around Jamaica and they normally subsist on seaweed, but when seaweed is not available, they can still survive. Chlorophyll eaten previously is not fully digested, but some of it is stored in the form of undamaged chloroplasts in leaf-shaped tufts on its back. These floral organelles are still functionally active and produce sugar when exposed to sunlight. This sugar is then distributed through its body to provide energy. It can now be stated that:

- The animal borrows the chemical factory of the plant, including its control information, and thus virtually changes itself into a plant.

- This snail ingests seaweed which then ensures sufficient nutrition for up to six weeks when exposed to sunlight. This is an amazing principle.

All human nutritional problems could be solved if only we could imitate these animals. Photosynthesis is such a brilliant information-controlled process that it is not really understood; it is also impossible to copy it chemotechnically. It has not yet been possible to imitate the above mentioned animals by utilizing and preserving chloroplasts (the chlorophyll organelles) with their functions intact, outside of leaf cells.

A3.4.2 Animals with "Lamps"

As far as energy is concerned, there is another extremely interesting phenomenon exhibited by many sea animals and some simple land animals (e.g., glowworms; see details in [G15]), namely bioluminescence (Latin *lumen* = light). These organisms can emit light of various colors (red, yellow, green, blue, or violet) and in different signal sequences. When technological light production is compared to bioluminescence, the former proves to be extremely inefficient as far as energy input is concerned. Normally, an electric light bulb only converts 3 to 4 percent of the applied energy into light, and the efficiency of a fluorescent tube is only about 10%. Our lamps could be considered to be heat generators rather than radiators of light.

Bioluminescence, being an invention of the Creator, involves the radiation of cold light — a reaction which no man has yet been able to copy. In this process, certain illuminative substances (luciferin) are oxidized by an enzyme called luciferase. Three fundamentally different types of luciferin can be distinguished, namely that of bacteria, that of fireflies, and that of the Cypridina. An American biochemist, professor W.D. McElroy, was able to quantify the efficiency of this type of light production. It was found that each and every quantum of energy transported to the light organ in the form of ATP[28] was converted to light. The number of oxidized luciferin molecules is exactly equal to the number of emitted light quanta. All the light emitted by a firefly is "cold" light, which means that there is no loss of energy through the radiation of heat. We are thus dealing with lamps which are 100% efficient because of the complete conversion of energy into light.

Many bacteria, tiny organisms, insects, and deep sea fishes especially, have been equipped with this method of producing light by the Creator. The best-known examples are the fireflies and the glowworms (*Lampyris* and *Phausis*). Most of the subtropical and tropical lampyrids can emit deliberate sequences of flashes; the European ones are not able to do this. In experiments with the black firefly *(Photinus pyralis)* it was found that the flying male emitted 0.06 second flashes at intervals of 5.7 seconds, and the female on the ground replied after exactly 2.1 seconds with the same rhythm.

These flashing signals are obviously understood by the prospective mate. There also are insects that have lamps which emit different colors, like the Brazilian train worm *(Phrixothrix)*. This beetle larva *(Driliden)* which lives on snails, normally carries two orange-red lights in front. At the approach of danger, two sets of 11 greenish lanterns are switched on, one on each side. This resembles a train, and the name "train worm" is quite apt.

During a visit to Israel in 1985, we went to the underwater observatory in Eilath and could watch the lantern fish *(Photoblepharon palpebratus steinitzi)* living in the Red Sea. This fish does not produce its own light, but obtains it from symbiotic luminescent bacteria. These bacteria are so small that the light of a single one is invisible, but the light of an entire colony can be observed. They congregate on an oval light organ situated below the eyes of the fish and are fed and provided with oxygen through a densely branching network of capillary blood vessels. They continuously generate light, but the fish can deliberately switch the light on and off. It does this by pulling a black skin flap over the luminescent organ like an eyelid, and is thus able to transmit different flashing signals. These signals attract the prey it requires for subsistence.

Bacterial emission of light is fundamentally different from that of other luminescent organisms. Other marine organisms only emit

---

28. ATP (= adenosin triphosphate) is a macro-molecule used for the storage and transportation of energy in living cells (see paragraph A3.3).

light when they are disturbed or stimulated (e.g., by the passage of a ship or of a mackerel school, or the breaking of waves), but bacteria continuously emit light of a constant intensity.

The bioluminescence of abyssal creatures, like glowing fishes, crabs, arrow worms, and jellyfishes, is quite impressive. Many kinds of fish have lamps along their sides, while others have several rows of lamps. The luminous organs can be arranged in curves, in oscillatory patterns, or quite irregularly. The five-striped star constellation fish *(Bathysidus pentagrammus)* has five beautiful shining lines on both sides of its body, each of which consists of a row of large pale yellow lights, surrounded by serrated bright purple "jewels."

Luminous shrimps *(Sergestes prehensilis)* have more than 150 light points, all of which can be quickly switched on and off. For one or two seconds yellow-green lights flash sequentially and quickly from head to tail, just like neon advertisements in cities. Many kinds of fish employ luminescent bacteria to generate light flashes, but others have highly specialized organs which produce their own luminous substances. Some fishes have intricately constructed light projectors, concentrating lenses, or other optical equipment which can, for example, direct a ray of light in a specific direction. The projectors are constructed in such a way that a mosaic of thousands of minute crystals acts as a perfect mirror behind the luminous tissues. Some creatures even have color filters (pigment membranes) for producing any shade of color.

The inventiveness of the Creator is infinite, and we can only stand amazed.

A3.4.3 The Lung, an Optimal Structure

As in the case of biological systems, the construction of an efficient technological plant requires that the consumption of energy should be a minimum. One should pay special attention to irreversible processes, since they determine the cost of the energy. In flow processes, friction is the decisive irreversible factor. Frictional losses can be reduced by having large diameter conduits and by decreasing the contact areas. There are constraints: the provision of generous dimensions in a processing plant increases investment costs considerably, and in living organisms much more basic energy would be required. The total quantity of energy required by an organ or a muscle consists of two parts, namely a certain minimum which is necessary for proper functioning, plus any increase needed for greater activity.

Continuing the work of Swiss physiologist and Nobel Laureate Walter R. Hess (1881), and using the human lung as an example, E.R. Weibel [W2] showed that this optimization problem is solved in a remarkable way. The lung is constructed in such a fashion that when the body tissues are relatively inactive and thus require a minimum of input material and energy, then only a small increase in the basic conversion process is involved to overcome pressure losses. The air passage branches into the well-known two bronchi, each of which again branches into two smaller passages having equal diameters. This pairwise furcation into smaller conduits continues until the 23rd level, which represents the finest air capillaries. The average ratio d_2/d_1 of two consecutive diameters (d_2 following d_1) is very nearly 0.8. When pressure decreases have to be a minimum for a given volume of conduits and laminar flow must be maintained, then the result obtained by optimization calculations in fluid dynamics is found to be $d_2/d_1 = (1/2)^{1/3} = 0.79370$. This is consistent with the measured value of 0.8 and this $(1/2)^{1/3}$ formula holds even more exactly for the furcations of the blood vessels supplying the lung. The more we study the details of biological systems, the stronger the impression becomes that their Creator is a brilliant constructor and inventor.

A3.4.4 The Flight of Migrating Birds

The flight of birds is one of the most fascinating kinds of propulsion seen in creation. It involves numerous solutions which cannot be imitated technologically [D2, R3, and S2]. Aerodynamically, birds' wings are highly specialized and optimized structures. Their curvature is especially important, otherwise they could not fly. An airplane has to have a fairly high minimum airspeed to stay airborne, but birds can utilize the updraught caused by their wing strokes to fly quite slowly. Their wings are carrier surfaces as well as propellers; the efficiency of the latter function is very high, and cannot yet be attained by technological means. We now discuss two of the numerous problems solved in the design of bird flight, namely the matters of *precise energy calculations* and *exact navigation*.

A3.4.4.1 The Flight of Migrating Birds: An Accurate Energy Calculation

Every physical, technological, and biological process strictly obeys the energy law, namely that a certain total amount of energy is required. Migrating birds have to carry enough energy in the form of fat to complete their journey, but birds' bodies have to be as light as possible, so unnecessary weight should be strictly avoided. It is also necessary that fuel consumption should be optimal. How did the Creator provide for enough fuel without having "reserve tanks" or overnight "pit stops"? The first aspect is to determine the most optimal speed. If a bird flies too slowly, it consumes too much fuel for propulsion. If it flies too fast, then more energy is required to overcome air friction. There is thus a certain optimum speed for minimum fuel consumption. If the bird knew this special speed, it could fly the most economically. Depending on the aerodynamics of its body and its wings, every bird has a specific optimal speed (it is 45 km/h in the case of the Aztec seagull, for example; and 41.6 km/h for a parakeet). It is known that birds keep exactly to their optimum energy-saving speed when traveling. How do they know this? It is just one of many puzzles which ornithologists cannot solve.

We now consider the energy problem in more detail in the case of the golden plover *(Pluvialis dominica fulva)*. These birds migrate from Alaska to spend the northern winter in Hawaii. They have to fly non-stop over the ocean without resting, because there are no islands en route, neither do they swim. During this 88-hour journey of more than 2,485 miles (4,000 km) (depending on the point of departure), they beat their wings an enormous 250,000 times without stopping at all. At the start, their average weight G_0 is 200 g, 70 g of which is padding (fat) which serves as fuel. It has been found that these birds consume 0.6% of their weight per hour (fuel consumption $p = 0.006/h$) to produce propulsion energy and heat. During the first hour the amount of fuel x_1 it thus requires

$$x_1 = G_0 \times p = 200 \times 0.006 = 1.2 \text{ g fat.} \qquad (1)$$

At the beginning of the second hour it weighs $G_0 - x_1 = 200 - 1.2 = 198.8$ g, so that it consumes somewhat less energy during the second hour:

$$x_2 = (G_0 - x_1) \times p = G_1 \times p = 198.8 \times 0.006 = 1.193 \text{ g} \qquad (2)$$
$$x_3 = (G_0 - x_1 - x_2) \times p = G_2 \times p = 197.6 \times 0.006 = 1.186 \text{ g} \qquad (3)$$

For the 88th hour the fuel consumption is down to

$$x_{88} = (G_0 - x_1 - x_2 - x_3 - \ldots - x_{87}) \times p = G_{87} \times p \qquad (4)$$

because of its reduced weight. We can now calculate its weight at the end of the journey, after subtracting the hourly weight reduction:

1st hour: $G_1 = G_0 - x_1 = G_0 - G_0 \times p = G_0(1-p)$ (5)

2nd hour: $G_2 = G_1 - x_2 = G_1 - G_1 \times p = G_1(1-p) = G_0(1-p)^2$ (6)

3rd hour: $G_3 = G_2 - x_3 = G_2 - G_2 \times p = G_2(1-p) = G_0(1-p)^3$ (7)

. . .

zth hour: $G_z = G_{z-1} - x_z = G_{z-1} - G_{z-1} \times p = G_{z-1}(1-p) = G_0(1-p)^z$ (8)

. . .

88th hour: $G_{88} = G_{87} - x_{88} = G_{87} - G_{87} \times p = G_{87}(1-p) = G_0(1-p)^{88}$ (9)

The hourly weights G_0, G_1, . . . , G_{88} form a geometric sequence with common ratio $q = 1 - p < 1$. This computation is somewhat over-simplified,[29] but, by substitution in (9) we find the final weight after 88 hours to be:

$$G_{88} = 200 \times (1 - 0.006)^{88} = 117.8 \text{ g} \qquad (10)$$

The total fuel consumption is given by

$$G_0 - G_{88} = 200 - 117.8 = 82.2 \text{ g} \qquad (11)$$

which is appreciably greater than the 70 g of fat the bird started out with! The bird's weight cannot go below 130 g (see Figure 45). In spite of flying at the optimum speed for minimal fuel consumption, the bird would not be able to reach Hawaii because it started out with too little fat. To determine the number of hours that the bird could fly with the given amount of fuel, we have to solve the following equation for z:

$$G_z = G_0 \times (1-p)^z = 200 - 70 = 130 \text{ g}.$$

The result is that the 70 g of fat will be consumed after 72 hours, which is 81% of the required flying time. This means that the bird would plunge into the ocean about 497 miles (800 km) short of its destination. Did we make some mistake, or has the bird been inadequately constructed by the Creator? The answer to both questions is "no." We regard the Creator's work with amazement. He employs the fundamental theorem which states that "energy input is optimized

---

29. A more exact calculation involves the differential equation $dG/dt = -G(t) \times p$ with $G(t=0) = G_0$ instead of the hourly steps considered above. The solution of this equation is a continuous function $G(t) = G_0 \times \exp(-px\,t)$ where $p = 0.006/h$, which differs only in a few insignificant decimal places from the result given in equation (10).

through information." In the case of the plover, this means that the bird has been given some important additional information, namely: "Do not fly *alone* (curve G_A), but fly in a *V formation* (curve G_V)! In the V formation, you will save 23% of your energy and will then safely reach your destination." Curve G_V in Figure 45 depicts the weight decrease in V formation. After 88 hours, the normal residual amount of fat is 6.8 g, which has not been carried along unnecessarily, but is a reserve to be used when head winds are encountered. The extremely low specific rate of fuel consumption, $p = 0.6\%$ of its weight per hour, is all the more amazing when we compare it with that of man-made aircraft which is many orders of magnitude greater (for a helicopter $p = 4$ to 5%; and $p = 12\%$ for a jet plane).

Somebody who does not regard these precise phenomena as the work of the Creator cannot answer the following questions:

- How does the bird know the exact energy requirement?
- How is it possible that the bird accumulates the exact amount of fat before the journey?
- How does the bird know the distance and the specific fuel consumption?
- How does the bird know the migration route?
- How does the bird navigate to reach its destination promptly?
- How does the bird know to fly in a V formation with other birds to reduce fuel consumption?

In my book *If Animals Could Talk* [G15], the golden plover acts as narrator involving the reader in an imaginary dialogue. The facts presented here are used as point of departure to draw the reader's attention to numerous wonders of creation.

Besides the Eastern Siberian golden plover mentioned above, there is also the North American golden plover *(Nominatrasse)*. These birds also undertake a non-stop long distance migration flight from the coast of Labrador across the Atlantic Ocean to Brazil. The western plovers follow the same route for both the outward and the return journey, but the American plovers use different routes in autumn and spring. On the northward leg, they fly back to Canada over Central America and the United States. Some further astonishing migration feats are:

- The Japanese snipe *(Capella hardtwickii)* flies 5,000 km to Tasmania.

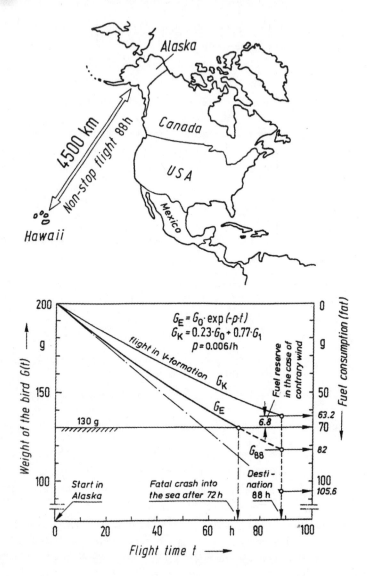

Figure 45: The flight of the East Siberian golden plover. For the migration of up to 4,500 km from Alaska to Hawaii, the amount of available fuel is 70 g. If this flight is undertaken by a single bird, it would consume all its fat reserves after 72 hours and would plunge into the ocean 800 km from its destination. On the other hand, flying in a V formation reduces the energy consumption by 23%, so that the birds reach their destination safely.

- The East Siberian spine-tailed swift *(Chaetura caudacuta)* migrates from Siberia to Tasmania.
- The migration route of the American sandpipers (e.g., *Calidris melanotus* = grey breasted sandpiper) covers 16,000 km from Alaska to Tierra del Fuego at the southern tip of South America.

A3.4.4.2 The Flight of Migrating Birds: A Navigational Masterpiece

Finn Salomonsen, a Danish ornithologist, writes the following about the in-flight orientation of birds [S2]: "The ability of birds to find their way while flying is a mystery and a puzzle. Few other questions have over the years given rise to so many theories and speculations as this one." This navigational ability is indeed a supreme wonder, since birds do not have complex gyroscopes, compasses, or maps, and environmental conditions like the position of the sun, wind direction, cloud cover, and day-night rhythms, keep changing all the time. When terrestrial birds have to cross an ocean, as we have seen in the case of the golden plover, a small error in direction would result in their floundering helplessly over the open ocean and finally plunging to their death. Setting an exact course is not a question of trial and error, because a large majority of the migratory birds would never reach their destination without exact navigation. No species could survive such great losses. Any evolutionistic view of this fact can be rejected out of hand. The idea that juvenile birds are shown the way by their parents plays a minor role at most, since many kinds of birds fly singly. We thus have to assume that migratory birds possess an inherent sense of direction which enables them to orient themselves with respect to geographical direction and to stay on course. This sense of direction is demonstrated by Salomonsen in the case of two kinds of small birds living in western Greenland and which both migrate to the south in autumn. The wheatear *(Oenanthe oenanthe)* and the snow canary live in the same region, and they often begin their migration at the same time, but their ways part after arriving in southern Greenland. The snow canaries continue directly south to spend the winter in America, while the others turn southeast and fly right across the Atlantic Ocean to western Europe and North Africa. Both kinds of bird have a specific sense of direction which determines their different courses.

Detailed results about navigational precision have been found by transporting different kinds of birds to distant locations. A noteworthy experiment was undertaken with two kinds of marine swallows *(Sterna fuscata* and *Anous stolidus*) which breed on the Tortugas Islands in the Gulf of Mexico. The birds were taken by ship in different directions and were released at distances of between 517 and 850 miles (832 and 1368 km) from their nesting place. Although they found themselves in, for them, unknown parts of the ocean, most of them returned home after a few days, flying unswervingly straight back to their eggs and their young on the Tortugas Islands.

Many experiments have been carried out with homing pigeons, and their navigational abilities have been extensively investigated and described. Salomonsen writes as follows about these breathtaking marvels of navigation [S2]:

> Even when pigeons have been transported while anaesthetized, or when their cage was rotated so that its orientation changed continuously, they were able to fly back home just as readily as undisturbed pigeons, when released. It can be asserted without a doubt that these birds possess a special ability for determining their geographic position; they have a real navigational sense. We know nothing about the actual nature of this sense, neither do we know where the special sense organ is located.

These birds have exceptional faculties: They can return home over great distances, even though deprived of any possibility of orientation when transported. Wherever they are released, they have the amazing ability to extract the required data from the environment to determine their position relative to their home. Even after having oriented themselves in this unknown way, the real problem arises, namely en route navigation. A simple sense of direction is inadequate for this purpose.

When crossing oceans, the birds have to take drift, caused by the perennial winds, into consideration. To avoid wasting energy on detours, such factors have to be determined and corrected continuously, as with a cybernetic control system. The Creator provided birds with a very precise "autopilot" which is obviously able to monitor environmental data continuously and compare it with the internally programmed home location and the envisioned geographic destination, to guarantee the quickest and most economical route. As yet, nobody but the Creator who devised it knows the location of this vitally important system, neither do we know how the operational information is encoded. We use a special term to cover our ignorance, we say the birds have "instinct."

REFERENCES

[B1] BAM — Informationsversorgung — neue Möglichkeiten in der Bundesanstalt für Materialforschung BAM-Information 6/81.

[B2] Bauer, F.L., Goos, G. — Informatik — Eine einführende Übersicht Springer-Verlag, Berlin, Heidelberg, New York 1971, 213 p.

[B3] Blechschmidt, E. — Die pränatalen Organsysteme des Menschen, Hippokrates Verlag Stuttgart, 1973, 184 p.

[B4] Born, M. — Symbol und Wirklichkeit I Physikalische Blätter 21 (1965), p. 53–63.

[B5] Brillouin, L. — *Science and Information Theory* (New York: Academic Press Inc., Publishers, 1963), 2nd edition, 351 p.

[B6] Broda, E. — Erfindungen der lebenden Zelle – Zwölf epochale bisher nicht nachgeahmte Prinzipien – Naturwiss. Rundschau 31 (1978): p. 356–363.

[B7] Buck, J.B. — "Synchronous Flashing of Fire Flies Experimentally Produced," *Science* 81 (1935): p. 339–340

[C1] Carr, D.E. — Geheimnisvolle Signale – Die Rätsel der vergessenen Sinne – Fischer Taschenbuch Verlag, 1972, 208 p.

[C2] Chaitin, G.J. — "Randomness and Mathematical Proof, *Scientific American*, 232 (1975): p. 47–52.

[D1] Dake, F.J. — *Dake's Annotated Reference Bible* (Lawrenceville, GA: Dake Bible Sales, Inc., 1961).

[D2] Dawkins, R. — Der blinde Uhrmacher – Ein Plädoyer für den Darwinismus – Kindler-Verlag, München, 1987, 384 p.

[D3] Dose, K. — Die Ursprünge des Lebens (Tagungsbericht über den ISSOL-Kongreß in Mainz vom 10. bis 15. Juli 1983) Nachr. Chem. Techn. Lab. 31 (1983), Nr. 12, pp. 968-969.

[D4] Dröscher, V.B. — Überlebensformel dtv-Taschenbuch, 2nd Edition 1982, 329 p.

[E1] Eigen, M. — Self-Organisation of Matter and the Evolution of Biological Macromolecules Naturwissenschaften 58 (1971), p. 465–523.

[E2]   Eigen, M.   Stufen zum Leben, – Die frühe Evolution im Visier der Molekularbiologie – Piper-Verlag, München, Zürich, 1987, 311 p.

[E3]   Elektrizitätswirtschaft Die Elektrizitätswirtschaft in der Bundes-republik Deutschland im Jahre 1984, Elektrizitätswirtschaft 84 (1985), No. 19, p. 1–45.

[F1]   Feynman, R.P.   *The Character of Physical Law* (Cambridge, MA: The MIT Press, 1995), 2nd Edition, 173 p.

[F2]   Fischer   Der Fischer Weltalmanach 1994 – Zahlen, Daten, Fakten – Fischer Taschenbuch Verlag, Frankfurt/M., Nov. 1993, 1215 p.

[F3]   Flechtner, H.-J.   Grundbegriffe der Kybernetik Wissenschaftliche Verlagsgesellschaft mbH, 4th Edition 1969, 423 p.

[F4]   Folberth, O.G.   Hürden und Grenzen bei der Miniaturisierung digitaler Elektronik Elektronische Rechenanlagen 25 (1983) H. 6, p. 45–55.

[F5]   Forrest, S.   "Genetic Algorithms: Principles of Natural Selection Applied to Computation," *Science*, vol. 261, August 13, 1993, p. 872–878.

[F6]   Fricke, J.   Biomasse Physik in unserer Zeit 15 (1984), H. 4, p. 121–122.

[F7]   v. Frisch, K.   Aus dem Leben der Bienen Springer-Verlag Berlin, Heidelberg, New York, 9th Edition 1977, 194 p.

[F8]   Fromkin, V.,   *An Introduction to Language* (New York, Chicago:
        Rodman, R., et al.   Saunders College Publishing, Holt, Rinehard and Winston, 1983), third edition, 385 p.

[F9]   Fucks, W.   Die mathematischen Gesetze der Bildung von Sprachelementen aus ihren Bestandteilen Nachrichtentechn. Fachberichte NTF, Band 3, "Informationstheorie" (1956), p. 7–21.

[G1]   Gierer, A.   Die Physik und das Verständnis des Lebendigen Universitas 36 (1981), p. 1283–1293.

[G2]   Gilbert, W.   DNA-Sequenzierung und Gen-Struktur (Nobel-Vortrag) Angewandte Chemie 93 (1981), p. 1037–1046.

[G3]   Gipper, H.   Sprache als In-formation (Geistige Prägung) in: O. G. Folberth, C. Hackl (Hrsg.): Der Informationsbegriff in Technik und Wissenschaft, R. Oldenbourg Verlag, München, Wien, 1986, p. 257–298.

[G4]   Gitt, W.   Information und Entropie als Bindegliederdiverser Wissenschaftszweige PTB-Mitt. 91 (1981), p. 1–17.

[G5]   Gitt, W.   Ordnung und Information in Technik und Naturin: W. Gitt (Hrsg.), Am Anfang war dieInformation, Resch-Verlag, Gräfelfing/München, 1982, 211 p.

[G6]   Gitt, W.   Am Anfang war die Information – Forschungsergebnisse aus Naturwissenschaft und Technik – Resch-Verlag, Gräfelfing/München, 1982, 211 p.

[G7]   Gitt, W.   Ein neuer Ansatz zur Bewertung von Information – Beitrag zur semantischen Informations-theorie – in: H. Kreikebaum et al. (Hrsg.),Verlag Duncker & Humblot, Berlin, 1985, p. 210–250.

[G8]   Gitt, W.   "Künstliche Intelligenz" – Möglichkeiten und Grenzen – PTB-Bericht TWD-34, 1989, 43 p.

[G9]   Gitt, W.   Information: "The Third Fundamental Quantity," *Siemens Review*, vol. 56, no. 6 (Nov/Dec 1989): p. 2–7.

[G10] Gitt, W.   In 6 Tagen vom Chaos zum Menschen – Logos oder Chaos – Aussagen und Einwändezur Evolutionslehre sowie eine tragfähige Alternative, 4th edition 1995, Hänssler-Verlag, Neuhausen-Stuttgart, 224 p.

[G11] Gitt, W.   Das biblische Zeugnis der Schöpfung, 6th Edition, 1996, Hänssler-Verlag,Neuhausen-Stuttgart, 190 p.

[G12] Gitt, W.   So steht's geschrieben– Zur Wahrhaftigkeit der Bibel, 4th edition, 1997, Hänssler-Verlag, Neuhausen-Stuttgart, 200 p.

[G13] Gitt, W.   *Questions I Have Always Wanted to Ask* (Bielefeld (Germany: CLV-Verlag, 1992), 1st edition, 158 p.; German version: Fragen, die immer wiedergestellt werden, 14th edition, 1996, 158 p.)

[G14] Gitt, W.   *Did God Use Evolution?* (Bielefeld, Germany: CLV-Verlag, 1993), 1st edition, 159 p.; German version: Schuf Gott durch Evolution? 4th edition 1997, 158 p.

[G15] Gitt, W.   *If Animals Could Talk* (Bielefeld, Germany: CLV-Verlag, 1994), 1st edition, 127 p.; German version: Wenn Tiere reden könnten, 9th edition, 1995, 123 p.

[G16] Gitt, W.   *Stars and Their Purpose — Signposts in Space* (Bielefeld, Germany: CLV-Verlag, 1996), 1st edition 1996, 217 p.; German version: Signale aus dem All — Wozu gibt es Sterne, 2nd edition, 1995, 222 p.)

[G17] Gitt, W.   "Information, Science and Biology," *Creation Ex Nihilo Technical Journal*, vol. 10 (Part 2) (1996): p. 181–187.

[G18] Gitt, W.   "Information — A Fundamental Quantity in Natural and Technological Systems," Second Conference on the Foundations of Information — The Quest for a Unified Theory of Information, Vienna University of Technology, June 11–15, 1996.

[G19] Guinness   Das neue Guinness Buch der Rekorde, 1994, Ullstein Verlag Berlin, 1993, 368 p.

[H1]   Hastead, B.   "Popper: Good Philosophy, Bad Science?" *New Scientist* (July 17, 1980): p. 215–217.

[H2]   Hassenstein, B.   Was ist "Information"? Naturwissenschaft und Medizin 3 (1966), p. 38–52.

[H3]   Holzhausen, A.   Übersetzern in die Werkstatt geschaut — Aus der Praxis der Bibelübersetzung in aller Welt, Wycliff-Bibelübersetzer, 1980, 32 p.

[H4]   Hoyle, F.   "The Big Bang in Astronomy," *New Scientist* (Nov. 19, 1981): p. 521–527.

[J1]   Jockey, H.P.   "Self Organisation, Origin of Life Scenarios and Information Theory," *J. Theor. Biology*, 91 (1981): p. 13–31.

[J2]   Jones, E.S.   Das frohmachende Ja — Das Vermächtnis des bekannten Missionars und Evangelisten, Christliches Verlagshaus GmbH, Stuttgart,1975, 95 p.

[J3]   Junker, R., Scherer, S. Entstehung und Geschichte der Lebewesen Weyel-Verlag, Gießen,3rd edition, 1992, 275 p.

[K1]   Kaplan, R.W.   Der Ursprung des Lebensdtv Georg Thieme Verlag, Stuttgart,1st edition, 1972, 318 p.

[K2]   Kuhn, H.   Selbstorganisation molekularer Systeme unddie Evolution des genetischen Apparats, Angewandte Chemie 84, 1972, p. 838–861.

[K3]   Küppers, B.-O.   Der Ursprung biologischer Information — Zur Naturphilosophie der Lebensentstehung, Piper-Verlag, München, Zürich, 1986, 319 p.

[K4] Küpfmüller, K.   Die Entropie der deutschen Sprache, Fernmeldetechn. Zeitschrift 7 (1954), p. 265–272.

[L1] Lehninger, A.L.   *Bioenergetics — The Molecular Basis of Biological Energy Transformations* (Menlo Park, CA: W. A. Benjamin, Inc., 1971).

[L2] Lwoff, A.   Virus, Zelle, Organismus Angewandte Chemie 78 (1966), p. 689–724.

[L3] Lyons, J.   Die Sprache, C.H. Beck-Verlag, München, 4th edition, 1992, 318 p.

[M1] Matthies, H.   Satellitenfernsehen ist Fingerzeig Gottes Christen in der Wirtschaft (1986). H. 1, p. 7–9.

[M2] Meixner, J.   Die Thermodynamik irreversibler Prozesse Physikalische Blätter 16 (1960), p. 506–511.

[M3] Meschkowski, H.   Mathematiker-Lexikon, Bibliographisches Institut, Mannheim, Wien, Zürich, B. I.-Wissenschaftsverlag, 1980, 342 p., 3. überarbeitete und ergänzte Ausgabe.

[M4] Michalewicz, Z.   Genetic Algorithms + Data Structures = Evolution Programs Springer Verlag, Berlin, Heidelberg, 3rd edition, 1996, 387 p.

[M5] Mini Bible   Slide with "The Smallest Bible in the World," Available: Ernst Paulus Verlag, Haltweg 23, 67434 Neustadt/Weinstraße, Germany.

[M6] Mohr, H.   Der Begriff der Erklärung in Physik und Biologie Naturwissenschaften, 65 (1978), p. 1–6.

[N1] Nees, G.   Künstliche Intelligenz und Expertensysteme, Automatisierungstechnische Praxis 27 (1985), p. 25–32.

[O1] Ohta, T.   "A Model of Evolution for Accumulating Genetic Information," *J. Theor. Biol.* (1987) 124, p. 199–211.

[O2] Osawa, S., et al.   "Recent Evidence for Evolution of the Genetic Code," *Microbiological Reviews*, March 1992, p. 229–264.

[O3] Osche, G.   Die Vergleichende Biologie und die Beherrschung der Mannigfaltigkeit Biologie in unserer Zeit 5 (1975), p. 139–146.

[O4] Oth, R.   Das große Indianer-Lexikon – Alles über Kultur und Geschichte eines großen Volkes – Arena-Verlag, Würzburg, 1979, 220 p.

[P1]   Peierls, R.E.   Wo stehen wir in der Kenntnis der Naturgesetze? Physikal. Blätter (19) 1963, p. 533–539.

[P2]   Peil, J.   Einige Bemerkungen zu Problemen der Anwendung des Informationsbegriffs in der Biologie, Teil I: Der Informationsbegriff und seine Rolle im Verhältnis zwischen Biologie, Physik und Kybernetik, p. 117–128; Teil II: Notwendigkeit und Ansätze zur Erweiterung des Informationsbegriffs, p. 199–213, Biometrische Zeitschrift Bd. 15 (1973).

[P3]   Planck, M.   Vorträge und Erinnerungen, S. Hirzel-Verlag, Stuttgart, 1949.

[R1]   Rentschler, W.   Die Erhaltungsgesetze der Physik Physikalische Blätter 22 (1966), p. 193–200.

[R2]   Rokhsar, D.S., et al.   "Self-Organisation in Prebiological Systems: Simulations of a Model for the Origin of Genetic Information," J. of Molecular Evolution, 23 (1986): p. 119–126.

[R3]   Rüppell, G.   Vogelflug Rowohlt Taschenbuch Verlag GmbH, 1980, 209 p.

[S1]   Sachsse, H.   Die Stellung des Menschen im Kosmos in der Sicht der Naturwissenschaft. Herrenalber Texte HT33, "Mensch und Kosmos," 1981, p. 93–103.

[S2]   Salomonsen, F.   Vogelzug, Aus der Serie: Moderne Biologie, BLV München, Basel, Wien, 1969, 210 p.

[S3]   Schäfer, E.   Das menschliche Gedächtnis als Informationsspeicher, Elektronische Rundschau 14 (1960), p. 79–84.

[S4]   Scherer, S.   Photosynthese – Bedeutung und Entstehung – ein kritischer Überblick, Hänssler-Verlag, Neuhausen-Stuttgart, 1983, 74 p.

[S5]   Schneider, H.   Der Urknall, Zeitschrift factum (1981), Nr. 3, p. 26–33.

[S6]   Schuchmann, H.R.   "Artifical Intelligence," als Informations-technologie — "Künstliche Intelligenz," auf dem Weg von der Wissenschaft zur industriellen Anwendung, data report 19 (1984), H. 3, p. 4–11.

[S7]   Shannon, C.E.,   The Mathematical Theory of Communication (Urbana, Weaver, W.   IL: University of Illinois Press, 1949).

[S8]	Sösemann, F.	Information, physikalische Entropie und Objektivität, Wiss. Zeitschrift der Techn. Hochschule Karl-Marx-Stadt 17 (1975), p. 117–122.
[S9]	Spurgeon, C.H.	Das Buch der Bilder und Gleichnisse — 2000 der besten Illustrationen, J.G. Oncken-Verlag, Kassel, 1900, 731 p.
[S10]	Spurgeon, C.H.	Es steht geschrieben — Die Bibel im Kampf des Glaubens, Oncken-Verlag, Wuppertal und Kassel, 1980, 94 p.
[S11]	Steinbuch, K.	Falsch programmiert, Deutscher Bücherbund, Stuttgart, Hamburg, 1968, 251 p.
[S12]	Strombach, W.	Philosophie und Informatik, Forschungsbericht Nr. 122 der Abteilung, Informatik, Universität Dortmund, 31 p.
[U1]	Underhill, R.	*Here Come the Navaho! – A History of the Largest Indian Tribe in the United States* (Tucson, AZ: Treasure Chest Publications, Inc., 1953), 285 p.
[V1]	Vollmert, B.	Das Molekül und das Leben — Vom makromolekularen Ursprung des Lebens und der Arten: Was Darwin nicht wissen konnte und Darwinisten nicht wissen wollen, Rowohlt-Verlag, 1985, 256 p.
[W1]	Waltz, D.L.	Künstliche Intelligenz, Spektrum der Wissenschaft (1982), H. 12, p. 68–87.
[W2]	Weibel, E.R.	Morphometry of the Human Lung Springer Verlag, Berlin, 1973.
[W3]	v. Weizsäcker, E.	Offene Systeme I — Beiträge zur Zeitstruktur von Information, Entropie und Evolution, — Ernst Klett Verlag, Stuttgart, 1974, 370 p.
[W4]	Wieland, W.	Möglichkeiten und Grenzen der Wissenschaftstheorie, Angewandte Chemie 93 (1981), p. 627–634.
[W5]	Wiener, N.:	Kybernetik—Regelung und Nachrichtenübertragung in Lebewesen und Maschinen — Rowohlt Verlag, 1968, 252 p.
[W6]	Wills, P.R.	"Scrapie, Ribosomal Proteins and Biological Information," *J. Theor. Biol.* (1986) 122, p. 157–178.
[W7]	Winograd, T.	Software für Sprachverarbeitung, Spektrum der

8ae ot

Wissenschaft (1984), H. 11, p. 88–102.

[W8] Wuketits, F. M.   Biologie und Kausalität, Verlag Paul Parey, Berlin und Hamburg, 1981, 165 p.

[X1]   Energie aus Sonne und Wind: Raum nicht in der kleinsten Hütte, Zeitschrift "tag+nacht" der Stadtwerke, Braunschweig, IV, 1983, p. 3.

Name Index

Adams, J.C. 40
Åkerblad 57
Attenborough, D. 137
Bach, J.S. 112
Bauer, F.L. 255
Bell, J. 66
Berger, K. 102
Berenice 57
Bezzel, H. 151
Bloch, B. 209
Boltzmann, L. 177
Bonhoeffer, D. 156
Born, M. 30, 100, 255
Braun, K.F. 129
Bresch, C. 137
Brillouin, L. 199, 255
Carrel, A. 150
Chaitin, G.J. 125, 255
Champollion, J.F. 57
Chomsky, N.A. 210
Clausius, R. 34, 42, 177, 231
Cleopatra 57
Cocteau, J. 51
Copernicus, N. 29, 100
Crick, F.H.C. 99
Dawkins, R. 101–103, 137, 255
De Gaulle , C. 59
Dommel, P. 216
Dose, K. 106, 255
Eigen, M. 29, 82, 99, 137, 255, 256
Einstein, A. 41, 52–53, 100, 238
Ester, M. 12
Faraday, M. 35, 128
Feitscher, W. 115
Feynman, R. P. 23, 33, 36, 256

Flechtner, H.-J. 51, 256
Fleming, J.A. 128
Folberth, O.G. 193, 256
v. Frisch, K. 73, 221, 256
Fromkin, V. 217, 256
Fucks, W. 201, 256
Galle, J.G. 40
Galilei, G. 100, 127
Gerlach, W. 230
Gierer, A. 243, 256
Gipper, H. 67, 256
Gitt, C. 224, 225
v. Goethe, J.W. 76, 167
Gödel, K. 32
Goos, G. 200
Grigg, R. 13
Haken, H. 125
Hall, R.A. 210
Hassenstein, B. 197–198, 258
Hausmann, M. 150
Hebel, J.P. 148
Heisenberg, W. 43
Hertz, H. 129
Hess, W.R. 248
Hewish, A. 66
Hilbert, D. 31
Hine 129
Holzhausen, A. 183, 258
Horapollon 57
Hoyle, F. 104, 258
Huxley, T.H. 207–208
Jeans, J.H. 36
Jockey, H.P. 101, 258
Junker, R. 98, 258
Kaplan, R.W. 99, 258

Kato, I. 22

Keim, D. 13

Kemner, H. 148, 168

Kessler, V. 13

Kies, Jaap 13

Kilby, J. St. C. 191

Klopstock, F.G. 213

Kornberg, A. 66

Küpfmüller K. 199, 204, 259

Küppers, B.-O. ...82, 102–103, 137, 258

Kuhn, H. 30–31, 258

Lamarck, J.-B. de 82, 99

Lavoisier, A.L. de 29

Le Chatelier, H.-L. 41, 128–129

Lehninger, A.L. 259

Leverrier, U.J.J. 40

Luther, M. 149, 160, 167

Lwoff, A. 105, 259

Markov 204

Matthies, H. 141, 259

Maxwell, J.C. 129–130

Mayer, R.J. 34, 230

McElroy, W.D. 245

Meixner, J. 231, 259

Miller, G.A. 105, 126

Mozart, W.A. 112

Napoleon 56

Newton, I. 40, 100, 122

Nietzsche, F. 149

Nilsson, H. 105

Osche, G. 51, 259

Pascal, B. 28, 73–74

Pasteur, L. 81, 106

Pauli, W. 128–129

Peierls, R.E. 32, 260

Peil, J. 51, 260

Penn, W. 215

Planck, M. 30, 100, 238, 260

Popper, K. 101, 258

Ptolemy 56–57, 62

Rodman, R. 217, 256

Rushton, W.H. 197

Sachsse, H. 27, 260

Salomonsen, F. 253–254, 260

Scherer, S. 98, 258, 260

Schneider, H. 104, 260

Scholz, H. 32

Seidl, T. 13

Shannon, C.E. 12, 49–50,
58–59, 80, 95, 115, 125, 171–175,
177, 180–181, 196–199, 203, 207,
260

Spair 209

Spurgeon, C.H. 142, 145, 147, 151,
162, 261

Stark 238

Steinbuch, K. 50, 261

Strombach, W. 51, 76, 261

Sübmilch, J.P. 217

Trager, G.L. 209

Truman, H.S. 75

Twain, M. 215

Vollmert, B. 105, 261

Watson, J. 99

Weaver, W. 50, 260

Weibel, E.R. 248, 261

Weizenbaum, J. 226

v. Weizsäcker, E. 50, 261

Wieland, C. 13

Wieland, W. 30, 261

Wiener, N. 51, 261

Wilberforce, S. 207

Wolff, A. 13

Wuketits, F. 100, 137, 262

Young, T. 57

Zuse, K. 184